T0353362

Applications and
Trends in Fintech II
Cloud Computing, Compliance, and Global Fintech Trends

Global Fintech Institute - World Scientific Series on Fintech

Print ISSN: 2737-5897
Online ISSN: 2737-5900

Series Editors: David LEE Kuo Chuen *(Global Fintech Institute, Singapore &*
Singapore University of Social Sciences, Singapore)
Joseph LIM *(Singapore University of Social Sciences, Singapore)*
PHOON Kok Fai *(Singapore University of Social Sciences, Singapore)*
WANG Yu *(Singapore University of Social Sciences, Singapore)*

In the digital era, emerging technologies such as artificial intelligence, big data, and blockchain have revolutionized people's daily lives and brought many opportunities and challenges to industries. With the increasing demand for talents in the fintech realm, this book series serves as a good guide for practitioners who are seeking to understand the basics of fintech and the applications of different technologies. This book series starts with fundamental knowledge in finance, technology, quantitative methods, and financial innovation to lay the foundation for the fundamentals of fintech, and understanding the trending issues related to fintech such as regulation, applications, and global trends. It is a good starting point to the fintech literature and is especially useful for people who aspire to become fintech professionals.

Published:

Vol. 5   *Applications and Trends in Fintech II: Cloud Computing, Compliance,*
and Global Fintech Trends
edited by David LEE Kuo Chuen, Joseph LIM, PHOON Kok Fai
and WANG Yu

Vol. 4   *Applications and Trends in Fintech I: Governance, AI, and Blockchain*
Design Thinking
edited by David LEE Kuo Chuen, Joseph LIM, PHOON Kok Fai
and WANG Yu

Vol. 3   *Fintech for Finance Professionals*
edited by David LEE Kuo Chuen, Joseph LIM, PHOON Kok Fai
and WANG Yu

Vol. 2   *Finance for Fintech Professionals*
edited by David LEE Kuo Chuen, Joseph LIM, PHOON Kok Fai
and WANG Yu

Vol. 1   *Foundations for Fintech*
edited by David LEE Kuo Chuen, Joseph LIM, PHOON Kok Fai
and WANG Yu

More information on this series can also be found at https://www.worldscientific.com/series/gfiwssf

Global Fintech Institute – World Scientific
Series on Fintech : 5

Applications and Trends in Fintech II

Cloud Computing, Compliance, and Global Fintech Trends

Editors

David LEE Kuo Chuen
Global Fintech Institute, Singapore
Singapore University of Social Sciences, Singapore

Joseph LIM
Singapore University of Social Sciences, Singapore

PHOON Kok Fai
Singapore University of Social Sciences, Singapore

WANG Yu
Singapore University of Social Sciences, Singapore

Published by

World Scientific Publishing Co. Pte. Ltd.

5 Toh Tuck Link, Singapore 596224

USA office: 27 Warren Street, Suite 401-402, Hackensack, NJ 07601

UK office: 57 Shelton Street, Covent Garden, London WC2H 9HE

and

Global Fintech Institute Ltd.

80 Robinson Road, #08-01, Singapore 068898

Library of Congress Cataloging-in-Publication Data

Names: Lee, David (David Kuo Chuen), editor. | Lim, Joseph, editor. |
 Phoon, Kok Fai, editor. | Wang, Yu, editor.

Title: Applications and trends in fintech II : cloud computing, compliance, and global fintech trends /
 editors, David Lee Kuo Chuen (Global Fintech Institute, Singapore, Singapore University of
 Social Sciences, Singapore), Joseph Lim (Singapore University of Social Sciences, Singapore),
 Phoon Kok Fai (Singapore University of Social Sciences, Singapore),
 Wang Yu (Singapore University of Social Sciences, Singapore).

Description: Singapore ; Hackensack, NJ : World Scientific Publishing Co., [2022] |
 Series: Global Fintech Institute - World Scientific series on fintech, 2737-5897 ; vol. 5 |
 Includes bibliographical references.

Identifiers: LCCN 2021062850 | ISBN 9789811247996 (hardcover) |
 ISBN 9789811249303 (paperback) | ISBN 9789811248009 (ebook) |
 ISBN 9789811248016 (ebook other)

Subjects: LCSH: Finance--Technological innovations.

Classification: LCC HG173 .A7542 2022 | DDC 332--dc23/eng/20220112

LC record available at https://lccn.loc.gov/2021062850

British Library Cataloguing-in-Publication Data

A catalogue record for this book is available from the British Library.

For any available supplementary material, please visit
https://www.worldscientific.com/worldscibooks/10.1142/12579#t=suppl

Desk Editors: Balasubramanian Shanmugam/Yulin Jiang

Typeset by Stallion Press
Email: enquiries@stallionpress.com

Printed in Singapore

Preface

Just a few years ago, the word "Fintech" did not mean much to members of the public. Some associated it with cryptocurrency while others thought of payment systems using the phone. However, over the past five years, the adoption of Fintech in the mainstream public life has increased in pace. Fintech startups have also proliferated as the low interest rate environment provided cheap and more easily available financing. Adoption of Fintech applications has also been accelerated by the changes in working and living brought about by the Covid-19 pandemic restrictions.

The fast pace of developments in Fintech has fostered a demand for professionals to work in this field. The problem is that someone who aspires to work in this field has little idea about the requisite knowledge and skills. It is to this end that the Global FinTech Institute (GFI) was established.

The Global FinTech Institute aims to serve as a hub for the following initiatives:

- A forum for Fintech professionals to meet and collaborate to develop best practices for the industry and serve as a focal point to advocate for the industry.
- A professional society to develop standards and governance frameworks.
- A center to share insights and advance knowledge through the promotion of research.
- A professional body to organize the Fintech body of knowledge, and promote Fintech education.

- A fiduciary to certify knowledge and proficiency in Fintech through the Chartered Fintech Professional (CFtP) designation.

The CFtP program is designed to equip the candidate with a set of tools and a body of knowledge to practice as a Fintech professional. The program starts with building the foundation to understand finance and computer technology through tools like statistics, quantitative methods, programming, and fundamentals of blockchain and cryptocurrency. These tools are used to facilitate the fundamental building blocks of finance, computing, and technology. Finally, the program ends with the application of the concepts learned earlier. A more detailed description of what the program covers is given in what follows, in the listing of the CFtP courses. The CFtP designation is attained by passing a series of exams as well as satisfying the relevant work experience requirement and attestation of good character. The CFtP exams are organized as follows:

- Level 1AB – Foundation
  o Ethics and governance; statistics; quantitative methods; financial innovations; blockchain and cryptocurrency
- Level 1A – Finance
  o Economics; financial statement analysis, financial management; investment management
- Level 1B – Fintech
  o Data structure, algorithms, and Python programming; big data and data science; artificial intelligence and machine learning; computer network and network security
- Level 2 – Applications and Professional Practice
  o Ethics and governance; machine learning and deep learning in Finance; blockchain design and programming; cloud computing, cyber security, and quantum computing; compliance and risk management; global Fintech trends

This book is the second volume of a set of materials used for the CFtP Level 2 exams. While the book is geared toward the body of knowledge for the CFtP Level 2 exams, nevertheless, it can serve as a quick guide and summary of the issues pertaining to the areas of Fintech related to cloud computing, cyber security and quantum computing, compliance and risk management, and global Fintech trends.

About the Editors

Professor David LEE Kuo Chuen is a professor at the Singapore University of Social Sciences and Adjunct Professor at the National University of Singapore. He is also the founder of BlockAsset Ventures, the Chairman of Global Fintech Institute, Vice President of the Economic Society of Singapore, Co-founder of Blockchain Association of Singapore, and Council Member of British Blockchain Association. He has 20 years of experience as a CEO and an independent director of listed and tech companies and is a consultant and advisor to international organizations on food supply chain, blockchain, fintech, and digital currency.

Associate Professor Joseph LIM is with the Singapore University of Social Sciences where he teaches finance. He has also taught at the National University of Singapore and the Singapore Management University. Joseph obtained his MBA from Columbia University and PhD from New York University. In between his stints in academia, he worked in various advisory positions in the areas of private equity and valuation. Joseph, who is a CFA charter holder, has served in various committees at the CFA Institute and as President of CFA Singapore. In addition, he was on the board and committees of various investment industry associations. In the non-profit sector, he was on the board of a pension fund and several endowment funds. He is a coauthor of several popular college finance textbooks.

Associate Professor Kok Fai PHOON teaches finance at the School of Business, Singapore University of Social Sciences (SUSS). He received his PhD in finance from Northwestern University, MSc in Industrial Engineering from the National University of Singapore, and BASc in Mechanical Engineering (Honours) from the University of British Columbia. His research interests focus on the use of technology in portfolio management, wealth management, and risk and complexity of financial products. In addition to his current position at SUSS, Kok Fai has taught at other universities in Singapore and at Monash University in Australia. He has worked at Yamaichi Merchant Bank, at GIC Pte Ltd, and as Executive Director at Ferrell Asset Management, a Singapore hedge fund. He has published in academic journals including the *Review of Quantitative Finance and Accounting* and the *Pacific Basin Finance Journal* as well as practice journals like the *Financial Analyst Journal*, the *Journal of Wealth Management*, and the *Journal of Alternative Investments*.

Ms Yu WANG (Cheryl) is a fintech research fellow at the Singapore University of Social Sciences FinTech and Blockchain Group. Her main research interests are fintech, machine learning, and asset pricing. Prior to SUSS, she worked at the National University of Singapore, Business School as a research associate on corporate governance and sustainability. She graduated with an MSc in Applied Economies from Nanyang Technological University and BSc in Financial Engineering from Huazhong University of Sciences of Technologies. She has multiple journal papers, including an empirical study on sustainability reporting and firm value published on an SSCI journal, *Sustainability*, and one investigating cryptocurrency as a new alternative investment published on *Journal of Alternative Investments* that has been cited for over 200 times and recommended by *CFA Institute Journal Review*. She also serves as referee for various journals such as *Singapore Economic Review, Quarterly Review of Economics and Finance,* and *Journal of Alternative Investments*.

Contents

Part A: Cloud Computing, Cybersecurity, and Quantum Computing

Chapter 1

Cloud Computing

1.1 Introduction to Cloud Computing

Cloud computing emerges as one of the essential services for businesses and individuals. This section introduces the evolution of cloud computing and the characteristics that define cloud computing. It provides the fundamental concepts to understanding various aspects of cloud computing covered in subsequent sections.

Learning Objectives
- Distinguish essential characteristics of cloud computing and relate them to its applicability for businesses and individuals.

Main Takeaways

Main Points
- ARPANET allows computers in different physical locations to share resources via the network.
- Cloud computing aims to provide its users with on-demand and convenient access to a shared pool of resources.
- The resources can be provisioned and customized with minimal interactions with the cloud service provider.

Main Terms
- **On-demand resources:** The provision of pooled resources to clients based on the clients' varying needs.

- **Pooled resources:** Resources (specifically, processing capacity, storage, memory, network bandwidth, and virtual machines) that serve multiple consumers and can be dynamically assigned to them.
- **Self-service:** Ability of clients to request cloud resources without interactions with the cloud service provider.
- **Broad network access:** Ability for clients to access cloud services through a heterogeneous set of network mechanisms and devices.

1.1.1 *Introduction*

In the 1950s, organizations would place one or two machines serving central mainframe computers that provide processing power. Employees would then access the central mainframe computers from connected stations based on a time-sharing schedule. The concept behind this underlies the premise of cloud computing.

In 1969, J.C.R. Licklider developed a primitive version of the Internet, known as the Advanced Research Projects Agency Network (ARPANET). ARPANET allows computers in different physical locations to share resources via the network. The Virtual Machine (VM) operating system was released by IBM in 1972. A VM is the virtualization or emulation of a computer system. It allows users to run an application that behaves like a real, fully operational computer. As the concept of VM popularized and the Internet infrastructure is gradually being more developed, companies began offering "virtual" private networks as a rentable service.

In the early 2000s, Amazon launched Elastic Compute Cloud (Amazon EC2[1]). The EC2 is a web service that provides scalable computing capacity in the Amazon Web Services (AWS) Cloud. It allows companies and individuals to launch virtual servers, configure the security and network settings, and manage their storage without investing in hardware upfront. Additionally, Google's Google Docs services launched in 2006 allow users to create, share, edit, and comment on documents stored in the cloud.

In 2007, Netflix launched its video streaming service, using the cloud to stream movies and other video content into the homes and onto the computers of thousands (and eventually millions) of subscribers worldwide.

---

[1]Adapted from source: https://docs.aws.amazon.com/AWSEC2/latest/UserGuide/concepts.html.

1.1.2 *Definition and Characteristics*

The National Institute of Standards and Technology (NIST) definition of cloud computing is:

> "A model for enabling convenient, on-demand network access to a shared pool of configurable computing resources (e.g., networks, servers, storage, applications, and services) that can be rapidly provisioned and released with minimal management effort or service provider interaction."[2]

It defines five essential characteristics of cloud computing:

- **On-demand self-service:** The client of a cloud supplier should obtain computing capabilities or resources such as processing capacity and network storage capacity on an on-demand basis. This process does not require the client to go through human interaction with the service provider.
- **Broad network access:** The cloud capabilities should be accessible over the network through standard mechanisms or protocols used by heterogeneous thin or thick client platforms such as mobile phones, tablets, laptops, and workstations.
- **Resource pooling:** Resources such as processing capacity, storage, memory, network bandwidth, and VMs serve multiple consumers. The assignment of these resources is dynamic and depends on the consumer's demand. The consumer would have no control or knowledge of the exact location of their assigned resources. However, he/she may be able to specify location at a higher level of abstraction (e.g., country, state, or datacenter).
- **Rapid elasticity:** The cloud capabilities can be scaled in and out by provisioning and releasing them elastically based on demand. This process can be made more efficient via automation. The quick responses to requests for resources appear to the consumer as access to infinite resources. Elasticity provides the flexibility to provide these resources on demand.
- **Measured service:** A cloud system should closely monitor the service usage and the health of services and automatically control and optimize resources via metering capability. Resource usage can be monitored, controlled, reported, and billed accordingly. This provides transparency for both the cloud provider and consumer.

---

[2]Adapted from source: https://nvlpubs.nist.gov/nistpubs/Legacy/SP/nistspecialpublication 800-145.pdf.

1.2 Cloud Computing Models

1.2.1 *Interpretation of Cloud Computing Models and Service Models*

The four main cloud computing models differ based on the geographical location of the cloud infrastructure and the entity responsible for administering access and maintaining the infrastructure. There are different pros and cons for each model, and businesses may adopt different cloud computing models based on their needs and type of data. Service models define how businesses or individuals may use cloud services. This may range from pure data storage to the development of software and the usage of the cloud as a computing platform.

Learning Objectives
- Differentiate the four main cloud computing models and appraise the nature of each model.
- Examine different service models in cloud computing.

Main Takeaways

Main Points
- The NIST defines four cloud deployment models: public cloud, private cloud, community cloud, and hybrid cloud.
- There are three main cloud service models, namely Software as a Service (SaaS), Platform as a Service (PaaS), and Infrastructure as a Service (IaaS).

Main Terms
- **Cloud computing models:** Concern different ways in which cloud infrastructure is deployed and access to the infrastructure is administered.
- **"as a Service":** A suffix describing a computing capability that supports all five essential characteristics of cloud computing.

(a) Cloud Computing Models
The NIST defines four cloud deployment models: public cloud, private cloud, community cloud, and hybrid cloud. These models differ based on the location of the cloud infrastructure and the entity responsible for administering access and maintaining the infrastructure (Rountree & Castrillo, 2013).

(1) Public cloud

A public cloud is where the services and infrastructure are housed at an external service provider (i.e., the cloud provider's premises). The service provider is responsible for managing and maintaining the infrastructure, and the cloud services are available to the general public on a subscription basis. Connections to public cloud providers are usually made through the Internet. Examples of public cloud include Alibaba Cloud, Microsoft Azure, IBM SoftLayer, and Amazon Cloud.

The value proposition for a public offering is very strong. According to PwC, the public cloud will become the dominant infrastructure model in the future. The advantages that the public cloud offers for its clients include the availability of services, scalability, accessibility, and cost-saving. Although some public cloud service providers may charge extra costs for increased availability, they have the hardware, software, and staffing requirements for a highly available cloud service; this is considered hard and costly to achieve for most organizations. The public cloud implementation is also based on a highly scalable infrastructure that can quickly scale based on its client's capacity or traffic. Public cloud services are also expected to be accessible through a wide range of platforms and client types. Service providers generally prioritize this to gain a wide range of clients. As a result, public clouds are attractive solutions to organizations due to the cost savings they offer.

However, there are several drawbacks. With data residing on an external location, performing data analytics may require organizations to download the data from the cloud server and use another application to analyze the data. Hence, whether the cloud application provides functionality that integrates two or more different applications is a performance concern to be considered. In addition, organizations do not control when the public cloud service provider performs upgrades or maintenance on the system. At such time, services may not be available to the clients.

(2) Private cloud

A private cloud is similar to a public cloud except that the services and infrastructure are housed and located internal to the company or organization using the cloud. The organization is responsible for the management, administration, and software/client application installed on the end-user's system. A private cloud is usually accessed through a Local Area Network

(LAN) or a Wide Area Network (WAN). Occasionally where users are remote, the access is provided through the use of a Virtual Private Network (VPN). A private cloud offers better privacy compared to a public cloud. An example of a private cloud is VMware.

A private cloud provides more control to the organization owning the infrastructure. Hence, it allows the organization to decide when to perform upgrades or maintenance based on its need. The service downtime is controllable. In addition, the private cloud allows the organization to have direct access to the environment, including access to logs, traces, and monitoring of accesses. The drawback of a private cloud is the upfront cost, maintenance cost, and staffing needed to support the organization's needs. The organization is solely responsible for the end-to-end solution, including addressing diverse platforms that may be used by its clients, securing the data on the server, controlling and updating users' access to the data, and performing its security and compliance audits.

(3) Community cloud
A community cloud is usually commissioned for exclusive use by a community of users, such as organizations sharing a common purpose, mission, security requirements, or policy. The cloud infrastructure may be located on or off-premise. A community cloud offers privacy to the organizations, and it is jointly maintained and administered by a group of organizations. The advantage of the community cloud is the ability to share.costs between the organizations and allow different organizations to take charge of different support and maintenance work based on the skillsets or expertise owned by each organization. The drawback, however, is the need to define ownership of resources clearly. It is also essential for each organization to control what data it wishes to store on the community cloud. The data is accessible by all organizations using the community cloud.

(4) Hybrid cloud
A hybrid cloud is a combination of two or more cloud models. Sensitive data could be hosted on a private cloud, while non-sensitive data could be hosted on the public cloud. Each cloud model is a separate model itself, and they are linked together by standardized or proprietary technology that enables data and application portability. A hybrid cloud is generally more complex but allows more flexibility in fulfilling an organization's objectives.

(b) Service Models

The NIST defines three main cloud service models, namely Software as a Service (SaaS), Platform as a Service (PaaS), and Infrastructure as a Service (IaaS).

(1) Definition of "as a Service" (aaS)

According to NIST: "The term 'as a [cloud] Service' is a suffix describing a computing capability that supports all five essential characteristics of cloud computing. The term 'as a service (aaS)' implies that SaaS, PaaS, and IaaS are delivered by way of software."[3]

(2) Software as a Service (SaaS)

Many organizations have shifted from on-premise installations to cloud-native subscriptions. This reduces the upfront capital requirements for new software deployment. In a SaaS environment, the cloud service provider controls everything about the application being deployed. This limits the amount of customization that the client can request. In addition, maintenance of the software is administered and controlled by the service provider and may present downtime to the client. The usage data and statistics of the software are shared between the service provider and the client.

Most SaaS providers offer their services in the form of a web-based application. The main advantages of SaaS are that they allow organizations to use the latest software at all times without incurring additional costs with a flexible subscription model. Prime examples of SaaS providers are outlook.com, Google Drive, Dropbox, and Cisco WebEx.

(3) Infrastructure as a Service (IaaS)

IaaS provides clients with services including computing power, storage, networking, and operating systems. The clients use IaaS to deploy and run arbitrary software and applications. In most cases, IaaS providers provide such services using VMs that could be running Windows, Linux, or other operating systems to take advantage of multitenancy. The service provider is solely responsible for maintaining the physical hardware, storage, and networking infrastructure; it does not need to act as an operating system administrator, giving more control and security to the

---

[3]Adapted from source: https://nvlpubs.nist.gov/nistpubs/SpecialPublications/NIST. SP.500-322.pdf.

clients. The clients are responsible for maintaining the operating system and all the applications installed on the operating system. Prime examples of IaaS providers are Amazon Web Services, Alibaba Cloud, and Rackspace.

(4) Platform as a Service (PaaS)

PaaS allows clients to use programming languages, libraries, services, and tools supported by the provider. In PaaS, clients use the platform to provide for computing needs without building their infrastructure. The service provider has no control over what application or service the client develops. Still, the data from the application will be stored in the provider's database and shared with the client. The client will then view the application usage, trends, and statistics. Generally, the client is responsible for everything beyond the operating system and development platform. In contrast, the service provider is responsible for maintaining and ensuring that the operating system is patched and up-to-date. Examples of PaaS providers are Windows Azure, Apache Stratos, and OpenShift.

1.3 Architecture

1.3.1 *Cloud Architecture*

At the cloud service provider, the cloud architecture comprises different components that made up a cloud infrastructure. The cloud service provider is responsible for administering and maintaining these components to ensure seamless and customizable services to its clients.

Learning Objectives
- Recognize the technology components that are essential in a cloud architecture.

Main Takeaways

Main Points
- Cloud architecture is how technology components are combined and connected to create a cloud.
- These components are allocated for a cloud provider to provide different service models.

Main Terms

- **Virtualization:** Creates a virtual representation of a resource and reduces the need for additional hardware to meet clients' needs.
- **Multi-tenancy:** Scenario where multiple clients of a cloud service provider using the same computing resources.
- **Web APIs:** Front-end application that provides interfaces required for cloud services.
- **Physical resource layer:** A layer that comprises the physical computing and facility resources.
- **Resource abstraction and control layer:** A layer where the cloud provider manages access to the physical computing resources through abstraction.
- **Service layer:** A layer where a cloud provider defines its service models.

(a) Architecture

Cloud architecture is how technology components are combined and connected to create a cloud. The fundamental components of cloud architecture include (but may not be limited to) the following:

- **Virtualization:** Virtualization plays a crucial role in cloud architectures and is the technology on which all cloud architectures are built. Virtualization works by separating IT services and functions from hardware; it creates a virtual representation of a resource and reduces the need for additional hardware to meet clients' needs. A hypervisor is a VM that abstracts a machine's resources (such as memory, I/O, computing power, and storage) and creates multiple virtual images; it provides features for dividing and allocating resources to the clients (see Figure 1.1).
- **Hardware:** Hardware components such as servers, computers (e.g., CPU and memory), storage, networking equipment (e.g., routers, switches, and load balancers), and backup devices form an essential part of the cloud infrastructure. It may also include facilities such as heating, air conditioning, power, and other aspects needed in a physical facility. This physical hardware may be located at different geographical locations. Typically, the cloud service providers are responsible for maintaining and administering the hardware components.

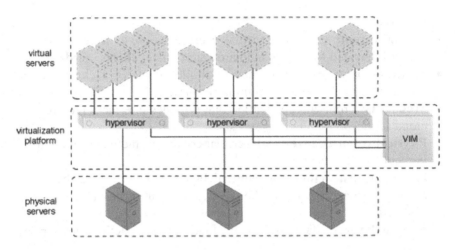

Figure 1.1:   Visual representation of hypervisor mechanism.

Source: https://patterns.arcitura.com/cloud-computing-patterns/mechanisms/hypervisor.

- **Applications or Middleware:** Software components that act as inter-mediaries are necessary to allow communications between servers, computers, or applications. It may also be used to relay information between the clients and the back-end servers/computers.
- **Mechanisms** for supporting multi-tenancy: Multi-tenancy refers to the scenario where multiple clients of a cloud service provider using the same computing resources. Each client's data is invisible to other clients, and the clients are not aware of each other's existence. The support for multi-tenancy is essential for a cloud service provider. Hence, a cloud service must provide for the virtual (or even physical) segregation of stored data on a per-client basis. Some cloud providers may use automation software to monitor usage in order to meet fluctuating market demand continuously.
- **Web APIs:** This is part of a front-end application that provides interfaces required for cloud services. It enables services to be accessible through the client's side applications (such as a web browser). User experience design (UX) is vital to create a navigable online experience.

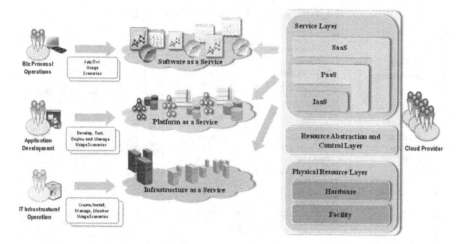

Figure 1.2: Illustration of three-layer cloud service.

Source: https://www.nist.gov/system/files/documents/itl/cloud/NIST_SP-500-291_Version-2_2013_June18_FINAL.pdf.

The NIST illustrated how cloud services could be orchestrated (see Figure 1.2). In this figure, the three-layered framework on the right-hand side shows how the components are allocated for a cloud provider to provide different service models.

At the physical resource layer, also considered the back-end layer, the physical computing and facility resources (i.e., hardware) are located. The back-end may also provide middleware to help connect devices to communicate with each other.

The resource abstraction and control layer is where the cloud provider manages access to the physical computing resources through abstraction. This includes hypervisors, VMs, and other software that ensure efficient, secure, and reliable service providers.

The service layer is where a cloud provider defines its service models. This requires some front-end or user/client-facing architecture such as web APIs. The front-end relays requests and data to the back-end via a network. The back-end layer protects data from the front-end and responds to queries.

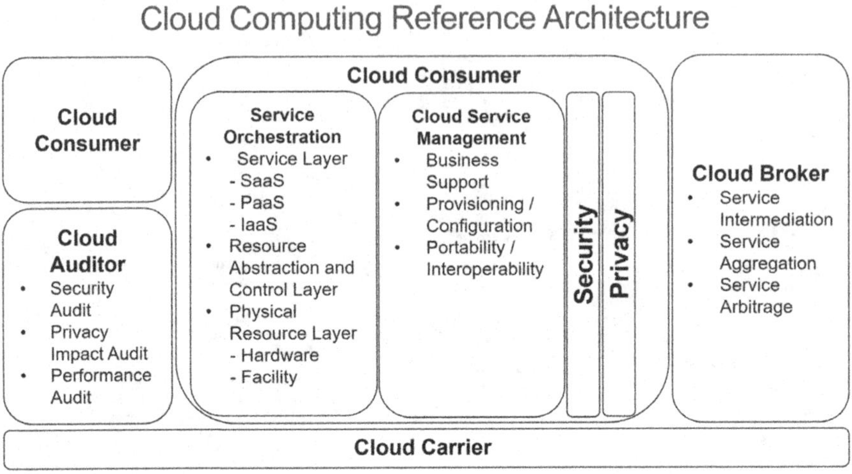

Cloud Computing Reference Architecture

Figure 1.3: NIST the conceptual reference model.

Source: https://www.itu.int/en/ITU-D/Regional-Presence/AsiaPacific/Documents/Events/2015/July-Could-Computing/S3_M_I_Deen.pdf.

The NIST cloud computing conceptual model presented in Figure 1.3 is depicted as "an integrated diagram of the system, organizational, and process components." Generally, the primary responsibility lies with the cloud service provider. Apart from managing all the hardware and software required in cloud architecture and their associated security and privacy issues, cloud providers are also responsible for cloud service management. Business support includes customer, contract, inventory management, accounting, billing, pricing, and rating. The cloud provider is also required to respond to resource changes, perform monitoring, reporting, metering, and ensure efficient data portability, service portability, and system portability.

1.4 Cloud Computing in Fintech

1.4.1 *Uses of Cloud Computing in Fintech*

This section describes the uses of cloud computing for financial institutions (FI) and Fintech firms. It discusses several possible ways that FIs or

Fintech firms may leverage cloud computing to enhance their business efficiency and generate additional revenue.

Learning Objectives
- Evaluate the impact of cloud computing in Fintech.

Main Takeaways

Main Points
- Cloud computing enables companies to outsource the administration of technology infrastructure to cloud service providers and access computing resources in a flexible, efficient, and secure manner.
- The costs saved from housing, administering, and maintaining own computing infrastructure can be invested to enhance business efficiency and generate additional revenue.
- This is embodied in benefits including data management opportunities, operational cost efficiencies, scalability and agility, automated services, business continuity, customer centricity, artificial intelligence (AI) capabilities, and environmental efficiencies.

Main Terms
- **Accelerated innovation:** The ability of businesses to innovate using different cloud service models without capacity constraints and the need for significant investment in infrastructure.
- **Scalability:** The ability to acquire additional resources on-demand without costly upgrades to on-premise technology infrastructure.

(a) Cloud Computing in FinTech
The cloud model enables companies to outsource the administration of technology infrastructure to cloud service providers and access computing resources in a flexible, efficient, and secure manner.

With cloud maturity becoming the hallmark of the world's best performing banks (Accenture, 2020), the financial services industry has observed steady cloud adoption, which has only been accelerated further by the Covid-19 pandemic. There are several ways in which companies — Fintech entrants and established incumbents — utilize cloud technology to expedite the process of innovation in financial services. This is embodied in benefits including data management opportunities, operational cost efficiencies, scalability and agility, automated services, business continuity, customer centricity, AI capabilities, and environmental efficiencies.

(1) Data management
The benefits of cloud computing are most pronounced in data management systems. Traditional data infrastructures in FIs are not only expensive to purchase, set up, and maintain, but they are also unable to scale to meet the variable and increasing volume of data.

Cloud technology enables Fintech companies to aggregate, store, and manage large quantities of data securely, without capacity constraints and the need for significant investment in infrastructure. With efficient data management on the cloud, businesses can harness innovative, data-centric approaches to improve existing products and services.

In 2020, Capital One became the first US bank to shift all of its operations into the public cloud by exiting its physical data centers. The movement away from infrastructure management has enabled the bank to manage data at a larger scale to take advantage of machine learning capabilities and deliver customer-centric innovation (Amazon Web Services, 2020).

(2) Operational costs
Cloud services enable Fintech organizations to reap considerable cost savings in developing and operating independent infrastructure for their data management needs. Migrating to the cloud allows companies to incur smaller, ongoing operational costs instead of significant up-front capital expenditure, channeled into more productive uses.

Further, cloud providers offer a utility-based model in which companies can scale up computing resources when required and scale down when demand subsides. As companies only pay for resources they utilize, cloud computing eliminates the need for costly over-provisioning (Blazheski, 2016). This dynamic cloud pricing captures considerable cost efficiencies and facilitates granular spending control.

A recent example of an enterprise data-lake migration in the financial services industry indicated a cost reduction of 30–40%. The reduction is driven by a combination of lower hardware costs and software consolidation cost reduction as required analytic tools became native to the cloud platform instead of being add-ons (Accenture, 2020).

(3) Scalability and agility
The ability to access a shared pool of configurable computing resources can increase a financial institution's ability to innovate by enhancing agility, efficiency, and productivity (Saluja & Sepple, 2018). For instance, it

provides Fintech companies with the flexibility to scale without the need for costly upgrades to on-premise technology infrastructure.

Cloud migration also enables shorter development cycles for new products, supporting an agile and efficient response to customers' needs. Fintech companies can test new scenarios and alternative configurations without a lengthy purchasing and provisioning process (Hon and Millard, 2018) alongside minimal upfront cost.

For Capital One, migration to the cloud through Amazon Web Services has enabled instant provisioning of infrastructure at scale and, consequently, rapid innovation. The bank has demonstrably improved from quarterly and monthly application updates to release new code multiple times per day.

Similarly, Atom Bank, the UK's first mobile-only bank, began developing a cloud-native banking stack on Google Cloud after encountering infrastructure limitations and scaling issues. Cloud migration has enabled enhanced agility for the bank, cutting its environment's lead time by up to 98%. The bank has also been able to improve development times drastically (Google Cloud, n.d).

(4) Automated services
Cloud technology enhances the capabilities of Fintech companies by allowing them to address the performance complexities of services such as AI, machine learning, and data analytic techniques. Companies can then reap the benefits of these services while keeping infrastructure costs low.

TD Securities, a leading provider of advisory and capital markets products, utilized massive computing power to price complex derivative products with its in-house software. Transition to an elastic and scalable cloud-based environment on Microsoft Azure has enabled rapid iteration of infrastructure configuration to meet its client's needs, allowing the firm to enhance performance at lower costs (Microsoft, 2019).

The multitude of sophisticated data analysis cloud software offered by major cloud providers can also provide Fintech companies with a real-time view of their portfolios, assisting risk monitoring and management.

(5) Business continuity
Ensuring business continuity during unprecedented times requires reliable and resilient infrastructure. Major cloud providers have invested significant funds to meet the highest security standards and necessary

regulations. They possess a demonstrable track record of performance within the financial services industry. Therefore, the adoption of cloud technology is highly reliable for businesses. It provides sophisticated systems for data storage that offer a much greater level of resilience to businesses, ensuring data security in the event of disasters.

Most companies experience improved disaster recovery times after migration to the cloud. S&P Global Ratings, the world's leading provider of independent credit ratings, experienced improvements of over 50% in its disaster recovery time and is confident that the resiliency of Amazon Web Services would allow the company to avoid SEC penalties during application downtime (Amazon Web Services, 2020).

The data saved in the cloud storage is also well encrypted to eliminate hacks and significant types of security threats. Therefore, it is arguably more secure than legacy infrastructure without cloud adoption.

(6) Artificial intelligence

Cloud can support the massive data storage capacity, scalable computing power, and embedded graphic processing units (GPUs) to handle the large data stores and algorithms that AI systems need to work on an ongoing basis. Coupled with its flexibility, it is deemed to be the most viable place for complex AI-driven business processes that drive rapid innovation (Finextra, 2020).

Public cloud providers have a variety of AI-based tooling to enhance the offering of Fintech Companies. For instance, Alibaba Cloud offers an AI Service solution that allows companies to build various types of multi-language customer service chatbots to enable text, voice, and image interactions (Alibaba Cloud, n.d).

Using the cloud in conjunction with AI enables companies to build new customer experiences, optimize operations, and manage talent through leveraging tools including machine learning, Internet of Things platforms, image recognition, and natural language processing. These capabilities are key drivers in increasing overall profitability, streamlining operations, and retaining talent.

(7) Customer centricity

Customer centrism is imperative to survival in the increasingly competitive, digitally transformed Fintech industry. By enhancing efficiency and personalization, the cloud can assist Fintech organizations in meeting the needs of their customers efficiently.

For instance, service providers such as Amazon Web Services and Microsoft Azure rely on server maintenance, technical support, and optimal performance. Fintech companies are hence able to redirect funds and manpower toward dedicated and innovative customer service.

In addition, personalized and predictive selling of products is a formidable advantage for Fintech companies by improving customer acquisition, satisfaction, and retention. The cloud offers better data-driven preparation for more predictable and optimal customization results by allowing real-time information updates. This maximizes the return on investment of the companies' decision strategies and enhances the customer experience.

The UK's Starling Bank has managed to turn large amounts of data into real-time actionable insights that have improved customer interactions at scale, using BiqQuery from Google Cloud. For instance, merchant identification and real-time notifications with Google Maps APIs have enabled the bank to offer personalized and convenient solutions for its customers, such as budget tracking and fraud detection.

(8) Environmental efficiencies
Through cloud migration, Fintech companies can also reduce the energy consumption and carbon footprint that comes with setting up physical infrastructure. With more efficient utilization of computing power and less idle time, companies can reap significant environmental efficiencies.

1.5 Risks, Challenges and Considerations

1.5.1 *Risk, Challenges, and Considerations of Cloud Computing*

Mass adoption of cloud computing presents risks and challenges to both cloud service providers and their clients. This section details essential risks that should be considered and presents several considerations for businesses planning to adopt cloud computing models.

Learning Objectives
- Appraise the risks and challenges faced by cloud service providers and their clients.
- Assess key considerations in the adoption of cloud computing for businesses.

Main Takeaways

Main Points

- Data breach/loss is devastating to both the cloud service provider and its clients. It can be due to reasons such as misconfiguration of services and change control, insider threat, or insecure APIs.
- Cryptojacking is slowly overtaking ransomware as the most preferred attack that generates more revenue for attackers.
- The key considerations for businesses before adopting a cloud solution include service provider management, security, legal and regulatory compliance, data sovereignty, and the ability to conduct incident detection and response.

Main Terms

- **Data breach:** The intentional or unintentional release of confidential information to an untrusted environment.
- **Data loss:** Incident where data were erased from the cloud storage due to hacking, virus, or system failure.
- **Cryptojacking:** The unauthorized use of resources to mine cryptocurrencies
- **Unauthorized access:** Incident where unauthenticated or unintended user gain access to privileged data.
- **Data sovereignty:** The idea that data are subject to the laws and governance structures within the nation it is collected.

(a) Risks, Challenges, and Considerations

(1) Data breach/loss

Data breach, or information leakage, is the intentional or unintentional release of confidential information to an untrusted environment. Data loss is an incident where data were erased from the cloud storage due to hacking, virus, or system failure. To the cloud service providers, the consequences of a data breach/loss may include regulatory implications that may result in monetary and reputational loss, legal and contractual liabilities, brand impact, customer churn, and unplanned expenses to fix security gaps. For business or individual clients, cloud data breach/loss may result in loss of intellectual property to competitors, compromise of private information, loss of competitive edge, decreased company valuation, change in leadership, and lawsuits.

The reasons for cloud data breach/loss can be due to:

- **Misconfiguration of services and change control:** The misconfiguration of services can happen in several ways. Common misconfigurations include weak authentication, incorrect security policy on data storage items, and over-privileged accounts. For instance, in 2017, the personal information of 123 million US households was exposed when the user access to an Amazon Web Services (AWS) S3 cloud storage bucket was incorrectly configured. Instead of allowing only authorized users to access the contents, the bucket was configured to allow any AWS "Authenticated Users" to download its stored data; this refers to any AWS account user. In another incident, the Capital One Financial Corporation data breach that happened in 2019 resulted in the personal data leakage of over 106 million customers. The breach that resulted in a fine of $80 million for the company was due to an ex-employee at AWS who illegally accessed Capital One's AWS cloud servers using a misconfigured web application firewall (Noonan, 2020). The inability of cloud service providers to patch or fix a software vulnerability or security flaw is also a cause for a data breach. Hackers exploit the vulnerability to gain access to the network. The Equifax hack reported in 2017 is due to an untimely fix of a vulnerability in its Apache Struts software (Fruhlinger, 2020).

- **Insider threat:** The Netwrix 2018 Cloud Security Report indicated that 58% of companies attribute security breaches to insiders. Insider threats can be intentional or unintentional. Unaware employees may fall victim to phishing attacks, ransomware/malware attacks, or social engineering. Insider data theft is also cited as one of the most common cloud security incidents by Netwrix in 2021, and it is particularly prominent in small organizations with less than 100 employees. Examples of insider threats include the Twitter scam in 2020 and the Cisco incident in 2018. In the Twitter attack in 2020, attackers targeted a small number of employees through a phone spear-phishing attack (BBC News, 2020). As a result, the attackers obtained the employees' credentials and gained 130 private and corporate Twitter accounts. They used 45 of the hacked accounts to promote a bitcoin scam which netted the scammers more than $100,000. The hacked accounts include those of Barack Obama, Elon Musk, Bill Gates, Apple, and other notable individuals or companies. The Cisco incident in 2018 saw a Cisco employee intentionally accessed Cisco's cloud infrastructure and deleted 456 VMs for Cisco's WebEx Teams application. The act resulted in the denial of WebEx services for approximately 16,000 users. Cisco spent roughly $1.4 million in employee time to audit and fixed the damage; it also had to pay a total of $1 million in restitution to affected users (BNP Media, 2020).

- **Insecure APIs (Application Programming Interface):** API is an interface that defines interactions between two or more applications. Businesses use APIs to connect services and to transfer data. In cloud computing, APIs are used to allow clients to manage and interact with cloud services. Hence, APIs security is essential to ensure that they are not misused or exploited by hackers to circumvent authentication and access control policies of services. The Instagram data breach in 2019, where almost 50 million user records were leaked and sold for bitcoin, was due to a security bug in its developer API (Ashford, 2017). Among the solutions are good API hygiene by cloud developers and compliance to standard API frameworks, such as the Open Cloud Computing Interface (OCCI) and the Cloud Infrastructure Management Interface (CIMI).

(2) Cryptojacking

Cryptojacking refers to the unauthorized use of resources to mine cryptocurrencies. Hackers plant cryptomining code on computing resources after unsuspected users click on a malicious link or visit a website with JavaScript code that auto-executes once loaded in a browser (Nadeau, 2021). An example of cryptomining software is the Smominru cryptomining botnet discovered in 2018 that infected more than a half-million machines to mine Monero. Hackers prefer cryptojacking as a cheaper and more profitable alternative to ransomware for several reasons. Firstly, not every user pays for ransomware-infected computers, whereas in cryptojacking, all infected computers help mine cryptocurrency. Secondly, the risks of being caught are much less with cryptojacking than with ransomware. Thirdly, victims have less incentive to trace back to the source because, in cryptojacking, no personal data was stolen or encrypted.

Cryptojacking cloud sources involve compromising container management platforms via misconfigured services and exposed APIs. A new variant of cryptojacking malware from threat group TeamTnT, named Black-T, targets AWS credential files on compromised cloud systems and mine for Monero (Coker, 2020). The malware will scan for exposed Docker daemon APIs. Upon successful identification and exploitation of the API, Black-T will be planted.

Ways to prevent cloud cryptojacking include increasing employee security awareness to thwart phishing attacks, deploying ad-blocking extensions on web browsers, using multi-factor authentication for cloud applications and IT assets, and promptly installing security patches and updates, and deploy cloud-based threat protection.

(3) Unauthorized access
Cloud infrastructure is outside the network perimeter of an organization, and it also makes it easier for an attacker to gain unauthorized access to the organization's cloud resources. Improperly-configured security or access control will enable an attacker to gain direct access. Phishing attack, where an attacker tricks an employee into clicking malicious links that ask for account credentials, is also one of the most commonly used tactics. A weak password by an organization's employee will give full access to data or functionality to an unauthorized user.

Among strategic considerations that banks (or any organizations) should consider when planning and implementing a cloud solution are:

(4) Service provider management
Cloud service providers may offer new, cloud-based services and capabilities regularly. Organizations should avoid vendor lock-in so that they do not need to re-platform when moving from one provider to another. Price flexibility moving workloads from one cloud to another to meet business needs should also be considered. As pointed out in a Deloitte report (Deloitte, 2019), "Adopting a multi-vendor/multi-cloud strategy can be complex and challenging; developing a shared understanding of architectural components and governance strategy enables optimal use of multi-cloud environments."

(5) Security
In the 2020 Cloud Security Report by (ISC)^2 (2020), most organizations are moderate to extremely concerned about cloud security. Among the biggest cloud security concerns include data leakage and data privacy/confidentiality. The three main cloud security controls that organizations use are encryption, auditing of user activity, and employee training (Netwrix, 2021).

The cloud providers are responsible for the security of the infrastructure layers, and the clients should be responsible for security and access management at the higher layer. This includes having proper employee security training and education, correct configuration of user access and identity management, conducting regular audit and monitoring of user activity, deploying multi-factor authentication, reviewing the type of data to be stored on the cloud, and performing proper data classification.

(6) Legal and regulatory compliance
Data protection regulations such as the Payment Card Industry Data Security Standard (PCI DSS), Health Insurance Portability and

Accountability Act (HIPAA), and General Data Protection Regulation (GDPR) require organizations to demonstrate correct handling of protected personal information. When such data is stored on the cloud, achieving and demonstrating regulatory compliance is essential. This mandates the compliance teams to track and enforce regulatory compliance continuously.

(7) Data sovereignty
The issue with data sovereignty lies in the fact that cloud infrastructure consists of geographically distributed data centers. This creates concerns around data sovereignty. Data protection regulations such as the GDPR limits the physical location where EU citizens' data can be sent to and stored. In 2021, Capgemini and Orange announced a plan to set up Bleu that provides an independent, trusted cloud platform in France. The critical concerns behind this act include providing immunity from all extraterritorial legislation, meeting data transfer requirements, and ensuring complete control of cloud-based applications from within an isolated infrastructure that uses data centers located in France. This move aligns with France's national cloud strategy in light of security and sovereignty pre-requisites (Capgemini, 2021).

(8) Incident detection and response
Incident detection and response concern the amount of time an organization needs to discover and respond to cloud security incidents. According to the survey by Netwrix (2021), the top three incidents that organizations find within minutes or hours are phishing, ransomware, and targeted attacks on cloud infrastructure. The incidents that took the longest to detect is data theft by insiders. Nevertheless, the survey also showed that data classification and user activity auditing reduced the organization's detection and response time. Data classification is where organizations tag sensitive files to exert more control and clarity on the data stored. On the other hand, activity auditing concerns monitoring malicious activity across the cloud environment and alerting to suspicious actions.

1.6 Global Cloud Market

1.6.1 *Global Cloud Market Overview*

The global cloud computing market is growing as it deepens the industry's transformation and enables more and more enterprises to seize innovation and opportunities. This section compares the cloud market in China and the US and how tech giants utilize cloud computing in their AI strategy.

Learning Objectives
- Compare the developments of the cloud market in China and the US.
- Illustrate the convergence of cloud computing and AI in the business strategy of tech giants in these regions.

Main Takeaways

Main Points
- Cloud computing has brought about fundamental changes in life, consumption, and business and triggers the entire industry's transformation.
- Organizations have their own cloud storage for Intentional, Unintentional, IoT/Car, and Cognitive Services data.

Main Terms
- **Intentional data:** Data that records choices and behaviors.
- **Unintentional data:** Data that was not collected with any specific analysis or purpose in mind.
- **Internet of Things (IoT):** The network of physical objects embedded with sensors and networking ability to connect and exchange data with other devices and systems over the Internet.
- **Cognitive Service:** A set of machine learning algorithms that Microsoft has developed to solve problems in AI.

(a) Global Cloud Market Overview
Cloud computing is regarded as the third IT wave after PC and Internet transformation and has become essential support for developing the information industry. Cloud computing is the main driving force for enterprise transformation. It has brought about fundamental changes in the way of life, consumption, and business; and triggers the entire industry's transformation. The development of cloud computing technology has entered a mature stage. Its application also moves towards a more core and critical area, paying more attention to security, stability, and risk prevention and control.

In 2017, Amazon AWS, Microsoft Azure, Alibaba Cloud, Google, and IBM ranked top five in the global market share of public cloud IaaS. Amazon had the highest market share of 51.8%, taking the absolute leading position. Patent filings in the cloud computing industry have more than doubled in the past five years. IBM, Microsoft, and Google, head-quartered in the United States, ranked in the top three, and Intel, Amazon, HP ranked in the top ten owners of cloud computing patents. This means that six of the top 10 cloud computing patents are in the US, further demonstrating that global cloud computing offerings are centered in the US. Huawei, a Chinese company, has been selected as one of the top 10 owners of cloud computing patents globally and ranked eighth, ahead of HP of the United States and SAP of Germany. As a technology company founded over 30 years ago, Huawei has a profound accumulation in cloud computing and infrastructure, attaching great importance to intellectual property and patent research.

Figures 1.4 and 1.5 show a comparison of AWS, Microsoft Azure, Alibaba Cloud, and Huawei Cloud and their respective available regions and countries. Their top business customers are shown in Figures 1.6 and 1.7.

As shown in Figure 1.8, eight out of the nine companies mentioned above (Figure 1.8) have their cloud for data storage in the form of Intentional, Unintentional, IoT/Car, and Cognitive Services data.

Cloud Services Comparison: Available Regions & Countries			
	amazon web services	**Azure**	**C-J** Alibaba Cloud	**HUAWEI**
Launch Time	Mar 2006	Feb 2010	Sept 2009	Mar 2017
Available Countries	190+	140+	150+	China & Hong Kong
Regions	18	42(plan for 54)	18(8 in China)	4

Figure 1.4: Cloud services comparison: Available regions & countries.

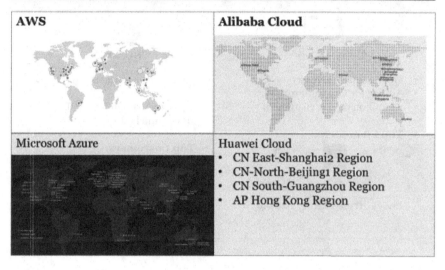

Figure 1.5: Cloud services comparison: Locations.

Cloud Services Comparison: Customers

- Begin with small customers
- Has increasingly taken on large customer deals

Top Customers:

- Most around its widely used software-as-a-service (SaaS) tools
- 50% of Top Fortune 500 companies

Top Customers:

Figure 1.6: Cloud services comparison: Customers (1).

Cloud Services Comparison: Customers

Alibaba Cloud

- Mostly small customers
- Aiming for large enterprises
- >1 million paying customers

- **Top Customers:**

HUAWEI

- Target at governments and large enterprises
- 238% increase in its user base since launched

- **Top Customers:**

Source: Sdx Central, ZD Net, Hwances, Schulte Research

Figure 1.7:   Cloud services comparison: Customers (2).

Company	Intentional Data	Un-intentional Data	IoT/Car	Cognitive Service	Cloud
Alibaba	AliPay, Taobao, Tmall, Alibaba.com, Alibaba Express, Yue'bao, Tmall, Alibaba Cloud (750 mn)	Youku, Weibo, UCWeb, Cainiao Logistics, Yahoo! China, SCMP, AliWangWang, LaiWang, PAI, Ding Talk	"Connected Car" with SAIC, AutoNavi, Ali Health, KFC	Platform for Artificial Intelligence (PAI 2.0), Tmall Genie	Ali Cloud
Tencent	WeChat Pay, 3rd Party Providers (JD.com, Didi, etc.)	WeChat (938 mn), QQ (700 mn), Qzone, WeChat Ecosystem, Gaming	Didi, Dianping review site	WeChat Voice/ Image, Tencent Video	Tencent Cloud
Ping An	Ping An Bank, Ping An Insurance, Ping An Asset Mgmt (350 mn)	Ping An Health, Ping An Securities	Ping An Auto Owner, Wanjia Clinics	Facial recognition, Voice print	Ping An Health Cloud
Baidu	Baidu Search, Baidu Wallet	Baidu Search	Food Delivery Service, Project Apollo	Little Fish	Baidu Cloud
Amazon	E-commerce (B2C, C2C)	Shopping search	Echo, Kindle, Whole Foods, Amazon Books, Logistics	Alexa, Rekognition, Polly, Lex, Amazon Video	AWS
Google	Google Play Store, Google Search	Google Search, Android OS, G-mail, Maps, Chrome, Snapchat (166 mn MAU), Youtube, Waymo	Android OS, Waymo	Health, Translation, Google Assistant, Google Face, Deep Mind	Google Cloud
Apple	iTunes (800 mn), Apple Music, Apple Pay (85 mn)	iOS, Safari	iPhone (1 bn), iPad, iPod, Mac, Apple Watch	Siri, Face Recognition	iCloud
Microsoft	Xbox, Microsoft Wallet (small)	LinkedIn, Office, Skype, Bing, IE	Kinect, Microsoft Surface, Windows Phone	Zo, Computer vision/ Speech/ Language API	Azure
Facebook	Messenger Pay	Facebook, Facebook Messenger (1.96 bn), Whatsapp(1.3 bn)	Oculus, Project Titan	Deep face, Deep text, Translation	/

Figure 1.8:   AI data source comparison.

According to Gartner, the global leader in cloud services is Amazon with 51.8% of the global market share than Microsoft with 13.3%, Alibaba with 4.6%, and Google with 3.3% in 2017. IBM has a global market share of 1.9%. In China, Alibaba leads, with Meituan and Tencent ranking second and third. Baidu is ranked 10th in China. Alibaba is leading the Asia market. Alibaba Cloud's international operations are registered and headquartered in Singapore. It is expanding its service into countries and regions involving the Belt and Road Initiative. Alibaba Cloud will have an integrated cloud technology and innovation platform for the Winter Olympics 2022. In March, it opened its first data center in Indonesia. In 2017, it launched 316 products and features; 60 were focused on high-value fields, including AI. Its reported revenue was 4.39 billion yuan (US$664.96 million) in 2018Q1, up 103% from the same period last year. Total revenue for the 2017 fiscal year reached 13.39 billion yuan, up 101%.

Tencent also has access to social media data generated by QQ, Wechat, and Wechat Pay stored in Tencent Cloud, possibly reaching a billion people's postings, chats, file transfers, photos, locations, and other personal information. Ping An provides Health, Real Estate, Transport, Smart City, Government, and Finance services, besides insurance. Thus, it has a massive database at its disposal via its cloud services. With Tencent, Alibaba, and Ping An as its largest shareholders, Zhong An provides pure online insurance services and has slowly expanded into many areas beyond e-commerce insurance. Zhong An is the largest pure online, cloud-based insurance company globally.

Baidu is also expanding its Baidu Cloud business. It has recently launched China's first cloud-to-edge AI chip — Kunlun. Using Kunlun, Baidu offers AI platforms and hardware for organizations to deploy AI-infused solutions. Baidu is also using its AI technologies in cars and more than 100 brands of refrigerators, TVs, and speakers. It is also partnering with Huawei to develop AI-powered smartphones and partnering with Qualcomm to optimize its DuerOS for IoT devices and smartphones.

Meanwhile, in the US, Amazon has transformed itself into the number one AI player in almost everything, including cloud and machine learning. Google's cloud services are also contributing to its revenue. In 2017, Google's advertising revenue amounted up to US$95.38.

The recent results showed that Google accounted for 86% of its parent Alphabet's 2018Q2 revenue of US$26.24 billion. Google's other revenues, including cloud services, hardware, and app sales, grew 37% to

US$4.4 billion over the same quarter a year earlier. Google Search, Street View, Google Photos; and Google Translate use Google's Tensor Processing Unit, or TPU, to accelerate their neural network computations behind the scene. The chip has been specifically designed for Google's TensorFlow framework, a symbolic math library used for machine learning applications such as neural networks. The third-generation TPU was announced on May 8, 2018, and Google "would allow other companies to buy access to those chips through its cloud-computing service."

Microsoft's recent growth has been spurred by its cloud services, including Azure, which has had its revenue growth above 70% over the previous year. Microsoft's focus on fast-growing cloud applications and platforms is helping it beat the slowing demand for personal computers that has hurt sales of its popular Windows operating system. However, unlike Microsoft, Apple's AI strategy continues to focus on running workloads locally on devices, rather than relying heavily on cloud-based resources.

From these studies, it can be seen that cloud computing is the foundation of AI strategy at this stage of the competition in the global cloud market. Alibaba dominates in Asia while Amazon dominates in the US.

References/Further Readings

Accenture. (2020). The Cloud Imperative for the Banking Industry. Cloud Services, Accenture Banking. https://images.info.accenture.com/Web/ACCENTURE/%7Be525da83-d3a8-44bf-bd38-b2fbc21399b0%7D_Accenture-Cloud-Imperative-Banking.pdf.

Alibaba Cloud. (n.d.). Artificial Intelligence Service for Conversational Chatbots. Alibaba Cloud Solutions. https://www.alibabacloud.com/solutions/ai-chatbots.

Amazon Web Services. (2020). Capital One on AWS. Amazon Solutions, Case Studies. https://aws.amazon.com/solutions/case-studies/capital-one/.

Ashford, W. (2017, August 31). Instagram Fixes API Blamed for Celebrity Data Leaks. ComputerWeekly.Com. https://www.computerweekly.com/news/450425513/Instagram-fixes-API-blamed-for-celebrity-data-leaks.

BBC News. (2020, July 31). Twitter hack: Staff tricked by Phone Spear-Phishing Scam. https://www.bbc.com/news/technology-53607374.

Blazheski, F. (2016). Banking Analysis: Cloud Banking or Banking in the Clouds? U.S. Economic Watch. https://www.bbvaresearch.com/wp-content/uploads/2016/04/Cloud_Banking_or_Banking_in_the_Clouds1.pdf.

BNP Media. (2020, September 4). Former Cisco Employee Pleads Guilty in Insider Threat Case. 2020–09-01 | Security Magazine. https://www.

securitymagazine.com/articles/93210-former-cisco-employee-pleads-guilty-in-insider-threat-case.

Capgemini. (2021, May 27). Capgemini and Orange announce plan to create "Bleu," a company to provide a "Cloud de Confiance" in France. Capgemini Worldwide.https://www.capgemini.com/news/capgemini-and-orange-announce-plan-to-create-bleu-a-company-to-provide-a-cloud-de-confiance-in-france/.

Coker, J. (2020, October 6). New Cryptojacking Malware Variant Targeting Cloud Systems Discovered. Infosecurity Magazine. https://www.infosecurity-magazine.com/news/cryptojacking-malware-variant/.

Deloitte. (2019). Cloud Banking: More than just a CIO Conversation. https://www2.deloitte.com/global/en/pages/financial-services/articles/bank-2030-financial-services-cloud.html.

Finextra. (2020). Natural Language Processing is the Next Step to Automation. Finextra Research. https://www.finextra.com/newsarticle/35053/natural-language-processing-is-the-next-step-to-automation.

Fruhlinger, J. (2020, February 12). Equifax Data Breach FAQ: What Happened, who was Affected, what was the Impact? CSO Online. https://www.csoonline.com/article/3444488/equifax-data-breach-faq-what-happened-who-was-affected-what-was-the-impact.html.

Google Cloud. (n.d.). Atom Bank: Empowering a Digital-only Bank to Transform the Way People Handle Their Finances. Google Cloud, Case Studies. https://cloud.google.com/customers/atom-bank.

Hon, W. K., & Millard, C. (2018). Banking in the cloud: Part 1 — Banks' use of cloud services. *Computer Law & Security Review*, 34(1), 4–24.

(ISC)². (2020). 2020 Cloud Security Report. (ISC)², Inc. https://www.isc2.org/2020-cloud-security-report.

Kahol, A. (2019, July 18). Cloud Cryptojacking: The Fastest-Growing Enterprise Cybersecurity Threat. Verdict. https://www.verdict.co.uk/cloud-cryptojacking/.

Microsoft. (2019). TD Securities transforms derivatives pricing and client experience using Azure. Microsoft Customers Stories. https://customers.microsoft.com/en-US/story/td-securities-banking-azure-canada.

Nadeau, M. (2021, May 6). What is cryptojacking? How to prevent, detect, and recover from it. CSO Online. https://www.csoonline.com/article/3253572/what-is-cryptojacking-how-to-prevent-detect-and-recover-from-it.html.

Netwrix. (2021). 2021 Cloud Data Security Report. https://www.netwrix.com/download/collaterals/2021%20Netwrix%20Cloud%20Data%20Security%20Report.pdf.

NIST. (2011). The NIST definition of cloud computing (No. 800–145). National Institute of Standards and Technology. https://nvlpubs.nist.gov/nistpubs/Legacy/SP/nistspecialpublication800-145.pdf.

NIST Cloud Computing Standards. (2013). NIST Cloud Computing Standards Roadmap (No. 500–291, Version 2). National Institute of Standards and

Technology. https://www.nist.gov/system/files/documents/itl/cloud/NIST_SP-500-291_Version 2_2013_June18_FINAL.pdf.

Noonan, L. (2020, August 6). Capital One fined $80m for data breach. Financial Times. https://www.ft.com/content/a730c6a0-c362-4664-a1ae-5faf84912f20.

Rountree, D., & Castrillo, I. (2013). The Basics of Cloud Computing: Understanding the Fundamentals of Cloud Computing in Theory and Practice (Basics (Syngress)) (1st ed.). Syngress.

Saluja, S., & Sepple, J. (2018). Cloud and Clear — Complete Your Journey to Cloud. Resounding Innovation Awaits. Accenture. https://www.researchgate.net/publication/331742827_How_Cloud_Computing_Is_Transforming_and_Benefiting_Financial_Institutions.

Seals, T. (2020, August 20). AWS Cryptojacking Worm Spreads Through the Cloud. Threatpost. https://threatpost.com/aws-cryptojacking-worm-cloud/158427/.

Schulte, P. (2019). Ai & Quantum Computing For Finance & Insurance: Fortunes and Challenges for China and America (Singapore University of Social Sciences — World Scientific F). WSPC.

Simmon, E. (2018). Evaluation of Cloud Computing Services Based on NIST SP 800–145 (No. 500–322). National Institute of Standards and Technology. https://nvlpubs.nist.gov/nistpubs/SpecialPublications/NIST.SP.500-322.pdf.

1.7 Sample Questions

Question 1

Which of the following describes the characteristics of cloud computing?

(a) Each client possesses its own dedicated cloud resources
(b) Cloud resources can be obtained on an on-demand basis
(c) Cloud capabilities can only be accessed via laptops and workstations

Question 2

Which of the following is false about the public cloud?

(a) The infrastructure is housed at an external service provider (i.e., the cloud provider's premises)
(b) The data stored on the cloud is public information
(c) The connection to the public cloud is through the Internet

Question 3
A cloud service provider is responsible for:

(a) Cloud service management
(b) Security audit of cloud services
(c) Service intermediation

Question 4
Data sovereignty refers to:

(a) The ability of an individual to analyze his/her own data
(b) The ability of an individual to securely possess his/her own data
(c) The ability of an individual to control usage of his/her own data

Question 5
Which of the following is not a benefit of using the cloud in conjunction with artificial intelligence?

(a) Optimizing operations
(b) Building new customer experiences
(c) Ensuring cloud data integrity

Solutions

Question 1

Solution: Option **b** is correct.

According to NIST's definition of cloud computing characteristics, resource pooling optimizes the usage of cloud resources, and cloud capabilities should be accessible over the network through standard mechanisms or protocols used by heterogeneous thin or thick client platforms.

Question 2

Solution: Option **b** is correct.

Whether it's a public, private, hybrid, or community cloud, information stored on the cloud is known only to the owner.

Question 3

Solution: Option **a** is correct.

Referring to the NIST Conceptual Reference Model, a specific auditor performs a security audit, and a cloud broker performs service intermediation.

Question 4

Solution: Option **c** is correct.

Question 5

Solution: Option **c** is correct.

Using the cloud in conjunction with AI enables companies to build new customer experiences, optimize operations, and manage talent through leveraging tools including machine learning, Internet of Things platforms, image recognition, and natural language processing. These capabilities are key drivers in increasing overall profitability, streamlining operations, and retaining talent.

Chapter 2

Fundamentals of Cybersecurity

2.1 Fundamentals of Cybersecurity

2.1.1 *Definition, Framework and Security Objectives*

As enterprises work towards digital transformation, the issue of cybersecurity becomes more prominent. This section describes several standard definitions of the term "cybersecurity" and the cybersecurity framework defined by the National Institute of Standards and Technology (NIST). An enterprise must distinguish the meanings of various security objectives and decide the security objective(s) they wish to achieve. After that, a proper security mechanism can be devised.

Learning Objectives
- Illustrate the elements of the NIST Cybersecurity Framework Core and the references examples to achieve those outcomes.
- Appraise different security objectives, including confidentiality, integrity protection, availability, authentication, and accountability.

Main Takeaways

Main Points
- Cybersecurity concerns the protection of data in electronic form, including data at rest and data in transit.
- The NIST Cybersecurity Framework Core specifies a set of activities to achieve specific cybersecurity outcomes.

- Five main security objectives guide the design and use of cryptographic techniques. They are confidentiality, integrity, availability, authentication, and accountability.

Main Terms
- **Information security:** Concerns protecting the integrity, confidentiality, and accessibility of all forms of information or data.
- **Cybersecurity:** The protection of data in electronic form, including data at rest and data in transit.
- **Data confidentiality:** The aim to shield data from unauthorized parties.
- **Data integrity:** The act of ensuring that data is not tampered with in transit.
- **Availability:** A system's ability to provide continuous and undisrupted services to legitimate users.
- **Data authentication:** The ability to verify the origin of a piece of data.
- **Accountability:** The ability to prevent users from falsely denying that they have sent or authorized a particular data.

(a) Definitions
According to H.R. 4246 "Cyber Security Information Act," cybersecurity is "The vulnerability of any computing system, software program, or critical infrastructure to, or their ability to resist, intentional interference, compromise, or incapacitation through the misuse of, or by unauthorized means of, the Internet, public or private telecommunications systems or other similar conduct that violates Federal, State, or international law, that harms interstate commerce of the United States, or that threatens public health or safety."[1]

According to S. 1901 "Cybersecurity Research and Education Act of 2002"[2]:

> Cybersecurity: information assurance, including scientific, technical, management, or any other relevant disciplines required to ensure computer and network security, including, but not limited to, a discipline related to the following functions:
>
> 1. Secure System and network administration and operations;
> 2. systems security engineering;

---

[1] Adapted from source: https://fas.org/sgp/congress/2000/cybersec.html.
[2] Adapted from source: https://www.congress.gov/bill/107th-congress/senate-bill/1901/text.

3. information assurance systems and product acquisition;
4. cryptography;
5. threat and vulnerability assessment, including risk management;
6. web security;
7. operations of computer emergency response teams;
8. cybersecurity training, education, and management;
9. computer forensics;
10. defensive information operations.

We can further distinguish between information security and cybersecurity according to the definition of Olcott (2019). The phrase "information security" concerns protecting the integrity, confidentiality, and accessibility of all forms of information or data. It concerns protecting the confidentiality of data in soft and hard copy, in data centers, or in cabinets. Examples of information security are locking all files and documents after use and the setting of multifactor authentication for data access on computers. On the other hand, "cyber security" concerns the protection of data in electronic form. This includes data stored on mobile, in computers, on the cloud, or in servers. Examples of ensuring cybersecurity include encryption and setting up firewalls.

(b) Cybersecurity Framework[3]
The Framework Core provides a set of activities to achieve specific cybersecurity outcomes and references examples of guidance to achieve those outcomes. The Core is not a checklist of actions to perform. It presents key cybersecurity outcomes identified by stakeholders to manage cybersecurity risk. The Core comprises four elements: Functions, Categories, Subcategories, and Informative References.

1. **Functions** organize basic cybersecurity activities at their highest level. These Functions are Identify, Protect, Detect, Respond, and Recover. They aid an organization in expressing its cybersecurity risk management by organizing information, enabling risk management decisions, addressing threats, and improving by learning from previous activities. The Functions also align with existing methodologies for incident management and help show the impact of investments in cybersecurity.

---

[3]Adapted from source: https://nvlpubs.nist.gov/nistpubs/CSWP/NIST.CSWP.04162018.pdf.

For example, investments in planning and exercises support timely response and recovery actions, resulting in reduced impact on service delivery.

2. **Categories** are the subdivisions of a Function into groups of cybersecurity outcomes closely tied to programmatic needs and particular activities. Examples of Categories include "Asset Management," "Identity Management and Access Control," and "Detection Processes."

3. **Subcategories** further divide a Category into specific outcomes of technical and/or management activities. They provide a set of results that, while not exhaustive, help support the achievement of the outcomes in each Category. Examples of Subcategories include "External information systems are cataloged," "Data-at-rest is protected," and "Notifications from detection systems are investigated."

4. **Informative References** are specific sections of standards, guidelines, and practices common among critical infrastructure sectors that illustrate a method to achieve the outcomes associated with each Subcategory.

The Informative References presented in the Framework Core are illustrative and not exhaustive. They are based upon cross-sector guidance, most frequently referenced during the Framework development process.

- **Identify:** Develop an organizational understanding to manage cybersecurity risk to systems, people, assets, data, and capabilities. The activities in the Identify Function are foundational for effective use of the Framework. Understanding the business context, the resources that support critical functions and the related cybersecurity risks enables an organization to focus and prioritize its efforts, consistent with its risk management strategy and business needs. Examples of outcome Categories within this Function include Asset Management, Business Environment, Governance, Risk Assessment, and Risk Management Strategy.

- **Protect:** Develop and implement appropriate safeguards to ensure the delivery of critical services. The Protect Function supports the ability to limit or contain the impact of a potential cybersecurity event. Examples of outcome Categories within this Function include Identity Management and Access Control, Awareness and Training, Data Security, Information Protection Processes and Procedures, Maintenance, and Protective Technology.

- **Detect:** Develop and implement appropriate activities to identify the occurrence of a cybersecurity event. The Detect Function enables the timely discovery of cybersecurity events. Examples of outcome Categories within this Function include Anomalies and Events, Security Continuous Monitoring, and Detection Processes.
- **Respond:** Develop and implement appropriate activities to take action regarding a detected cybersecurity incident. The Respond Function supports the ability to contain the impact of a potential cybersecurity incident. Examples of outcome Categories within this Function include Response Planning Communications; Analysis, Mitigation, and Improvements.
- **Recover:** Develop and implement appropriate activities to maintain plans for resilience and to restore any capabilities or services that were impaired due to a cybersecurity incident. The Recover Function supports timely recovery to normal operations to reduce a cybersecurity incident. Examples of outcome Categories within this Function include Recovery Planning, Improvements, and Communications.

(c) Security Objectives

The five objectives of confidentiality, integrity, availability, authentication, and accountability guide the design and use of cryptographic techniques.

Confidentiality may refer to data confidentiality or user confidentiality. Data confidentiality aims to shield data from unauthorized parties. This is similar to the original objective of classical cryptography and is achieved through data encryption. User confidentiality is concerned with untraceability — the ability to conceal data paths — and unlinkability — to hide the connection between multiple pieces of data that may be original from the same user.

Data integrity is concerned with ensuring that data is not tampered with in transit. Integrity can be achieved using the hash function, message authentication codes, or digital signature. Integrity is closely associated with authentication and accountability — two security objectives have evolved above and beyond the traditional "CIA triad."

Availability as a security objective is associated with a system's ability to provide continuous and undisrupted services to legitimate users. It is closely associated with a malicious activity known as a Denial-of-Service (DoS) attack or Distributed DoS (DDoS) attack.

Authentication may refer to data or user authentication. Data authentication aims to verify that the origin of a piece of data is what it claims to be. Provision of data authentication can be achieved using a digital signature. User authentication aims to verify that a user is who they claim to be, and this is commonly enforced by asking users to provide authentication factors to a login system based on what the user knows (e.g., username/password), what the user has (e.g., access card), who is the user (e.g., fingerprint).

Accountability aims to prevent users from falsely denying that they have sent particular data. It is analogous to the concept of non-repudiation and can be provided by creating a digital signature on the piece of data. Generally, the provision of accountability and data authentication implicitly ensures data integrity.

2.2 Cryptography

2.2.1 *Understanding Cryptography*

Cryptographic techniques are a set of mathematical algorithms used to achieve security objectives. Each cryptographic technique can be used to achieve one or more security objectives. For instance, encryption achieves only data confidentiality and no others, whereas a digital signature achieves data integrity protection, data authentication, and accountability. This section provides a brief overview of cryptography and the type of data that should be protected.

Learning Objectives
- Describe modern cryptography.
- Distinguish different types of data that should be protected.

Main Takeaways

Main Points
- Modern cryptography is a science and a mathematical discipline.
- Existing modern cryptographic algorithms are not unconditionally secure — they can be broken given enough time and computing power.
- The main types of data include data at rest and data in transit; they exhibit different characteristics and are present under different adversarial environment.

Main Terms
- **Classical cryptography:** The art of writing or solving codes.
- **Modern cryptography:** A science and a mathematical discipline that relies on rigorous proofs of security.
- **Computationally secure:** The state of existing cryptographic schemes that does not assume them to be unconditionally secure and unbreakable.
- **Data at rest:** Data in storage that are not moving from devices to devices.
- **Data in transit:** Data that actively moves from one location to another across the network.

(a) Cryptography

If we look up cryptography in the dictionary, we will likely find a definition is "the art of writing or solving codes." This definition accurately describes the historical evolution of classical cryptography up until the 1970s and 1980s. Classical cryptography has been around for millennia — the earliest known uses of codes have been recorded as far back as ancient Egypt. What made classical cryptography an art was that there was little theory behind the construction or decryption of codes and no systematic way of thinking about the requirements a secure code had to satisfy. Its purpose was primarily to achieve secrecy, and because of the great expense involved, its use was limited to governments and military organizations. Perhaps the most famous example is the Enigma machine invented by the Germans in the early 20th century and used by Nazi Germany to encrypt military communications during World War II.

The field of cryptography has evolved a lot since then. Unlike classical cryptography, modern cryptography is an art and a science and a mathematical discipline. Instead of ill-defined, intuitive notions of complexity or cleverness, the field now relies on rigorous proofs of security. Cryptographic techniques cannot be proven unconditionally secure, as that would require breakthroughs in the analysis of computational complexity that are not yet within our reach.

We can think of modern cryptography as a suite of algorithms based on the intractability of complex problems, which are problems that cannot be solved in a "reasonable amount of time." This phrase is deliberately vague, as the speed of computing and, therefore, the requirements of what we consider to be a code that is secure enough are ever-changing.

Compared to classical cryptography, modern cryptography is also much more pervasive. Its use now extends beyond secret communication to the protection of the user, data at rest (in storage), and data in transit (sent over a network), and it is integral to nearly all computer systems. In one form or another, most of us are users of cryptography daily, whether we are sending an e-mail or paying for a ride with our transportation card.

Refining our earlier statement, we say that a cryptographic scheme is computationally secure if no efficient attacker can break it in a reasonable amount of time. An "efficient attacker" can be understood as an attacker with a reasonable amount of computing power. In contrast, "a reasonable amount of time" can be understood as a time frame during which the ability to solve a problem has ceased to be useful or interesting. Cryptographic techniques that meet these conditions have a negligible probability of being broken.

(1) Data at rest

Data at rest refers to data stored on a hard drive, flash drive, or server and are not moving from devices to devices. Data at rest may be considered less vulnerable than data in transit as the hardware and network that these data reside in are protected by security mechanisms. However, attackers often find data at rest a more valuable target than data in transit.

(2) Data in transit

Data in transit refers to data that actively moves from one location to another across either a public network (e.g., the Internet) or a private network. As data is transmitted through the network, it is exposed to eavesdropping, modification, deletion, or even malicious insertion.

There are multiple approaches to protecting data at rest and data in transit. Encryption is a popular tool for securing both types of data. Common encryption methods for data at rest include cryptographic techniques such as DES and AES standards. For data in transit, either end-to-end encryption is used, or encrypted connections such as the SSL and TLS protocols are used.

Apart from ensuring that the confidentiality of data is not compromised, it is also essential to ensure that data integrity and authentication are preserved. Existing encrypted connection protocols are designed such that authenticated encryption is provided.

Besides using cryptography to secure the data, additional security mechanisms should also be in place. Network security solutions like firewalls, intrusion detection, and antivirus secure the networks against malware attacks or intrusions. Proper access control mechanisms that create policies for classifying user roles and data sensitivity ensure adequate data protection against unauthorized access.

"While data in transit and data at rest may have slightly different risk profiles, the inherent risk hinges primarily on the sensitivity and value of your data; attackers will attempt to gain access to valuable data whether it's in motion, at rest, or actively in use, depending on which state is easiest to breach. That's why a proactive approach including classifying and categorizing data coupled with content, user, and context-aware security protocols are the safest and most effective way to protect your most sensitive data in every state."[4]

2.3 Cryptocurrency and Cybersecurity

2.3.1 *Cryptocurrency and Cybersecurity*

The cryptocurrency and blockchain area is closely related and may require a rethink of our existing cybersecurity settings. Cryptocurrency and blockchain brought forward the idea of a wallet. Wallet technologies (based on public key infrastructure) enable users to have sole control of their funds without relying on a trusted third party (TTP). However, a cryptocurrency exchange in a "centralized" setting exposes them to some cybersecurity risks. Also, apart from providing a secure and authenticated public ledger, blockchain is considered a technique to boost cybersecurity. This section will discuss the relationship between cryptocurrency, blockchain, and cybersecurity.

Learning Objectives
- Appraise the security of cryptocurrency wallet and cryptocurrency exchanges.
- Examine the usage of blockchain to boost cybersecurity.

Main Takeaways

Main Points
- Existing wallet standards define several types of a cryptocurrency wallet and how a user's private keys are generated.
- There are two types of wallets, namely hot and cold wallets; each type of wallet differs in terms of security and usability.

---

[4]Lord, N. (2019, July 15). Data Protection: Data In transit vs. Data At Rest. Digital Guardian. https://digitalguardian.com/blog/data-protection-data-in-transit-vs-data-at-rest.

- Cryptocurrency exchanges must secure their private keys as well as their users' KYC information.
- Blockchain's data structure and decentralized infrastructure could potentially serve as new ways to boost cybersecurity.

Main Terms
- **Wallet:** A piece of software application or hardware that store a user's private key.
- **Mnemonic code words:** A list of words (in English or another language) that can be used to recover a user's master private key when presented in a correct order.
- **Air-gapped system:** A computing device that is completely cut-off from any form of connectivity.

(a) Cryptocurrency and Cybersecurity
(1) Cryptocurrency storage

In the decentralized world of cryptocurrencies, the onus for protection is often placed on the cryptocurrency holder. Each holder of a cryptocurrency wallet possesses a private key that unlocks and allows the holder to spend cryptocurrencies in that specific wallet. Generally, there are two types of wallets: A JBOK (Just a Bunch of Keys) wallet, also called a non-deterministic wallet, and a deterministic wallet.

A non-deterministic wallet generates keys independently, each time using a different random number. A deterministic wallet derives all the private keys from a single master private key known as the seed. The prime difference between the two is that a non-deterministic wallet requires its holder to keep a list of independent keys. In contrast, a deterministic wallet allows its holder to regenerate the set of keys as long as the seed is available. To preserve user privacy, it is recommended to use a new key for every transaction so that cryptocurrency transactions are not traceable.

Mnemonic codewords are a list of words (in English or another language) that can be used to recover a lost seed when taken in the correct order. As cryptocurrency wallet technology matures, industry standards have emerged to make wallets interoperable, useable, and secure. For instance, the generation of mnemonic codewords is based on the BIP-39 standard. The method of generating a list of keys from a seed is specified in BIP-32 as the Hierarchical Deterministic (HD) wallet. BIP-44 defines a multicurrency multi-account structure for HD wallets.

There are two basic forms of cryptocurrency storage: hot wallet and cold wallet. Hot wallets are connected to the Internet and are generally perceived to be more convenient to use. However, they face higher risks as it is exposed to online threats such as malware and viruses. Cold wallets are offline wallets. They are usually in the form of physical devices that require the holder to plug into a computing device before being able to unlock and spend the cryptocurrencies.

Cryptocurrency exchanges use cold storage of private keys for their daily trades. Private keys are kept in devices that are cut off from any form of connectivity. Such devices are also called air-gapped systems. For reserves designated to cover anticipated withdrawals in a day, only the corresponding private keys are kept on the online server while the rest are secured in cold storage. A master public key is used to create a watch-only wallet and provide addresses for receiving cryptocurrencies.

However, cold storage does not fully guarantee the security of cryptocurrencies when its users lack security awareness and are negligent. In published research in 2020, academics from an Israeli university detailed a technique to convert a RAM card on an air-gapped computer into an impromptu wireless emitter. The air-gapped computer can subsequently transmit sensitive data at speeds of up to 100 bytes per second to devices up to several meters away (Cimpanu, 2020).

The infamous Mt. Gox hack resulted in $460 million stolen in the form of bitcoin and realized that the fully decentralized, digital nature of cryptocurrency attracts an increased risk of attack. The $28 million hack on crypto exchange Bitpoint in July of 2019 affected half of its customer base through a compromise in Bitpoint's hot wallets.

Interestingly, the funds (of more than $760 million worth of bitcoin) stolen in the Bitfinex hack in 2016 were closely monitored by the cryptocurrency community. Using data from blockchain tracking services, the stolen funds were moved in tens of transactions ranging from 1 to as much as 1,200 bitcoin at a time. Cryptocurrency exchanges intervened to blacklist the attackers' addresses to prevent them from converting the stolen bitcoins into fiat or altcoin.

This raises the concern about the regulations of cryptocurrency exchanges. A sound regulation will subject cryptocurrency exchanges to enforce comprehensive controls on transaction reporting, suspicious activity monitoring, Anti-Money Laundering (AML) requirements, and Know-Your-Customer (KYC) regulations.

Another concern with hacked cryptocurrency exchanges is the leakage of personal data due to leaks of KYC information. While the loss of private keys results in the loss of funds, the leakage of KYC information is deemed more dangerous and may subject the cryptocurrency exchange to legal implications. In 2019, Binance openly pointed fingers at its KYC vendor after customer information was leaked. These examples, along with the recent attack on the crypto tax reporting service, show that personal data safety measures must keep up with the implemented safety measures for the custody of assets (Viglione, 2020).

(2) Blockchain for cybersecurity
There are also discussions on how blockchain can be used to boost cybersecurity. Some of the aspects identified are:

- Data integrity protection — The data structure on a blockchain is secured using a hash chain and/or Merkle Hash Tree. These structures create a cryptographic link between data and facilitate data existence and integrity verification. For instance, the "chain of blocks" concept in many blockchain designs creates an immutable record of timestamped data as long as the majority of the miners are honest. It is difficult for an attacker to change, add, remove, or reorder the data without significant economic loss. The use of Merkle Hash Tree to secure transactions within a block (such as in Bitcoin) or to register timestamped data (such as in Diem) provides a simple manner to validate a transaction; any changes to data in the tree's leaf nodes would cause an error to propagate to the root and will be detected.
- Decentralized infrastructure — Blockchain is a form of distributed ledger where transactions are recorded and maintained by a large network of globally distributed nodes. As such, blockchain is decentralized in nature; a single node's failure will not cause the system to come to a standstill. Such an architecture with no central point of control helps to mitigate against a single point of failure in the network, which addresses the security objective of "availability."

Forbes suggests promising use cases of blockchain in cybersecurity could include decentralized storage solutions, IoT security, safer DNS, and private messaging.

DARPA is also exploring blockchain applications in areas related to cybersecurity, such as economics-driven security models and how centralization may impact the cybersecurity posture of permissionless distributed consensus protocols.

2.3.2 *Definition of Zero Trust vs. Trustless*

Our existing societal structure, including security framework, often relies on a TTP. A TTP with a good reputation saves users from doing much research or bearing other costs associated with making subjective judgments. In other words, the user's mental transaction cost is low. However, the assumption of a TTP often results in high costs and becomes a risk in a security protocol. As such, it is important to plug the security hole by minimizing the role of the TTP.

Learning Objectives
- Differentiate the concepts of "zero-trust" and "trustless".

Main Takeaways

Main Points
- The basic idea of zero trust systems is to protect a core of assets (data, services, whatever) with a digital perimeter (or perimeters) that checks every operation.
- Trustless, as demonstrated in Satoshi Nakamoto's way, is to protect only the ledger through cryptography and a consensus mechanism.
- The TTP minimizing protocols essentially aim to distribute trust.

Main Terms
- **Trusted third party (TTP):** An entity that facilitates interactions between two parties who both trust the third party.
- **Zero trust system:** A system that protects a core of assets by requiring user authentication and authorization.
- **Trustless system:** (in Bitcoin context) A system that protects only the ledger and does not assume inherent trust in the users.

(a) Zero-trust versus Trustless
The basic idea of zero trust systems is to protect a core of assets (data, services) with a digital perimeter (or perimeters) that checks every operation. In particular, every user must authenticate their identity and authorization to the perimeter. This translates to an extremely "centralized" approach, with the "centralized" component being the authorization mechanism.

On the other hand, as demonstrated in Satoshi Nakamoto's way, Trustless is to protect only the ledger. Such protection is achieved through cryptography and a consensus mechanism. All the ledger users are equally trusted, and all operations are transparent. The validity of operations is then determined by the majority of the user population. Hence, users, or peers, must establish trust among themselves. It is necessary for a peer in the network to authenticate the other party it is communicating with.

It is then interesting to notice that a zero-trust system does not trust any users, whereas a trustless system trusts the users and nothing else.[5]

Expanding on the issue of trust, Nick Szabo, in his infamous paper, noted that the introduction of a "TTP" controlled by a third party constitutes the introduction of a security hole into the design of any security protocol. One of the most well-known requirements of a TTP is the introduction of a certificate authority (CA) in public-key cryptography. A CA is given the responsibility to vouch for the identity of participants, and it has proved to be the most expensive component of the centralized public key infrastructure.

Naturally, TTPs play a very important role in our day-to-day activities for many years. This is attributed to several reasons. Firstly, it is far easier to design protocols that rely on TTPs than those that do not, and it is also tempting to become a TTP, particularly a successful one. Using a TTP reduces the initial design cost. A TTP with a good reputation will free the users from doing much research or bearing other costs associated with making judgments on whether to trust a specific party. In a similar nature, companies like Visa, Dun and Bradstreet, and Underwriter's Laboratories connect untrusting strangers into a common trust network, and our economy benefited from "trusting" these companies.

However, as proven in the public key infrastructure (using CAs) and the Internet (the DNS), the largest long-term cost of the systems is the cost of implementing the TTPs, which occurs in the implementation of costly physical security techniques, auditing, compliance, and securing business relationships.

Nick Szabo identified several TTP minimizing protocols that show promises in improving trust:

- Chaum mixes;
- multiparty private computations;
- byzantine resilient replicated databases.

---

[5]Adapted from source: https://robertmcgrath.wordpress.com/2020/10/15/zero-trust-versus-trustless/.

It is straightforward to notice that the phrase "TTP" could be easily replaced with "vulnerable to a third party," which is a security hole. As concluded by Szabo, "The best 'TTP' of all is one that does not exist, but the necessity for which has been eliminated by the protocol design, or which has been automated and distributed amongst the parties to a protocol."

2.3.3 *Anonymity and Privacy*

The ability to maintain anonymity and privacy on the open network is desirable for businesses and individuals. This section breaks down the notion of anonymity and user privacy into "untraceability" and "unlinkability" and illustrates them using a cryptocurrency transaction. It introduces zero-knowledge proofs (ZKP) as ZKP is widely perceived as an advanced and promising technology in realizing complete user privacy.

Learning Objectives
- Examine the notion of anonymity and user privacy in a blockchain system.
- Describe zero-knowledge proof and its properties.
- Appraise the concept of surveillance capitalism and assess the future development of user privacy and self-sovereignty.

Main Takeaways

Main Points
- The notion of user privacy includes untraceability and unlinkability.
- Zero-knowledge proof allows one to prove knowledge of a statement without revealing any information about that statement.
- The concern on user data collected by giant tech companies gives rise to the issue of surveillance capitalism.

Main Terms
- **Unlinkability:** A condition in which two events occurring under the observation of an attacker should appear unrelated to the observer.
- **Untraceability:** The ability to conceal the details of a transaction so that an observer cannot follow the trail.
- **zk-SNARKs:** A variant of zero-knowledge proof that provides user anonymity and transaction untraceability, and unlinkability in a more efficient manner.

(a) Anonymity and Privacy

User privacy in a blockchain rests on the untraceability and unlinkability of transactions. Untraceability means we should be able to conceal the details of a transaction so that an observer cannot follow the trail. Unlinkability, in general, means that two events occurring under the observation of an attacker should appear unrelated to the observer. Earlier, we said that blockchain technology is pseudonymous instead of anonymous. There is no identifying information linked to the wallet addresses or transactions by simply observing the blockchain. However, we can trace the source of every transaction, and therefore, able to obtain a graphical visualization of transaction paths. It is possible to link an identity to a wallet address through prior knowledge or social engineering. We, therefore, need security schemes in place to protect user privacy.

Furthermore, suppose an attacker observes the following transaction traces (Figure 2.1) at time *t*.

At time *t* + 1, a new transaction, as shown in Figure 2.2, occurs.

Such an attack is similar to a dusting attack, where an attacker sends users tiny amounts of cryptocurrencies to their wallets. After that, the attacker analyzes these wallet addresses to identify which ones belong to the same user. An observer can deduce that addresses 2, 3, and 4 belong to the same user with a certain probability.

Understanding user privacy as a form of confidentiality might lead us to considering encryption as a solution. The two main types of data in a Bitcoin transaction are the transaction amount and the addresses of the sender and receiver. Immediately, some problems are evident with encrypting this information. Encryption alone does not allow blockchain to function properly or securely as a decentralized P2P payment system,

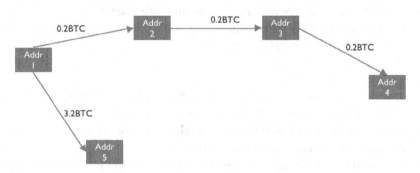

Figure 2.1:   Trace of transactions that can be obtained from a public blockchain.

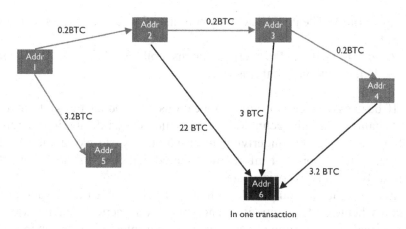

Figure 2.2: A new transaction that takes user's inputs from three different addresses may reveal user's private information.

and encryption alone does not ensure untraceability and unlinkability. For example, encrypting transaction data or wallet addresses does not provide untraceability if the same wallet is reused. Furthermore, encrypting transaction data and wallet addresses without providing additional information will impede miners in the effort of validating transactions (e.g., check for double-spending and proof of ownership).

Blockchain developers have managed to develop algorithms that ensure user privacy while addressing these concerns. Among the methods used include: CoinJoin, stealth addresses, ring signature, and Ring Confidential Transaction (RingCT) in Monero and ZKP.

(b) Zero-knowledge Solutions

Typically, when we want to convince someone that we possess knowledge of a secret statement, such as a password, we do so by exchanging the statement with a verifying authority or user who also possesses knowledge of it. But what if the user verifying the information does not — and should not, for privacy — possess knowledge of the secret statement itself? ZKP allow us to prove to a verifier that a secret statement we hold is true without revealing any information about that statement to the verifier. Such proofs have three properties:

1. **Completeness:** If the prover is honest, the prover will eventually convince the verifier.

2. **Soundness:** The prover can only convince the verifier if the statement is true.
3. **Zero-knowledge:** The verifier learns nothing about the statement aside from the fact that it is true.

If businesses were to build applications or conduct transactions on blockchains using this technology, they could verify information validity without revealing the underlying information. By shrinking the attack surface, or the amount of information shared, hackers will have a much more difficult time exposing data.

Zcash is the first public blockchain to implement a full privacy protection scheme on transactions. It encrypts all transaction data and uses a scheme called "zero-knowledge succinct non-interactive arguments of knowledge" (zk-SNARKs) to provide user anonymity, transaction untraceability, and unlinkability. The zk-SNARKs scheme is more efficient than the traditional zero-knowledge proof.

A good illustration of ZKP can be found in (Quisquater *et al.,* 1989). The traditional design of a zero-knowledge proof is interactive and requires multiple iterations to be convincing. The non-interactive zk-SNARKs algorithm used in Zcash is more succinct in terms of proof size and efficient in terms of verification time.

(c) Surveillance Capitalism

"Surveillance is the business model of the Internet," said Bruce Schneier at a conference in the year 2014 (Schneier, 2014). This is quickly becoming a reality. The concern and awareness on user data privacy elevated in recent years when companies and data brokers' personal data leakage and monetization broke the news. In a publication by Shoshana Zuboff, such a phenomenon known as surveillance capitalism is where giant tech companies obtained their users' data and made a fortune by analyzing and selling it (Zuboff, 2020).

The estimated $200 billion per year data broker industry primarily operates in the shadows. California's Assembly Bill 1202 (AB 1202) defines a "data broker" as a "business that knowingly collects and sells to third parties the personal information of a consumer with whom the business does not have a direct relationship." This inherently means that anyone can buy data from a data broker.

Once personal data is accessed, it can be easily copied, shared, and traded without much cost.

Compared to the information available to data brokers, the data available to tech companies such as Google, Facebook, and Apple are massive. User data are transformed into user behavioral data and offer a complete profile on each of their users. In 2017, a journalist asked the dating app Tinder to access her data and was surprised to receive 800 pages containing information on everything from her preferences in men to her tastes in music (Fong, 2020).

Information about a user can be obtained as easily as a data access request. As pointed out by Zuboff, "Once we searched Google, but now Google searches us. Once we thought of digital services as free, but now surveillance capitalists think of us as free." (Naughton, 2019).

The wealth of data collection underpinning surveillance capitalism fundamentally undermines security as it enables much more effective targeting and attacks.

A recent set of opinions pointed to an area to look into for answers: blockchain. With its combination of decentralization, encryption, and public key infrastructure, blockchain technology may be a solution to the self-sovereignty of data, eliminations of intermediaries, and a single point of failure. Cryptocurrency wallet technologies that allow users to have sole control of their funds could be extended in concept to allow individuals to choose what data to share and with whom.

The issue with surveillance capitalism could be an opportunity for pro-privacy developers. As pointed out by CoinDesk's Michael J. Casey, "Those building zero-knowledge-proof systems and other privacy-protection layers can talk to a vision of decentralized protocols that both empower individuals to control their data and prevent the public ledger from becoming a new behavior extraction tool. That's one potential answer to surveillance capitalism" (Casey, 2019).

References/Further Readings

Casey, M. J. (2019, February 4). The Crypto-Surveillance Capitalism Connection. CoinDesk. https://www.coindesk.com/blockchain-crypto-surveillance-capitalism-shoshana-zuboff.

Cimpanu, C. (2020, December 15). Academics turn RAM into Wi-Fi cards to steal data from air-gapped systems. ZDNet. https://www.zdnet.com/article/academics-turn-ram-into-wifi-cards-to-steal-data-from-air-gapped-systems/.

Davis, T. M. (2000, April 12). Introduction of the Cyber Security Information Act of 2000. https://fas.org/sgp/congress/2000/cybersec.html.

Fong, M. (2020, November 4). The Lurking Security Risks of Surveillance Capitalism. 2020–11-05 | Security Magazine. https://www.securitymagazine.com/articles/93835-the-lurking-security-risks-of-surveillance-capitalism.

Lord, N. (2019, July 15). Data Protection: Data in Transit vs. Data at Rest. Digital Guardian. https://digitalguardian.com/blog/data-protection-data-in-transit-vs-data-at-rest.

Lo, S. W., Wang, Y., & Lee, D. K. C. (2021). Blockchain and Smart Contracts: Design Thinking and Programming for Fintech (Singapore University of Social Sciences — World Scientific Future Economy Series). World Scientific Pub Co Inc.

Olcott, J. (2019, September 15). Cybersecurity vs. Information Security: Is there a Difference? Retrieved from www.bitsight.com: https://www.bitsight.com/blog/cybersecurity-vs-information-security.

McGrath, R. (2020, October 12). "Zero Trust" versus "Trustless"? Robert McGrath's Blog. https://robertmcgrath.wordpress.com/2020/10/15/zero-trust-versus-trustless/.

Naughton, J. (2019, January 20). "The Goal is to Automate Us": Welcome to the Age of Surveillance Capitalism. The Guardian. https://www.theguardian.com/technology/2019/jan/20/shoshana-zuboff-age-of-surveillance-capitalism-google-facebook.

NIST. (2018, April). Framework for Improving Critical Infrastructure Cybersecurity (1.1). National Institute of Standards and Technology. https://nvlpubs.nist.gov/nistpubs/CSWP/NIST.CSWP.04162018.pdf.

Quisquater, J.-J., Quisquater, M., Quisquater, M., Quisquater, M., Guillou, L., Guillou, M., ... Guillou, S. (1989). How to Explain Zero-Knowledge Protocols to Your Children. Advances in Cryptology — CRYPTO' 89.

Schneier, B. (2014). News: Surveillance is the Business Model of the Internet: Bruce Schneier — Schneier on Security. Schneier on Security. https://www.schneier.com/news/archives/2014/04/surveillance_is_the.html.

Szabo, N. (2001). Trusted Third Parties are Security Holes | Satoshi Nakamoto Institute. Satoshi Nakamoto Institute. https://nakamotoinstitute.org/trusted-third-parties/.

Viglione, R. (2020, October 6). Prioritizing security on cryptocurrency platforms. Security Infowatch.Com. https://www.securityinfowatch.com/cybersecurity/article/21157330/prioritizing-security-on-cryptocurrency-platforms.

Zuboff, S. (2020). The Age of Surveillance Capitalism: The Fight for a Human Future at the New Frontier of Power (Illustrated ed.). PublicAffairs.

2.4 Sample Questions

Question 1
Which of the following is not an element of the NIST Cybersecurity Framework Core?

(a) Functions
(b) Categories
(c) Classes

Question 2
Data authentication refers to:

(a) Ability to verify that the origin of a piece of data is what it claims to be
(b) Ability to verify that the sender of a piece of data is who he/she says he/she is
(c) Ability to verify the data trail

Question 3
Which of the following has a higher security risk?

(a) Data at rest
(b) Data in transit
(c) Both have the same security risk

Question 4
The reason that blockchain can be used to boost cybersecurity include:

(a) The hash chain structure in the blockchain
(b) The use of Merkle Hash Tree to validate the transaction
(c) Both of the above

Question 5
Which of the following is false?

(a) Bitcoin transactions are traceable
(b) Bitcoin users are identifiable
(c) Bitcoin addresses can be linked

Solutions

Question 1

Solution: Option **c** is correct.

The elements include Functions, Categories, Subcategories, and Informative References.

Question 2

Solution: Option **a** is correct.

Option b refers to user authentication.

Question 3

Solution: Option **b** is correct.

Data in transit has a higher security risk because it is sent from devices to devices through an open, insecure network. Hence, more protection, including encryption, authentication, and integrity verifications, are needed.

Question 4

Solution: Option **c** is correct.

Question 5

Solution: Option **b** is correct.

Bitcoin users are anonymous, hiding behind wallet addresses. However, all bitcoin transactions can be traced due to the public nature of the block-chain; with some social engineering or prior knowledge, it is possible to link two apparently unrelated bitcoin addresses to the same user.

Chapter 3

Quantum Computing

3.1 Introduction to Quantum Computing

The difference between quantum computers (QCs) and our existing computing devices (i.e., digital computers) is how information is represented. This section reviews the fundamentals of quantum computing and how data is represented on a QC.

Learning Objectives
- Illustrate the fundamental physics of quantum computing and how it works.
- Describe the applications of quantum computing in various industries.

Main Takeaways

Main Points
- The computational advantage of QCs is derived from the idea that quantum computer (QC) bits (or qubit) can represent information not only as 0's or 1's but as a superposition of both 0 or 1.
- A qubit is a physical system that serves as the most basic memory block for a QC. They are the quantum equivalent of classical bits (transistors) used in today's computers and smartphones.
- QCs would be able to engage our current computational needs with more speed and accuracy.

Main Terms
- **Superposition:** The idea that subatomic particles like electrons can exist at different places at once.
- **Entanglement:** The idea that subatomic particles like electrons appear to affect one another across seemingly empty space.
- **Qubit:** The most basic memory block for a QC.

3.1.1 *Introduction*

The development of the computer starting in the 1930s has allowed us to create economic, social, and technological models for all walks of life. These computers are based on a binary system. This means that information is represented as a string of 0's or 1's where each character MUST **unambiguously** be a binary choice of 0 or 1. To represent this information, computers must have a corresponding physical system. Imagine this system as a series of switches with one direction representing a 1 and the other direction as a 0. Today, billions of these switches exist on the microprocessors in computers.

While information is stored as strings of 0's and 1's, these strings are processed, evaluated, and calculated through logic gates. These are made up of connected transistors. Logic gates are the fundamental building blocks toward the large computations we ask of our computers. When chained together hundreds of millions of times, they build up the capacity to perform advanced algorithms.

3.1.2 *How Quantum Computing Works*

Quantum computing is perhaps the most expensive innovative technology and the most difficult to understand because it has been on the Gartner Hype Cycle up-slope (Figures 3.1 and 3.2) for more than 10 years. Since 2005, Quantum computing has been mentioned as an emerging technology, and in 2017, it is still considered emerging. The foundation of quantum computing is the understanding that theoretical computing methods cannot be separated from the physics that governs instruments of computing. Specifically, the theory of quantum mechanics presents a new paradigm for computer science that drastically alters our understanding of information processing and what we have long assumed to be the upper limits of computation. If quantum mechanics rules nature, we should simulate it by creating quantum computers (QCs).

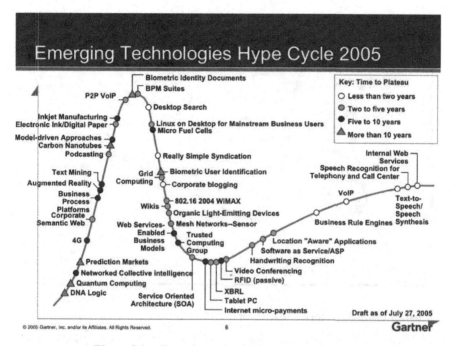

Figure 3.1: Emerging technologies Hype Cycle 2005.

Long before computers were miniaturized into the MacBooks and PCs that flood commercial use today, they were a jumbled mess of wire, tubing, and metal that weighed tons and occupied large rooms. They began as calculators designed for specific tasks. These computers, called analog computers, vary from tools as rudimentary as abacuses to devices with a more remarkable resemblance to modern computers. They could calculate the range, trajectory, and deflection data of gunfire and, for example, automated temperature and pressure flow in factories and airplanes.

The fundamental difference between an analog computer and a digital one is how information is processed (Figure 3.3). Analog computers represent information using a physical model that mimics the problem it is meant to solve. Because the problem is hardwired into the design of the machine, analog computers are limited to single tasks. On the other hand, digital computers represent quantities and information symbolically. Because that symbolic nature is flexible, it can constantly be restructured for different problems. The difference between an abacus, which represents numbers with beads and slides, and the calculator application on a smartphone, crunches numbers as binary values sent through a processing chip.

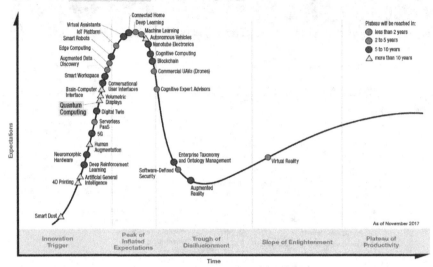

Figure 3.2: Gartner Hype Cycle for emerging technologies.

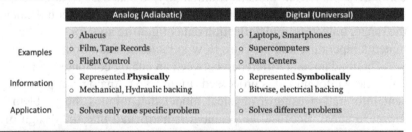

Figure 3.3: Classical analogy.

It is important to note that digital computers were not immediately superior to their analog counterparts. Indeed, digital computers are the standard today and are inherently designed to have far more potential than the many restrictions that come with analog computers. However, until that potential was fully reached, analog computers were considered a competing alternative to digital computers in many fields, especially industrial process control. Before digital computers were advanced enough to outpace analog, the frontier of technology was based on digital-analog hybrid systems like those implemented in the NASA Apollo and Space Shuttle programs. Both technologies were constantly in a race for improvement. It was not until the 1980s when digital revolution ignited the discovery and subsequent mass production of silicon transistors and microprocessors. This process, from pure analog to pure digital, took 25 years.

Today, the journey to develop the first functional QC mimics a similar evolutionary narrative. The analog equivalent of QCs is a paradigm known as Adiabatic QCs (or AQCs), with research and development lead by a Canadian company D-Wave Systems, and the United States Intelligence Advanced Research Projects Activity (IARPA). On the other end are computers that, as digital computers now, employ logic gates on different qubits to effect computation. These are so named Universal QCs (or UQCs).

3.1.3 *Physics of Quantum Computers*

As advanced as computers have become in the past century, they still depend on binary choices between 0 and 1 to make sense of the chaos around us. Yet as our understanding of the world deepens, we are more conscious of the limitations in this paradigm.

Developments in quantum mechanics are continuing to remind us of the unexplained complexities of our universe. At the core of this expanding branch of physics are the theories of superposition and entanglement. Simply put, this is the idea that subatomic particles like electrons can exist at different places at once (**superposition**) and also appear to affect one another across seemingly empty space (**entanglement**). These phenomena present a unique physical system to analyze and store information at speeds that are faster by a large order of magnitude compared to classical computers. QCs, first imagined in 1980, are now championed as the technology to fulfill this purpose. Figure 3.4 shows the potential of QCs.

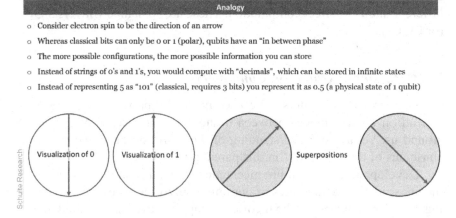

Introduction : Quantum Computers have exponential advantage		
	Classical Computer	**Quantum Computer**
Information	o Represented by binary bits o 0 or 1	o Represented by quantum bits (qubits) o 0 or 1, **superposition** of 0 & 1 (infinite)
Physical Systems	o Silicon based switches o Transistors	o Single Electrons, Diamonds o Must engage in quantum phenomena o **Superposition** and **Entanglement**
Calculations	o Deterministic	o Probabilistic

Quantum Advantage
o Qubits can store more information   o Computational capacity increases exponentially (2^n)   o Qubits can interact with one another (entanglement) and effect computation more efficiently

Schulte Research

Figure 3.4: Introduction: QCs have an exponential advantage.

Qubits : How does it represent information?
Analogy
o Consider electron spin to be the direction of an arrow   o Whereas classical bits can only be 0 or 1 (polar), qubits have an "in between phase"   o The more possible configurations, the more possible information you can store   o Instead of strings of 0's and 1's, you would compute with "decimals", which can be stored in infinite states   o Instead of representing 5 as "101" (classical, requires 3 bits) you represent it as 0.5 (a physical state of 1 qubit)

Visualization of 0   Visualization of 1   Superpositions

Schulte Research

Figure 3.5: Qubits: How does it represent information?

The computational advantage of QCs is derived from the idea that QC bits (or qubits) can represent information not only as 0's or 1's but as a superposition of both 0 or 1—potentially infinite variations of numbers between 0 and 1 (Figure 3.5). So, each quantum-bit is empowered with phenomenal amounts of information. If computers today can already accomplish so much with just two states, imagine the possibilities of a machine that can access millions of superpositions between 0 and 1. QCs will be able to calculate information exponentially quicker and will shatter our current limits of information processing. They are the vehicle to artificial intelligence, risk analysis, optimization, and the litany of technologies we have long imagined. For many new tasks, they are the natural successor to the modern computer that has defined the information age. This has important implications for understanding brain degenerative diseases, energy, agriculture, finance, biochemistry and many other branches of science. Figures 3.6 and 3.7 show the challenges.

3.1.4 *What is a Qubit?*

While the notion of a qubit has already been touched upon, it is important to understand that the fundamental technology of any quantum computation paradigm—whether adiabatic or universal—is this concept of a qubit. A qubit is a physical system that serves as the most basic memory block for a QC. They are the quantum equivalent of classical bits (transistors) used in today's computers and smartphones.

The information in both bits and qubits share a common goal: physically capturing the information that each computer is processing.

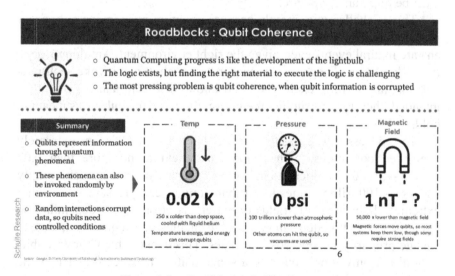

Figure 3.6: Roadblocks: Qubit coherence.

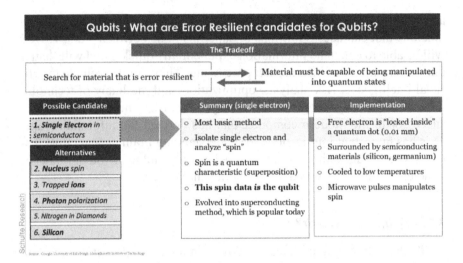

Figure 3.7:   Qubits: What are error resilient candidates for qubits?

As information is changed during computation, the bit or qubit must also be manipulated to represent that change. This is the only way the computer can keep track of what is happening. Because QCs store information in quantum states (superpositions and entanglement states), qubits themselves must physically represent these quantum states, so in turn, qubits must be quantum by nature.

This is challenging, mainly because quantum phenomena only occur in extremely fringe conditions. To worsen the problem, quantum phenomena are natural events even given the right environment. Anything from a ray of light to a change in pressure or temperature can invoke such phenomena, and in turn, excite the qubit into a different quantum state than intended, therefore corrupting the information that the qubit was meant to hold.

To address these issues, researchers place QCs in extremely controlled conditions, with temperatures held at no more than 0.02 Kelvin—20,000 colder than outer space—in nearly an empty vacuum—100 trillion times lower than atmospheric pressure—and either extremely light magnetic fields or extremely strong ones, depending on circumstance. Ultimately, all this trouble enables such a qubit candidate to engage primarily in superposition states. This event, which allows qubits to hold not only 0 or 1 but also a superposition between 0 and 1, is the crux behind quantum computing.

By enabling multiple states—possibly infinite states—these memory blocks can hold much more information than their binary cousins (classical bits) for each qubit. And in turn, QCs can affect computation much faster.

3.1.5 *Applications of Quantum Computing*

(a) Biochemistry—Drug Discovery

The implications of understanding how molecules interact with one another—and their behavior with the environment—have the power to unlock an understanding of a new generation of medicine. Proteins, for example, can perform their role in biological processes through their shape. These shapes, in turn, are governed by the interactions between different parts of their amino acid chain. They fold over on themselves to form three-dimensional structures. This enables them to perform some duties such as carrying isotopes around cells, blocking harmful infections, etc. The destructive side of this "folding" leads to malfunctioning proteins. This creates conditions and diseases ranging from general allergies to Alzheimer's and Mad-Cow (Figure 3.8).

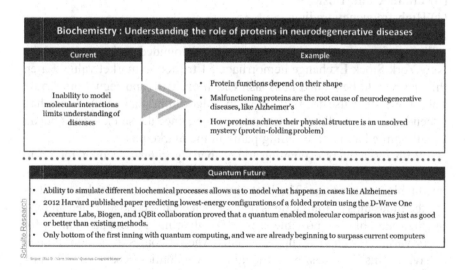

Figure 3.8: Biochemistry: Understanding the role of proteins in neurodegenerative diseases.

While the chemical components of proteins are well known, how they interact with one another and how they achieve their physical structure is poorly understood. Having access to a computer that can simulate the minute interactions within proteins that may cause these diseases would inform a generation of medical researchers and enable a revolution in drug discovery and patient treatment. Researchers are now proving just that. In 2012, Harvard Professor Alan Aspuru-Guzik published a paper predicting the lowest-energy configurations of folded proteins using the D-Wave One computers.

On the corporate side, Accenture Labs' researchers collaborated with Biogen, the third-largest biotechnology company, and 1QBit to prove that a quantum-enabled molecular comparison method was just as good as or better than existing methods. (Molecular comparison is one of the first steps in developing a new drug). Their quantum process provided more contextual information about shared traits between compared molecules and the traditional method, which only infers such trait matches. Furthermore, it enabled researchers to see precisely how, where, and why molecule bonds matched, offering hope for more expedited drug discovery, trials, and effectiveness.

(b) Finance and Business
(1) High-frequency trading

In the meager 36 minutes between 2:32 and 3:08 pm on May 6, 2010, millions of people around the globe were confounded as they watched the New York Stock Exchange hemorrhage $1 trillion in market value. Later, this day would be named the Flash Crash of 2010, and regulators would trace the root cause to a spoof in the algorithms that many firms had depended on for trading—a dependency that, once the stock market began to fall, ignited a massive selling panic in the marketplace.

With researchers estimating today that algorithms account for up to 70% of the high-frequency trading on Wall Street, algorithms have become invaluable commodities. The best algorithms achieve results by monitoring the thousands of transactions that happen each second and then analyzing their variables for possible profit through arbitrage. But accounting for every variable is challenging, especially when it comes to random human behavior. This is especially challenging in economics because, unlike any other scientific field, economics is unique in its lack of a controlled environment where researchers can run experiments and test hypotheses. As a result, researchers can only grasp models for the future based on what has happened in the past. Attempts to predict the future are governed by probability and many past variables. Dictating this exact pursuit is the class of algorithms known as Monte-Carlo Simulations. Because of their computational weight, it is a field that molds particularly well around the advantages of a QC. The ability to process more variables and draw conclusions from more extensive data sets could provide a more accurate accounting of projected returns, risk assessments, and other factors necessary in evaluating baskets of investments.

The research engaged in this particular study has already proven quantum speedup. In 2018, a team in Toronto presented a quantum algorithm for the Monte Carlo pricing of trading derivatives that demonstrated an $O(\sqrt{N})$ run time instead of the classical $O(N)$ run time. Different teams worldwide investigate and discover new parts of what is now considered "quantum finance" (Figure 3.9).

1QBit recently published two papers. One explored the calculations of optimal arbitrage opportunities using a Quantum Annealer like the D-Wave system. Another analyzed the impact of Brexit on financial markets. Investment firms are in a kind of financial arms race as well. DE Shaw, Renaissance Technologies, Two Sigma, and JP Morgan are adding quantum computing to their quantitative investment arms.

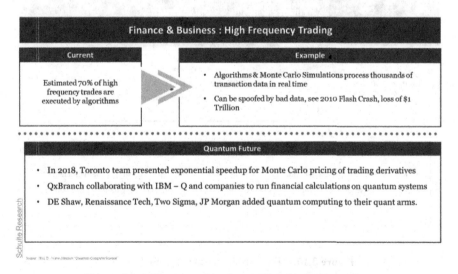

Figure 3.9:   Finance and business: High-frequency trading.

So long as the financial industry depends on computation to aid or even power investments, quantum computing will be one of the most important factors in developing future financial technology and, ultimately, ways to beat the market.

(2) Optimization

While Adiabatic QCs may never be able to run Shor's Algorithm, their ability to compute optimization algorithms has merit. Nearly every industry has to deal with a notion of optimization: (1) what are the best flight routes for optimizing passenger seat miles; (2) what is the most economical sourcing of materials for manufacturing cars; (3) what are the best communication routes to maximize advertising? The list is endless. Virtually anything that depends on a choice that will minimize loss and maximize gain requires optimization. Figure 3.10 shows the possible future.

The implications are tremendous if this technology is industry-scalable, especially for retail companies like Amazon, whose slim profit margins depend entirely on supply chain efficiency. The promise of even a 1% improvement can translate to millions of dollars in gained profit. Researchers examining the role of quantum computing in transportation operations are already making progress. Volkswagen is leading a study on how to tackle

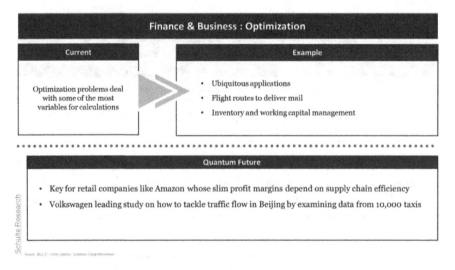

Figure 3.10: Finance and business: Optimization.

traffic flow in Beijing by analyzing data from 10,000 taxis. The sheer amount of movement data, destination points, and alternative routes can lead to what is known as a "combinatorial explosion" for traditional computers and is precisely why QCs are necessary as an industry tool.

(c) Artificial Intelligence

While researchers debate the varying methods for reaching a functional AI system, everyone agrees that artificial intelligence is a technology built on massive amounts of data. Luckily, our society in the information age produces on average 2.5 quintillion bytes of data every single day (this is the number of neurons in every single adult brain in Europe). Massive amounts of information are traversing our countries and seas, and the ability to learn from this data is the burgeoning interest of the information age.

Advances are being made in laboratories worldwide. None are more impressive than the team at Regitti Computing that successfully uses one of its 19-qubit UQC chips to run a clustering algorithm. This method sorts different things into similar groups that operate as a benchmark for unsupervised machine learning.

AI has always been the natural candidate positioned for a quantum revolution, and many experts consider quantum computing to be the ark upon which such a technology could be delivered. So, naturally, research and funding for this growing field of "Quantum Machine Learning" isn't lacking. In 2013, Google, NASA, and the Universities Space Research Association launched the Quantum Artificial Intelligence Lab to explore the D-Wave AQC.

Similarly, IBM has committed $240 million to open the Watson AI Lab in Cambridge, MA, to study the possibilities and applications of quantum machine learning. Interest is mainly concentrated in a possible hybrid classical-quantum solution, where the computationally heavy problems are offloaded to a QC while the classical computer analyzes the data. This may be promising because short calculations may evade dealing with errors still prevalent in current QCs, and such quantum-classical solutions could be realized within the next decade.

(d) Government

Because of its computational difficulty, large-number factorization is the foundation for security procedures like ECC encryption and its older brother, RSA encryption. RSA is the gold standard in cryptography and is used ubiquitously, including securing online banking, protecting file transfers, fire-walling systems software like Microsoft Windows, and encrypting sensitive government information.

The promise of QCs poses a dangerous threat to the validity of these encryption procedures. According to Market Research Medium, the fear of decryption is revitalizing the cybersecurity industry, and startups are already increasing this market space—a market space that is expected to be worth $25 billion by 2025. Concurrently, "Quantum Encoding" is emerging to combat this future, and proposals like Quantum Key Distribution (QKD) provide quantum-safe alternatives. ID Quantique is an example founded in Switzerland and uses QKD to protect data. It was acquired in early 2018 by SK Telecom for $65 million. SK Telecom, the largest cell carrier in South Korea, plans to use the technology to guarantee security for a 5G broadband expected to roll out as early as March 2019.

3.2 Blockchain and Quantum Computing

QCs are powerful machines that take a new approach, built on the principles of quantum mechanics, to processing information. Quantum computing technologies have been advancing very rapidly, and their strong processing capabilities pose a threat to the cryptographic technologies that underpin the security properties of blockchains.

Learning Objectives
- Appraise the impact of quantum computing on blockchain security.

Main Takeaways

Main Points
- The application of quantum technologies in blockchains is a potential means to mitigate the security issues that the realization of quantum computing itself will bring about.
- Active research is ongoing in blockchains to ensure that their security properties are not compromised in the quantum era.

Main Terms
- **Shor's algorithm:** A quantum algorithm optimized to solve for prime factors.

- **Grover's algorithm:** A quantum algorithm that allows a user to search through an unordered list for specific items.

3.2.1 *Blockchain and Quantum Computing*

The application of quantum technologies (e.g., quantum random number generators (QRNGs), QKD, etc.) in blockchains is a potential means to mitigate the security issues that the realization of quantum computing itself will bring about. MIT summarizes this eloquently: "If quantum computers break blockchains, quantum blockchains could be the defense."

A blockchain is secured by two primary mechanisms: (1) digital signature via asymmetric cryptography and (2) hashing.

(a) Impact on Asymmetric Cryptography

In 1994, Peter Shor published a paper and coined Shor's Algorithm. This would spark the entire industry of quantum computation. It was designed to reduce numbers into their prime factors, a pursuit that may seem trivial but is the foundation of a wide range of cyber-security protocols. Today, Shor's algorithm is still considered the landmark discovery in quantum computation and is frequently considered a benchmark for quantum computation.

The public and private keys used to secure blockchain transactions are large numbers, hashed into a group of smaller numbers. Asymmetric cryptography algorithms depend on computers to find the prime factors of these enormous numbers.

Shor's algorithm is a quantum algorithm optimized to solve for prime factors. Using the most common encryption standard, it takes a classical computer 2^{128}, that is to say 340,282,366,920,938,463,463,374,607, 431,768,211,456 basic operations, to find the private key associated with a public key. On a QC, it would take 128^3 (i.e., only 2,097,152) basic operations to find the private key associated with a public key.

Elliptic curve digital signatures, which form the foundation of current blockchain security, are vulnerable to Shor's algorithm.

(b) Impact on Hash

In 1996, this very challenge of searching for a superposition of "results" from a quantum calculation was solved by Lov Grover, an

Indian–American computer scientist from Bell Laboratories. Sparing the mathematical details of the algorithm, Grover's is an iteration that, when applied to a superposition of output states, helps to express the desired output with greater probability while eliminating undesired outputs. Especially with large data sets, Grover's algorithm can search the data set for the desired result at an exponential speedup from its classical counterpart.

The first important use of Grover's Algorithm occurs when $n = 4$, or when there are four inputs. In this case, it takes exactly one invocation of Grover's algorithm to determine the solution, while a classical computer can do no better than test each of the four possible solutions in random order, solving it in a mean time of 2.25 iterations. This simple example highlights the capacity for Grover's to shorten run times and provide efficient calculations.

Scaling such a demonstration to a more meaningful size, Grover's algorithm is expected to solve with no more than $\sqrt{N}$ where N is the input size. Conversely, a classical computer needs N iterations to do the same thing. While this may seem like a small improvement, industry calculations often consider millions of data points, and such an algorithm is not only valued for its efficiency but it can also raise the upper limit of how many data points we can handle. This provides more efficient and accurate machine learning procedures as the data from AI proliferates.

Grover's algorithm is a quantum algorithm that allows a user to search through an unordered list for specific items. It requires 2^{256} (a 78-digit number) of basic operations with a classical computer to find the correct hash. A QC using Grover's Algorithm would only take 2^{128} (a 39-digit number, broken out above in the Shor's Algorithm section) of basic operations to solve the correct hash.

A comparison between Grover's algorithm and Shor's algorithm is shown in Figure 3.11.

Recognizing that the quantum era is near, there is active research ongoing in blockchains to ensure their security properties are not compromised, even in the quantum era.

(c) Quantum-Proofing New Blockchain
Using Post-Quantum Cryptographic Schemes: Designing quantum-resistant blockchains from scratch would involve applying post-quantum cryptographic schemes and quantum cryptography.

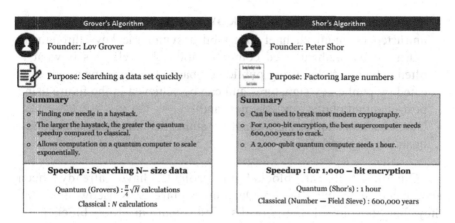

Figure 3.11: Comparison between Grover's algorithm and Shor's algorithm.

In 2016, the US National Institute for Standards and Technology (NIST) initiated a multi-year standardization project to identify candidates for quantum-resistant cryptosystems. It cites estimates made by Dr. Michele Mosca, University of Waterloo, that: "There is a 1 in 7 chance that some fundamental public-key crypto will be broken by quantum by 2026, and a 1 in 2 chance of the same by 2031."

NIST has shortlisted 26 potential algorithms that could be quantum-resistant, and draft NIST standards for quantum-resistant cryptographic algorithms are estimated to be ready in 2023–2025.

The most cost-effective way of making the blockchain resistant against quantum attacks is to replace the currently deployed digital signature schemes based on RSA or EC-DSA with post-quantum ones.

Examples of post-quantum schemes are lattice-based schemes (learning with errors, LWE), supersingular isogenies schemes, multivariate-polynomial schemes, code-based schemes, or Merkle tree-based signatures.

Blockchains Using Quantum Cryptography: Quantum cryptographic tools may also be used to make blockchains more secure. Examples include:

- **Quantum Random Number Generators (QRNGs)** — They avoid the cryptanalytic risks associated with pseudo-random number generators and promise a more fundamental and more reliable source of randomness than conventional entropy-based random number generators;

- **Quantum Key Distribution (QKD) systems** — This method uses an untrusted quantum channel to establish symmetric keys through an untrusted but authenticated communication channel. This is what is often achieved today using public key-based key agreement authenticated by public key signatures and can be achieved in the future using post-quantum public-key schemes; and
- Other quantum tools, e.g., quantum authentication, quantum money, quantum fingerprints.

Quantum-resistant blockchain projects have already been announced, e.g., the Russian Quantum Centre in Moscow indicated they had developed the world's first quantum-proof blockchain, Quantum Resistant Ledger by the QRL Foundation, which was launched in June 2018. Ethereum is also said to achieve quantum resistance around 2022–2024.

Replacement of Vulnerable Algorithms: Patching existing blockchains against quantum attacks may be significantly more complex than designing quantum-safe blockchains from scratch. The first step is to replace the vulnerable cryptographic primitives with quantum-resistant ones. For example, there is a need to replace the digital signature scheme with a quantum-resistant scheme in the Bitcoin network and use the latter to sign new transactions. This approach would provide security for future transactions.

Specific to Bitcoin, there is also research to examine the risk of Bitcoin to attacks by QCs, with findings indicating that the Proof of Work used by Bitcoin is relatively resistant to substantial speedup by QCs in the next 10 years; however, the elliptic curve signature scheme used by Bitcoin is much more at risk and could be completely broken by a QC as early as 2027. The same research study also reviewed available post-quantum signature schemes, suggesting that the candidates that would best meet the security and efficiency requirements of blockchain applications hash and lattice-based schemes (see Table 3.1).

Secure Transition Strategies: Research is also ongoing to examine secure transition strategies for existing blockchains, e.g., a commit-delay-reveal approach where a sufficiently long delay period of 6 months is proposed for consensus to be reached.

Table 3.1: Comparisons of the public key and signature lengths of post-quantum signature schemes in kilobits (kb).

Type	Name	Security level (bits)	PK length (kb)	Sig. length (kb)	PK + Sig. lengths (kb)
I.1	GPV	100	300	240	540
I.2	LYU	100	65	103	168
I.3	BLISS	128	7	5	12
I.1	DILITHIUM	138	11.8	21.6	33.4
II.1	RAINBOW	160	305	0.244	305
III.1	LMS	128	0.448	20	20.5
III.2	XMSS	128	0.544	20	20.5
III.3	SPHINCS	128	8	328	336
III.1	NSW	128	0.256	36	36
IV.1	CFS	83	9216	0.1	9216
IV.2	QUARTZ	80	568	0.128	568

Note: The security level given is against classical attacks. Type I are lattice based, type II based on multivariate polynomials, type III hashing based, and type IV code based.

IBM suggests that the hardware transition from GPUs to the quantum era will happen in three stages:

- Current–2022: Utilize GPUs, build new accelerators with conventional CMOS.
- 2022–2026: Overcoming the von Neumann bottleneck, Analog devices can combine memory and computation, neuromorphic computing.
- Beyond 2026: Quantum computing.

3.3 Current Developments and the Future

3.3.1 *Overview*

While quantum computing holds immense promise for the future, the technology is still far from being actualized for commercial use. The leading companies in the field of quantum computing include D-Wave, Google, IBM, Intel, 1QBit, and QxBranch.

Learning Objectives
- Examine the current development of quantum computing and identify essential traits for QCs.

Main Takeaways

Main Points
- Information stored in the qubit can be corrupted by environmental factors such as temperature, magnetic flux, or a random ray of light.
- The ability to correct errors or to function at low error rates is important for QCs.
- AQC is less flexible compared to UQC.

Main Terms
- **Error correction:** The method used to add error-tolerant qubits to retain information stored in the qubit.
- **Adiabatic Quantum Computer (AQC):** An analog equivalent to general QCs and is suited for optimization algorithms but suffer from qubit de-coherence.
- **Universal Quantum Computer (UQC):** A system upon which many quantum algorithms are intended to operate; the computation is realized by sequences of logic operators acting on different qubits.

(a) Current Development and the Future
At the same time, the academic world makes headway on potential algorithms that could be run on such a device. D-Wave is working on producing quantum annealers while Google, IBM, and Intel are pushing the frontier on Universal QCs (UQC). Startups like 1QBit and QxBranch are focused on the applications of this technology to industries. Finally, other startups like Rigetti are trying to bridge all teams by building processors, designing software for the processor, and applying it to industries.

The ultimate goal of all these computers is when QCs can surpass classical computers, a finish-line aptly named Quantum Supremacy. It is estimated that 50 logical qubits on a UQC operating at below a 0.5% error rate are all that's required, but reaching such a goal may be 5–10 years away. The most significant roadblock on this path is the notion of environmental noise and errors, which is explained next.

(1) Error correction

Much of the quantum computing landscape today resembles the discovery of the filament for the lightbulb. The general logic of the technology exists, but we still struggle to find the materials to deliver that technology.

As has been repeated, the biggest challenge facing QCs is retaining information. QCs operate using quantum phenomena as a source of data and storage. A change in temperature, a magnetic flux, or a random ray of light can also invoke these kinds of quantum behaviors and corrupt the information stored in the qubit. Furthermore, the possible physical candidates for qubits are limited. Whatever is used must (a) be capable of being manipulated into quantum states like superpositioning and (b) being stored and have that information accessed. Leading candidates include electrons, photons, superconductors, and even diamonds, but none have proven to be the perfect fit.

Aside from a candidate qubit that is relatively error-tolerant, researchers are also working on ways that a computer can actively correct errors. The leading solution was proposed by Peter Shor (who also discovered Shor's Algorithm). This involves coupling multiple qubits and ancillary qubits to have fault-tolerant redundancy within the design. If one qubit is corrupted, its ancilla would hypothetically be uncorrupted and restore the corrupted qubit to its original state. Such a solution has distinguished physical qubits and operational logical qubits.

Of course, there are still issues with this design. Namely, an incredible number of physical qubits would need to contribute to a logical qubit, with estimates as high as 10,000 of today's physical qubits for a single logical qubit, according to Alan Aspuru-Guzik of Harvard University. Moreover, the overhead computational costs of error-correcting require almost as much power as today's QCs can handle in total, thus leaving little room to run the actual algorithm.

It's not just a race for adding new qubits, but a race for adding error-tolerant qubits, and evaluating the progress of technology requires benchmarking both metrics. The current goal is a 0.5% coherence rate. At those levels, computational power is expected to increase exponentially. The growth of performance decreases significantly at higher error rates, and beyond 1% error rates adding more qubits does not add any computational power at all.

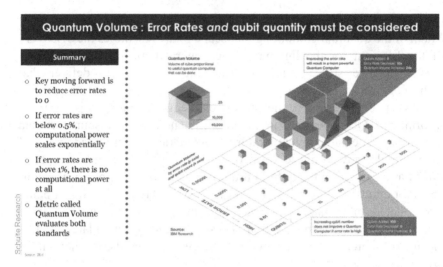

Figure 3.12:   Quantum Volume infographic courtesy of IBM research.

This cannot be a race to add qubit quantity. IBM has proposed a metric called **Quantum Volume** that scales with both error tolerance and qubit count (Figure 3.12). It reduces errors as qubits are added. In other words, the reduction in errors is as important as the addition of computing power.

(2) Adiabatic quantum computers

Adiabatic QCs (AQC) can be considered analog equivalent to general QCs. AQCs are particularly suited for optimization algorithms to calculate the best choice for all possible solutions in a specific, given scenario. The promise of efficient optimization is particularly rewarding since it is necessary for nearly every industry and one of the most noticeable limitations in modern computation. While this paradigm for calculation works well in certain situations, it cannot complete many of the algorithms envisaged for Quantum Computation. More pressingly, AQC's suffer from qubit decoherence and lack any infrastructure for error correction.

Another issue AQCs face is that the nature of these computations requires multiple interactions between qubits occurring simultaneously. However, the more interactions there are between qubits, the more vulnerable the qubits are to errors and the harder it is to keep track of each interaction. The problem is two-fold. To reduce noise, interactions between qubits must be limited. However, this would in turn limit what the particular AQC can accomplish.

Hypothetically, a fully connected AQC could operate competitively with a UQC. Such AQCs, also called general AQCs, would approximate the operations done in a UQC, albeit at a slower computational speed. Realizing such a technology may be years away, but AQCs still holds the most promise as the first experimentally realizable QCs. Research is focused now on finding a way to minimize errors and scale up current technology. The two ways to accomplish this are either finding physical material that is naturally error-tolerant or conceiving a way to error correct during computation.

(3) Universal quantum computers
Unlike AQCs, which specialize only in optimization calculations, Universal QCs are a form of quantum computation that holds greater promise and potential. In this paradigm, computation is realized by sequences of logic operators acting on different qubits. Because of its flexibility, UQC is the system upon which many quantum algorithms are intended to operate. This means that there is already much academic infra-structure surrounding UQCs and their potential applications.

While this technology is the more flexible of the two options, UQCs also face the most development problems. These systems rely on their qubits to store information, while logic gates access that information and draw conclusions. Thus, the preservation and processing of information as a whole is the fundamental building block of UQCs. However, as quan-tum superposition is a delicate phenomenon, the physics of maintaining multiple qubits in independent superpositions is challenging. This is aggravated by the fact that quantum mechanics is not just a laboratory-generated phenomenon. All of nature operates by quantum mechanics, so any interaction of the qubits with their environment can corrupt the qubit and, therefore, the information they represent.

The seeming impossibility of preventing these kinds of errors, called error correction or qubit coherence, has long been the greatest argument against the feasibility of QCs. However, rapid developments in this study of quantum error correction are helping realize the possibility of a UQC that is error-resilient. The basic solution is to couple many qubits together and to treat this group of qubits as the sum of its majority. If one qubit is corrupted, it is overshadowed by the remaining qubits that are still stable.

This is fundamentally the failsafe redundancy method used in the development of classical computation as well.

(4) D-Wave 2000Q

D-Wave is the leading producer of QCs, with their most recent model housing an impressive 2000 qubits. Their numerous collaborations with research institutes, companies, and universities are testament to their progress in the field, but their 2000 qubits are still far from Quantum Supremacy. Most importantly, their system aims at AQC, not UQC, and thus does not qualify for the 50 qubit benchmark. Furthermore, there is controversy on whether D-Wave computers actually engage in quantum calculations or simply perform calculations with a potentially quantum infrastructure. The main point is that even though D-Wave originally planned to move toward Adiabatic Quantum Computation (AQC), they have since grounded their technology in quantum annealing systems. This quantum computation paradigm is a subset of AQCs but lacks the potential to scale into a general AQC that enables it to compete with UQCs. Instead, quantum annealing is a limited technology, with significant controversy on whether such computation can reach speeds faster than classical computation. Namely, researchers at USC have already proved that classical computers can outperform D-Wave's 2000Q. Moreover, if D-Wave intends to continue scaling its technology, it must deal with errors (Figure 3.13). While UQCs have the infrastructure for building physical vs. logical qubits, AQCs cannot do so, hence its research primarily focuses on finding material for a fault-tolerant qubit.

Despite all the skepticism, D-Wave is engaging in numerous projects and collaborations. Even if they are not producing profoundly advanced QCs, their $200 million funding is at least a testament to their potential to do so.

(5) Google Bristlecone

In March of 2018, Google announced its newly minted 72 qubit QC that they are "cautiously optimistic" can demonstrate quantum supremacy. The technology comes after Google's trial run with their 9-qubit device, which shown only 0.6% error rates, just 0.1% from the generally accepted threshold of 0.5% error rates. Their 72-qubit device is a scaled-up version of their 9-qubit device, and they hope to preserve such error rates, though benchmarks for this new chip have not been released yet.

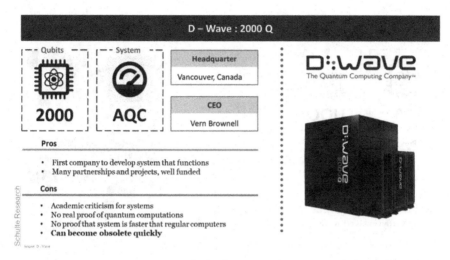

Figure 3.13: D-Wave: 2000Q.

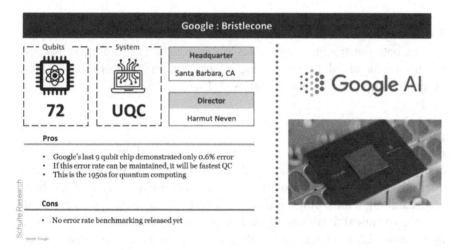

Figure 3.14: Google: Bristlecone.

Google has also released plans considering hybrid Adiabatic — Universal QCs, though no system has been produced yet (Figure 3.14).

(6) IBM
In November of 2017, IBM released a 50-qubit QC that can preserve its quantum states for 90 milliseconds — an industry record. In addition to its

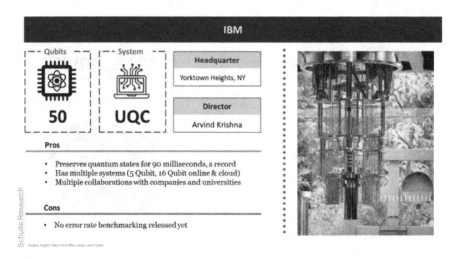

Figure 3.15:   IBM.

50-qubit system, it also has a fully functional five qubit system and 20 qubit system, both functioning at error rates low enough that researchers can access and use on the cloud. Benchmarking information on the error rates for their 50-qubit computer has not been released (Figure 3.15).

(7) Intel Tangle Lake

Despite a relatively late start in production, Intel produced a 49 qubit chip codenamed Tangle Lake displayed at the 2018 CES. While such a chip does not bring any breakthroughs in quantum computing technology, Intel is researching a kind of qubit that could be built out of single electrons in silicon. Technical details aside, such a qubit is beneficial because it can be mass-produced with the same fabrication methods as transistors today. Unsurprisingly, this is a similar fabrication method that Intel has become particularly good at after mass manufacturing the microprocessor for the past few decades (Figure 3.16).

(8) Global race

As different private companies quickly advance toward quantum suprem-acy, a similar race is taking hold of countries worldwide. In 2015, China's largest retailer Alibaba teamed up with the state-backed Chinese Academy

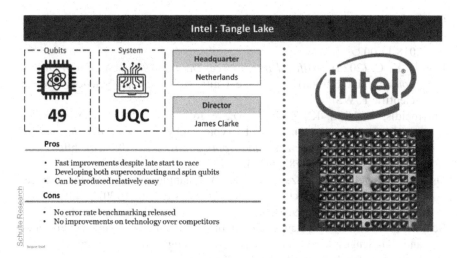

Figure 3.16: Intel: Tangle Lake.

of Sciences to research the field. In February 2018, the first prototype 11 qubit chip became available for cloud testing, and the Chinese government has since pledged $10 billion for research and development in a new national quantum lab. Similarly, the European Union is planning a $1.1 billion investment in research.

References/Further Readings

Corcoles, A. D., Kandala, A., Javadi-Abhari, A., McClure, D. T., Cross, A. W., Temme, K., Nation, P. D., Steffen, M., & Gambetta, J. M. (2020). Challenges and Opportunities of Near-Term Quantum Computing Systems. *Proceedings of the IEEE*, 108(8), 1338–1352. https://doi.org/10.1109/jproc.2019.2954005.

Cusumano, M. A. (2018). The business of quantum computing. *Communications of the ACM*, 61(10), 20–22. https://doi.org/10.1145/3267352.

Egger, D. J., Gambella, C., Marecek, J., McFaddin, S., Mevissen, M., Raymond, R., Simonetto, A., Woerner, S., & Yndurain, E. (2020). Quantum Computing for Finance: State-of-the-Art and Future Prospects. *IEEE Transactions on Quantum Engineering*, 1, 1–24. https://doi.org/10.1109/tqe.2020.3030314.

Fernandez-Carames, T. M., & Fraga-Lamas, P. (2020). Towards Post-Quantum Blockchain: A Review on Blockchain Cryptography Resistant to Quantum Computing Attacks. *IEEE Access*, 8, 21091–21116. https://doi.org/10.1109/access.2020.2968985.

Gyongyosi, L., & Imre, S. (2019). A survey on quantum computing technology. *Computer Science Review*, 31, 51–71. https://doi.org/10.1016/j.cosrev. 2018.11.002.

Lee, D. K. C. (2020). *Artificial Intelligence, Data and Blockchain in a Digital Economy* (1st Edition). Singapore University of Social Sciences—World Scientific F, WSPC.

Mavroeidis, V., Vishi, K., Zych, M. D., & Jøsang, A. (2018). The impact of quantum computing on present cryptography. *International Journal of Advanced Computer Science and Applications*, 9(3), 405–414. https://doi. org/10.14569/ijacsa.2018.090354.

Orús, R., Mugel, S., & Lizaso, E. (2019). Quantum computing for finance: Overview and prospects. *Reviews in Physics*, 4, 100028. https://doi. org/10.1016/j.revip.2019.100028.

Schulte, P. (2019). AI & Quantum Computing for Finance & Insurance: Fortunes and Challenges for China and America (Singapore University of Social Sciences—World Scientific F). WSPC.

3.4 Sample Questions

Question 1

Which of the following is false?

(a) Information is stored as strings of 0's and 1's in analog, digital, and quantum computers (QCs)

(b) Analog computers are limited to single tasks

(c) Digital computers can constantly be restructured for different problems

Question 2

Which of the following is true about classical computers and QCs?

(a) Both represents information in only strings of 0's and 1's

(b) Both produce deterministic calculations

(c) Classical computers have a smaller computational capacity than QCs

Question 3

What is quantum finance?

(a) The use of QCs in financial transactions

(b) The use of quantum algorithms in the finance context

(c) The investment in the development of quantum computing

Question 4

The Shor's algorithm:

(a) Breaks existing cryptographic hash functions
(b) Was used to search through an unordered list for specific items
(c) Was designed to reduce numbers into their prime factors

Question 5

An adiabatic quantum computer (AQC) is:

(a) Suited for optimization algorithms
(b) More error resilient than a universal quantum computer (UQC)
(c) Able to handle different quantum algorithms

Solutions

Question 1

Solution: Option **a** is correct.

Analog computers represent information using a physical model that mimics the problem it is meant to solve. Quantum computers (QCs) represent information in qubits.

Question 2

Solution: Option **c** is correct.

QCs represent information in qubits, in 0 or 1, or superposition of 0 and 1. The calculations for a QC is probabilistic.

Question 3

Solution: Option **b** is correct.

Question 4

Solution: Option **c** is correct.

Shor's algorithm breaks the digital signature scheme. Grover's algorithm is the algorithm that speeds up the breaking of the cryptographic hash function.

Question 5

Solution: Option **a** is correct.

UQC is more error-resilient compared to AQC. Option **c** describes a UQC.

Part B: Compliance and Risk Management

Chapter 4

Technology Risk Management (TRM)

4.1 Technology Landscape, Geo-Politics, and the Imperative for Technology Risk Management (TRM)

Learning Objectives
- Understand why Technology Risk Management (TRM) is important, especially for financial institutions.

Main Takeaways

Main Points
- Technological innovations in the business world are an ongoing evolutionary process.
- The rise of e-commerce, mobile banking, and digital payments leads to increased technology risk.
- Competition between countries to the lead in key technologies results in geopolitical risk for technology deployment in enterprises.

Main Terms
- **ABCD:** This is an abbreviation for AI, Blockchain, Cloud, and Data.
- **Core banking system (CBS):** This is a critical piece of technology that controls nearly all of a bank's significant operations.

- **Digital banking:** Refers to the automation of traditional banking services.
- **Distributed ledger technology (DLT):** Refers to the technology associated with the communication and update of immutable records in a network of users.
- **Mobile banking:** Is the making of financial transactions on mobile devices.
- **Neural processing unit (NPU):** Is a specialized circuit on which the fundamental logics for implementing machine learning algorithms.
- **Open source:** Refers to software and related developmental activities whose source code belongs to the public domain in virtue of its license.
- **Smart cognition:** Refers to computational processes that mimic human behavior or reasoning in problem-solving.
- **Technology risk management (TRM):** Is the discipline of planning for and monitoring risks that arise from the use of technologies and the setup and control of mitigating processes. This goes beyond information security and data protection but includes managing technology controls and technology management.

4.1.1 *Technology Innovations in Finance and the Economy*

Digital Business Transformation (DBT) is a source of innovative transformations in the current business world. The definition of DBT is the "use of technology to radically improve the performance or reach of enterprises" (Westerman *et al.*, 2014). Executives employ a suite of technological tools to improve over existing use of traditional technologies, such as Customer Relationship Management (CRM) systems, Enterprise Resources Planning (ERP) systems, and others covering internal processing and delivery of value propositions. DBT has a profound impact on business entities.

However, the continual reliance on digital technology exposes companies to new types of risk. These, known as technology risks, encompass cybersecurity, data and privacy theft, and intrusion. In response to the threat, authorities have responded by setting forth carefully crafted TRM guidelines for companies to guide them to manage and minimize their risks.

This section discusses relevant developments in technology, the reliance of financial institutions on the new technologies and how such reliance leads to technology risks.

Figure 4.1 shows key milestones in technological inventions or disruptions. Each milestone leads to the further need for TRM across the board.

(a) Core Banking System: Centralizing the Branch-Based System

An early massive technological disruption phase for financial institutions (FIs) occurred during the core banking system (CBS) replacement wave. The CBS is a critical piece of technology that sits at the heart of nearly all of a bank's major operations. Heidmann (2010) describes the CBS in analogy to a nervous system. Architecturally, the CBS links all bank services across business units, together with customers, onto a common network. This is comparable to the anatomical network of nerves. Data storage and processing are handled in a centralized manner. This is comparable to the brain. The CBS system is also a platform on which new features are developed and capable of organic growth.

Before the advent of the CBS, typically, each bank branch had its own server and was autonomous from central control. At the end of each day, data from each branch is physically collated and sent to the data center. This system is known as the "branch-based system" (www.diffen.com, n.d.). The system was rather inadequate. The resulting operational lags in time and information cause banks to seek new ways to improve the efficiency of their networks. The solution was found in centralization. A successor to the CBS was first introduced in the US in the 1970s. In the 1980s, it spread to Europe and India.

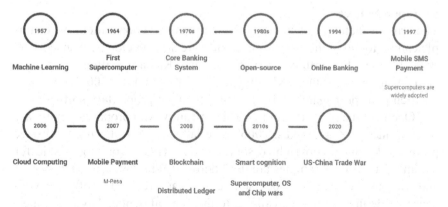

Figure 4.1: Timeline of key milestones on technological inventions or disruptions.

The CBS has the following advantages (Moreno and Sindhu, 2012):

(1) Opens up a more customer-centric business strategy by offering a holistic bird's eye view of the relationship with customers through a single database.
(2) Provides a cost-efficient database.
(3) Permits more agile business lines by decoupling production creation from product distribution while splitting up internal processes.
(4) Reduces costs.
(5) Enhances system flexibility.

Moreover, a centralized platform allows formerly decentralized branches to connect quickly. This is particularly significant in a global setting as it helps FIs expand globally. A centralized database also allows global trading to be conducted, potentially linking up the equity markets and the foreign exchange market.

Because of such stated benefits, FIs have become reliant on the CBS. However, this reliance has instead led to different types of threats. As CBS is based on a technological platform and centralized, technology threats loom as the target becomes more concentrated and attractive. The traditional system connecting the branches had been a rather closed one that could be secured physically on-premise with limited point-to-point connections. With the CBS, the banking network became more exposed in a wide-area configuration. In addition, centralized data storage at the bank's data center is an attractive target for potential attackers.

(b) Open Source
The crux of inclusive technology is openness and cooperation. An example can be found in the open-source software and development space. The year 1985 saw the birth of open source when Richard Stallman wrote the GNU Manifesto for the GNU Project (Carilllo & Okoli, 2008). This was an attempt to propagate the legal mechanisms of proprietary software.

Open-source software contrasts significantly with proprietary software (Econimides & Katsamakas, 2006). The latter refers to licensed software products that have copyrighted source codes. This is commonly sold for commercial profit. Examples are the Microsoft Windows operating system and various PC games. Open-source software refers to software with source code that is openly available to the general public. Any public person can access, use, study, modify and distribute the source code. Examples include the Linux Operating System (What is open source?, n.d.) and Bitcoin (Bitcoin is an innovative payment network and a new kind of money, n.d.). Recently, major FIs have begun to contribute to open source to attempt to carve out a share of the enormous revenue pie, according to FinTech Futures (Killing four myths about open source in financial services, 2019).

While open source is attractive, it is also susceptible to attackers planting malicious code and backdoors and programmers unwittingly posting code into the public domain that exposes the inner workings of confidential operations.

(c) Digital/Mobile Banking and Payment Solutions

E-payment systems began almost as early as the internet itself. The first FI to offer online banking services — the Stanford Federal Credit Union — was established in 1994 (Rapport, 2004). Other companies that provide alternative solutions to electronic cash included Milicent (1995), ECash (1996), and CyberCoin (1996) (5 turning points in the history of e-payments, n.d.). These solutions include digital cash, e-money, or tokens. During this period, pioneering companies like Amazon and Pizza Hut played a decisive role in popularizing online payment and delivery for consumers (5 turning points in the history of e-payments, n.d.). E-commerce websites, such as eBay, were established in 1995 (Our history, n.d.). Mobile payment arrived on the scene soon after that. In 1997, Coca Cola introduced vending machines that allowed coke to be purchased via text messages (Martins, 2015).

These events indicate a clear trend that shows that online banking and online transactions are not only recently invented. The recent upthrust in the usage of smartphones, apps, and social media helped to improve the adoption of online transactions and the platforms for online banking. One prominent example is M-Pesa (What is M-Pesa, 2007). The company carried out the first mobile-to-mobile transactions. It is illuminating to ask why FIs and commercial entities favor online or mobile payment methods. Some reasons mentioned by McKinsey & Company (McKinsey, 2019) include the growing importance of cross-border business-to-business (B2B) transactions, growing revenue from the online payment sector, and lower barriers of entry. The online payment as a sector has experienced a 6% growth in CAGR since 2018 (McKinsey, 2019). Another point mentioned is that payment solutions are becoming more digitalized. Management of these payment services must rely on advanced technologies and incorporate digitalization features to improve data analytics capabilities. Further reasons (Cudjoe *et al.*, 2015) are the speed and efficiency of mobile payment and the easier access to money it represents.

The mid-1990s marked a series of growth for e-commerce and payment technologies. On one hand, there was the rise of the internet and the rise of e-commerce giants Amazon and eBay. Laudon and Traver (History of Ecommerce, 2008) even go to the extent of proclaiming that Amazon and eBay are the initiators of e-commerce. However, this would not have been possible without the internet as an underlying infrastructure and the rise of internet payment in 1994. Since then, e-commerce giants have witnessed impressive growth in their annual revenue (see Figure 4.2).

The adoption of e-payment for e-commerce that the US tech giants offered was simple. Most customers already had credit cards, so they simply had to register their credit cards with the e-payment service provider to start making their payments. However, this situation was not present in China and other developing countries.

The rise of e-commerce is not unique to the US. Developing countries, particularly China, have their own e-commerce industry and the corresponding giants. As Klein (2020) explains, while the US was focused on developing better credit cards with advanced chips and magnetic strips,

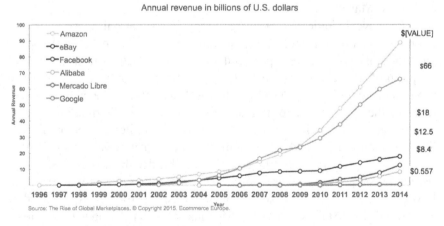

Figure 4.2:   Rise of E-commerce giants.

Source: Bigcommerce.com (Moore, n.d.).

China's e-commerce giant, Alibaba, focused on the more notable technology, QR-code, and digital wallets. The Chinese government had protected their domestic bank card industry by disallowing entry to the US credit card service providers. This meant that the number of Chinese citizens who used credit cards for e-payment had been small. It was also expensive to establish a wireless or wired debit card payment system from scratch in China. The Chinese merchants were hence motivated to search for a cheaper alternative. This arrived in the form of a smartphone. The Chinese mobile payment volume skyrocketed (see Figure 4.3). The wide adoption was also due to the economies of scale and positive feedback.

The immense Chinese market quickly lifted revenue from e-payment. In addition, the economy of scope strategies was widely practiced among the Chinese e-commerce giants. They are willing to expand their range of services once they have accumulated enough users (China: A Digital Payments Revolution, 2019).

The rise of e-payment follows a similar pattern in other developing countries. While there may not be protectionist measures resulting in a dearth of credit cards, many developing countries do not even have adequate banking services, making the ground favorable for the use of mobile technologies (see Figure 4.4) for payment services.

World Trade Organization (WTO) (WTO, 2013) argues that the lack of banking infrastructure but presence of adequate smartphone and data coverage led to the proliferation of e-payment. To illustrate, M-Pesa

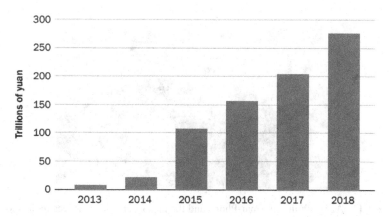

Figure 4.3: Volume of mobile transaction in China.
Source: Klein (2020).

started in Kenya in 2007 to provide banking and mobile payment services. It is one of the first companies to utilize a mobile wallet, and it became a leader in micro-financing (Graham, 2010). In 2012, the number of M-Pesa users had increased to 17 million in Kenya alone. This was attributed to the lack of accessible banking facilities.

Technology risk saw an exponential increase with the massive rise of digital/mobile banking and payments, especially in cyber risk and information or identity theft. Pegueros (2012) and Bankable (2008) pointed out that online banking and mobile transactions carry with them several risks. A vital issue was malware. According to some studies, malware samples on Android platforms alone increased from 400 in June 2011 to 13,000 in December 2011 (Jackson W., 2012). Other types of risks include POS vulnerabilities for payment technology, vulnerabilities of a data center for wireless carriers, and privacy concerns.

Bankable Frontier Associates LLC (2008) highlights several other conventional mobile Financial Services (m-FS) risks. For example, the level of independence from the Mobile Network Operator and low-security functionality on handsets in developing countries are forms of technology risks inherent with the mobile phone. Hackers may potentially exploit these vulnerabilities.

(d) ABCD

"ABCD" is an abbreviation for AI, Blockchain, Cloud, and Data (GovTech, 2018). They are the fundamental building blocks of digitization for the

Figure 4.4: Accessibility of SmartPhone and the lack of banking services in developing countries.

Source: World Trade Organization (2013).

future. For example, they constitute the basis for the next generation of CBS and transaction services.

A brief overview of each term is provided below:

- **AI:** AI stands for artificial intelligence. AI has a profound impact in the world of business, with applications in automation support, data analysis, and engagement with customers and employees. Generally speaking, AI technology empowers a machine to derive outputs from inputs, from a given set of algorithms, or to derive the algorithms using input-output pairings. Today's most popular form of AI is machine learning (ML), as introduced in Part B. Business management, a field of AI known as Neural Processing, is the technology behind the most advanced processing chips globally (Qualcomm Neural Processing SDK for AI, n.d.).
- **Blockchain:** In Bitcoin and some other cryptocurrency networks, the form of Distributed Ledger Technology (DLT) is known as blockchain (see Part C for more details about blockchain and DLT). Its application potential greatly exceeds the domain of cryptocurrency. Simply put, blockchain is an immutable and transparent data ledger. Due to its open and immutable nature, blockchain promotes trust and has the power to transform businesses from the removal of layers of monitoring through its use. According to IBM (What is blockchain for business? n.d.), blockchain is currently disrupting the financial services, food distribution, government, and retail sectors, as well as supply chains. However, blockchain has its fair share of risks, such as 1/3 attacks, Denial of Service Attacks and the breakdown of coordination that is commonly referred to as the Byzantine Generals Problem. In addition, the anonymous nature of public blockchain could be exploited by malicious elements to conduct money laundering or financial frauds.
- **Cloud:** Cloud refers to a readily accessible centralized data bank. The innovation of cloud computing transforms how data is stored and processed. According to Harvard Business Review (Hardy, 2018), cloud computing dramatically improves business process management (BPM). Refer to Part D on the risks, challenges and considerations in cloud computing.
- **Data:** Data forms the fundamental block behind AI, blockchain, and the cloud. According to McKinsey (Hurtgen & Mohr, 2018), large, accurate data sets have a profound impact in enhancing analytics

capabilities, predictive maintenance, fraud detection capabilities, demand planning, and supply chain optimization of business entities. We currently live in the age of "big data." This has a profound impact on our ability to predict. However, data collection and their subsequent distribution lead to privacy concerns from various stakeholders. In addition, valuable data stored on cloud servers raises cybersecurity issues.

(e) Distributed Ledger Technology (DLT)

In essence, DLT is inclusive by doing away with a central authority. Mills *et al.* (2016) argue that a combination of the characteristics of DLT can have a profound impact on the way digital assets are stored, monitored, and transferred. This will, in turn, make our current clearing payments and settlement processes more efficient. Collomb *et al.* (2017) argue that all company shareholders can be traced effectively with DLT to ensure dividend payments are made accurately.

DLT holds promise in automation and compliance enforcement through its immutable ledger in terms of financial reporting and compliance. One application of this is the fulfillment of the more stringent compliance set under Basel III for banks or under Solvency II for insurers to facilitate the enforcement of capital or liquidity requirements under these two regulatory frameworks. Lastly, lending and settlement can be accomplished more effectively as DLT can track lenders and payments, respectively. All these indicate the potential of DLT and the profound impact it can have when it comes to transaction, lending, and compliance.

(f) Smart Cognition

Knowledge is power, but conventional computers do not process knowledge. Recent developments in data science and AI can help mitigate this limitation through learning algorithms. ML, being one such form of learning, is widely adopted today. ML can be classified into two types: supervised learning and unsupervised learning.

In unsupervised learning, patterns are derived by extracting key features from unlabeled data sets. An example of an unsupervised learning algorithm is the K-mean clustering. In supervised learning, one has to rely on labeled data sets. The machine will learn using different labeled data sets to improve its accuracy over learning trials. Supervised learning includes algorithms such as K-nearest neighbors.

Supervised learning is applied in fraud detection and market forecasting in the business domain. Another typical example is predictive models for stock prices with regression (see Figure 4.5). Companies such as Netflix use predictive models to recommend shows to their users (Schatsky *et al.*, 2015), accounting for 75% of all usage. In contrast, unsupervised learning is used in customer feedback analysis and data visualization, where there are no fixed responses to given data sets. Nevertheless, unsupervised ML can allow the machine to extract patterns in general.

Besides the above learning mechanisms, there is also the advanced field of learning known as deep learning. Deep learning refers to the ability to learn in an unsupervised fashion from unstructured data sets by mimicking the human mind and its neural networks in multiple layers (Marr, 2018). Examples of deep learning applications include natural language processing, pattern recognition, image recognition, and voice recognition. Advancement in this area can have profound impacts on the world. Deep learning is currently investigated and developed by companies such as Samsung Bixby, Apple, and Huawei's Kirin chipset (Faggella, 2019).

Huawei is a leading player in this domain. It has developed charitable programs, such as StorySign, which improves literacy for deaf

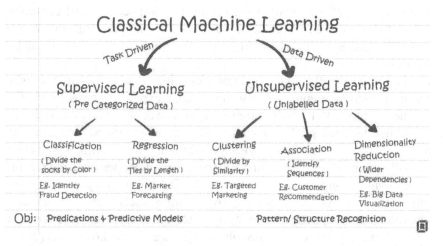

Figure 4.5: Types of machine learning and their functions.

Source: Medium.com (Io, 2019).

children using AI. Deloitte (Schatsky *et al.*, 2015) highlights the use of smart cognition in building driverless cars and automation of business processes, which can significantly transform our way of life and work.

However, there are risks to applying smart cognition. Some threats specific to technology risks include the following (Waterman & Bruening, 2014):

- Source data containing errors may introduce erroneous results.
- Data protection and boundaries are not established on how data can be collected and used.
- Corporate, social, and ethical responsibility when it comes to decision making: e.g., an InsurTech firm may be faced with the dilemma of who deserves the credit. If AI with smart cognitive power is making the decision, will it be ethical? These are important issues to resolve as loans and credits define the number of opportunities their recipients can potentially have.

The impact of social media has been witnessed in politics where candidates facing criticisms from internet users were forced to withdraw their candidature or to resign.

Social media can also be exploited to sway public sentiments during elections, such as during the UK Brexit Referendum and the 2016 US presidential election, highlighting the adverse impact of smart cognition when it is used in a manipulative way, and thus the need for governance and risk management that are imposed on potential technology firms by governments.

In particular, ML, smart cognition technology has been used in website recommendation engines. As Wang (2020) explains, recommendation engines employ ML to analyze user profiles. The analyses help the websites to publish targeted product recommendations to the users. Gomez-Uribe and Hunt (2015) have found evidence suggesting that Netflix's predictive algorithms can allow the organization to perform more personalized recommendations, saving Netflix an estimated USD 1 billion per year in marketing costs. With over 800 million active monthly users, Tik Tok uses such algorithms as well, according to Wang (2020), to ensure the success of Tik Tok's marketing. It leverages heavily on ML (see Figure 4.6). Davis (2019) outlines how Tik Tok, through ByteDance's ML tools, analyzes its active

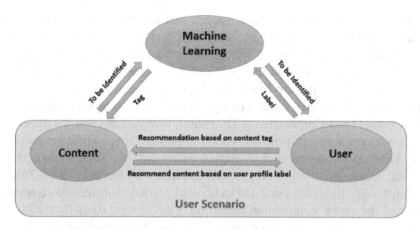

Figure 4.6: Predictive Algorithm deployed by Tik Tok.
Source: Toward Data Science (Wang, 2020).

users' behavior to promote targeted videos to these users. Besides videos, advertisements are also carefully targeted for the users.

Makers of videos also benefit from ML with recommendations on enhancements and video edits that cater to users' preferences. The reliance on ML and data analytics by web-based companies raises issues on data privacy. The large volume of data accessible to these firms can potentially be a lucrative target for hackers. As such, TRM needs to be put in place to protect these data from being exploited.

(g) The Tech War
Conventional microeconomics theory states that competition promotes productive efficiency in firms. Firms then become more productive as scarce resources are utilized more efficiently. However, certain recent developments contradict this. Chin (2019) argues that, instead of competing for efficiency, recent geopolitical developments have led to the competition for dominance. In the same article, Chin (2019) states that countries today throw their support behind key technologies to compete and ultimately dominate on a global stage.

Recently, the fight against the COVID-19 pandemic featured some examples of the application of supercomputers (Japanese supercomputer, crowned world's fastest, is fighting coronavirus, 2020). These supercomputers can calculate at speeds that are over 1,000 times faster than a regular computer and are capable of performing fast analytics. The fastest supercomputer, as of 2020, is the "Fugaku" (Japan's new supercomputer ranked fastest in the world, 2020), located in Kobe, Japan (see Figure 4.7). The other top five fastest supercomputers are from China and the United States (Jackson & Alering, 2020). The first supercomputer was the Control Data Corporation (CDC) 6600, invented in 1964. Its development was primarily driven by corporate funding for scientific purposes.

From 1997, events took a change as funding for supercomputers in China, Japan, and the US became driven mainly by the state (Bell, 2015). Almost every field of science and technology started to utilize supercomputers and the states' competition heated up. Fast-forward to 2010, the "warfare" for supercomputers has intensified as China unveiled the fastest supercomputer in the world (Jarvis, 2010). Two years later, in 2012 (McMillan, n.d.), US supercomputers unveiled the "Titan," which processed at a speed that is ten times faster than the supercomputers in 2010. This rivalry continues till today and was brought into the spotlight by the US-China trade war (Tao & Perez, 2019).

Figure 4.7: Fugaku, world's fastest super computer (at the time when this article was written).

Source: Kyodo News (Japan's new supercomputer ranked fastest in world, 2020).

Apart from supercomputers, smartphones have become a quintessential gadget for almost everyone. The reliance on smartphones has sped up the competition for the next operating system (OS). With the US prohibiting its companies from working with Huawei, Huawei unleashed its HarmonyOS (Sin, 2020) in direct competition against the incumbent Android and iOS operating systems. The HarmonyOS is an addition to the current Huawei home business ecosystem with its own set of supporting hardware and software for Chinese-made phones. There are other mobile operating systems in the market. The intense competition has led to the failure of some of these, including WebOS, MeeGo, Window Phone, BlackBerry 10, and FirefoxOS (C., 2017).

"Chip war" is an extension of geopolitical tension, lying beyond the domain of conventional business competition. . The most notable chip war that we witness is the US attempting to heavily regulate and ultimately defeat Huawei (America is determined to sink Huawei, 2020). Such a tactic deployed by the US is based on several considerations. Firstly, advanced chip manufacturing is comparable to oil supply (Blank, 2020). It has a profound impact not only on technology but also on economics and the military. Thus far, the US has led the world in chip technology (Wong & Gallagher, 2020). Then in 2018, Huawei unveiled, during the IFA electronics show in Berlin, its Kirin 980 core processor chips (Cheng & Li, 2018). This is the first mobile chip in the world with two neural processing units (NPU). It empowers Huawei with significantly faster processing speed and ML capabilities in smart imaging, facial recognition, and voice recognition.

In contrast, the most advanced chip in the US is the Apple A11 core processor, which has only one NPU. This has a severe impact on the US. Following recent developments, Chinese chip technology is likely to overtake the US, not to mention that China has the world's largest reserve of rare earth at 44 MT (McLead, 2019), which is essential for advanced chip making. Hence, it makes sense from the US perspective to adopt aggressive protectionist measures against Huawei by restricting their use of US technology.

Supercomputers and smartphones have become an essential part of our lives. The market value alone is lucrative enough to move powerful institutions, not to mention political motives. The state and large corporations' actions to control essential technology are a cause for concern. Issues of state surveillance have surfaced (Mitchell & Diamond, 2018), raising the risk of privacy loss. Another type of risk arises when the state collects data leaked as a result of whistle-blowing, as the examples of Edward Snowden and Julian Assange have shown. The same issue arises when major technology companies dominate the supply of OS and chips. What if hackers break into these companies and access personal data? The threat for this is very real as Facebook has experienced such a disaster before (Silverstein, 2019). Recently, Android reported a suspected data breach by hackers (Winder, 2020) which further intensified the level of risk for users.

Trade war and potential tariffs are manifestations of geopolitical risks. Taiwan Semiconductor and Samsung Electronics have been caught in the conflict arising from the chips war between the US and China (Mellow, 2020). Therefore, appropriate measures are required to ensure that business entities diversify their risks across the region. The incident highlights the need to establish a sound business continuity plan in the event of disruption.

4.2 Importance of TRM

Learning Objectives
- Review the importance of TRM for companies.

Main Takeaways

Main Points
- TRP is needed by everyone living in the digital economy.
- TRP comprises cybersecurity, information security, data privacy, and change management.
- The essence of TRP is captured by BCBS' Seven Principles of Operational Resilience: governance, operational risk management, business continuity planning and testing, mapping interconnections and interdependencies, third-party dependency management, incident management, and ICT with cybersecurity.

Main Terms
- **BCBS:** This is an abbreviation for Basel Committee for Banking Supervision. It is the primary organization that sets global standards for the prudential regulation of banks, and it provides a forum for the regular cooperation of banks on supervisory matters.

4.2.1 *Introduction to TRM*

The world is highly digitally connected. The economy, in particular the finance industry, is shifting from a physical cash-based system to a digital payments-based system. Physical barriers are coming down as money and transactions move to bits and bytes. Securing a financial institution (FI) is no longer simply about the physical premises. FI professionals, regulators, and consumers alike need to understand the technologies impacting the world and defend against the resulting risks. It is reasonable to say that a rudimentary understanding of the TRM is necessary for everyone living in this digital economy.

Greater digitalization and connectivity have made us more vulnerable and exposed to threats as we become increasingly reliant on technology. An example is given in Figure 4.8, which illustrates just the prevalence of data breaches.

4.2.2 *Differences Between Information Security, Cyber Security, Data Privacy and TRM*

In lieu of such threats, it is essential for everyone, especially from the management, to understand more about TRM.

TRM refers to the management of risks in the technology area. It is not simply information risk, cyber risk, or data privacy risks, typically grouped together. These terms are often used loosely and interchangeably.

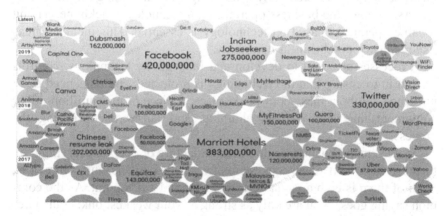

Figure 4.8: The world's biggest data breaches (snapshot, refer to the website for the latest).

Source: World's Biggest Data Breaches & Hacks (n.d.): Information Is Beautiful.

Nevertheless, distinctive differences between them exist and can be thus described:

(1) Information security concerns protecting the integrity, confidentiality, and accessibility of all forms of information or data (Olcott, 2019). It concerns protecting the confidentiality of data in soft and hard copy, in data centers, or cabinets. Examples of information security are locking all files and documents after use and the setting of multifactor authentication for data access on computers.

(2) Cybersecurity concerns the protection of data in electronic form (Olcott, 2019). This includes data stored on mobile, in computers, on the cloud, or in servers. Examples of ensuring cybersecurity include encryption and setting up firewalls.

(3) Data privacy concerns the ability to protect, collect, share and retain sensitive information (Dean, 2017). It is different from security as this, be it information or cyber, targets protection. Some concerns governed under data privacy that are not part of cybersecurity or information security include how data might be collected, with whom collected data may be shared, and how long collected data can be retained.

While most of the attention is on cyber-attacks and information leakages (these being most attention-grabbing and newsworthy), to operate a business in the digital economy is not simply about fending off the attackers. As much of the business operates on a technology backbone, having reliable operations based on technology is essential. This includes areas like resiliency and business continuity.

Processes are used to develop and manage the technology, controls are put in to ensure that the technology is protected, and risks need to be mitigated. Without these controls in place, a piece of multimillion-dollar equipment may blow up as shortcuts and lapses occur during the process.

Today, many businesses do not manufacture or operate everything by themselves but rely on an ecosystem of vendors, partners, and contractors. Each of them is both a valuable component and a risk point. As the common saying goes, "you are only as strong as your weakest link," outsourcing management is an important consideration of TRM. As we will see later, many weaknesses are presented through lapses of the FI's partners and vendors.

Without understanding and managing your outsourced processes correctly, internal processes and controls will be futile regardless of how robust they are.

Another vital aspect of TRM is business continuity in the face of disasters. For technology, it means two-aspects — (1) the technology deployed must be resilient and be able to recover in a reasonable time frame when a disaster happens (i.e., disaster recovery planning), and (2) technology used to support a non-technological disaster must be robust and enable the business to continue operating. The recent Covid pandemic has illustrated the importance of (2) for all industries and businesses. It emphasizes on companies to ensure that (1) is done well and the importance of technology is amplified.

TRM is therefore much broader in the scope of applicability and relevance, and many regulators have taken a similar stance when it comes to regulating a FI. Under the Monetary Authority of Singapore (MAS) guideline (2013) (Guidelines on Risk Management Practices — Technology Risk, 2013), TRM is referred to as a guideline that sets out 1) principles of risk management and 2) standards of best practice as guidance for FIs in the following aspects:

(1) establish a robust and sound TRP framework;
(2) strengthen system recoverability, reliability, resilience, and security;
(3) deploy strong authentication to protect customer data, transactions, and the entire system.

Areas of technology risks for the FIs to be cognizant includes, but is not limited to:

(1) information security/cybersecurity;
(2) application development;
(3) testing (of systems and technology);
(4) access control;
(5) change management;
(6) privilege access;
(7) patch management;
(8) software development lifecycle management;
(9) technology lifecycle management;
(10) insider attack;
(11) governance (of technology/operations);
(12) outsourcing (of technology/operations).

An FI needs to focus on TRM as the broader super-set. It also accounts for operations, change management, and resiliency to manage all the risks present in the rapidly evolving technological space. Figure 4.9 shows a Venn diagram that summarizes the different concepts — cybersecurity, information security, data privacy, change management, and TRM, showing that they are related but not identical.

4.2.3 *Basel — Definition of Operational Risk*

The Basel Committee on Banking Supervision (BCBS) is the primary organization that sets global standards for the prudential regulation of banks. It provides a forum for the regular cooperation of banks on supervisory matters (The Basel Committee — overview, n.d.).

In Basel's 1998 paper on Operational Risk Management (Operational Risk Management, 1998), it was noted that there was no definition of operational risk that is universally in consensus then. Still, many banks have defined operational risk as any risk that is not regarded as market risk or credit risk. Some banks described it as the risk of loss from various human or technical errors.

By Basel II, seven types of operational risk were projected (Barakat, 2014):

(1) internal fraud;
(2) external fraud;
(3) employment practices and workplace safety.

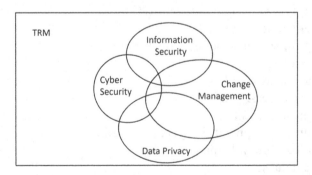

Figure 4.9: Venn diagram on the differences between cyber security, information security, data privacy, change management, and TRM.

(4) clients, products and business practice;
(5) damage to physical assets;
(6) business disruption and systems failures;
(7) execution, delivery and process management.

In 2020, Basel produced a consultative document to refine operational risk guidelines (Principles of Operational Resilience, 2020). BCBS sought to promote a principles-based approach to enhancing operational resilience through the publication. The paper contained seven principles as listed below:

(1) **Governance:** *Principle 1: Banks should utilize their existing governance structure to establish, oversee and implement an effective operational resilience approach that enables them to respond and adapt to, as well as recover and learn from, disruptive events in order to minimize their impact on delivering critical operations through disruption.*
(2) **Operational Risk Management:** *Principle 2: Banks should leverage their respective functions for the management of operational risk to identify external and internal threats and potential failures in people, processes, and systems on an ongoing basis, promptly assess the vulnerabilities of critical operations and manage the resulting risks in accordance with their operational resilience expectations.*
(3) **Business continuity planning and testing:** *Principle 3: Banks should have business continuity plans in place and conduct business continuity exercises under a range of severe but plausible scenarios in order to test their ability to deliver critical operations through disruption.*
(4) **Mapping interconnections and interdependencies:** *Principle 4: Once a bank has identified its critical operations, the banks should map the relevant internal and external interconnections and interdependencies to set operational resilience expectations that are necessary for the delivery of critical operations.*
(5) **Third-party dependency management:** *Principle 5: Banks should manage their dependences on relationships, including those of, but not limited to, third parties or intra-group entities, for the delivery of critical operations.*
(6) **Incident management:** *Principle 6: Bank should develop and implement response and recovery plans to manage incidents that could disrupt the delivery of critical operations in line with the bank's risk tolerance for disruption, considering the bank's risk appetite, risk*

capacity, and risk profile. Banks should continuously improve their incident response and recovery plans by incorporating the lessons learned from previous incidents.

(7) **ICT including cybersecurity:** *Principle 7: Banks should ensure resilient ICT, including cybersecurity that is subject to protection, detection, response, and recovery programs that are regularly tested, incorporate appropriate situational awareness, and convey relevant information to users on a timely basis in order to fully support and facilitate the delivery of the bank's critical operations.*

Thus, in the 2020 consultative paper on the seven key principles (Principles for the Sound Management of Operational Risk, 2020), Basel has incorporated the essence of TRM.

References/Further Readings

5 turning points in the history of e-payments. (n.d.). Retrieved from www. securionpay.com: https://securionpay.com/blog/5-turning-points-history-e-payments/.

America is determined to sink Huawei. (2020, May 23). Retrieved from www. economist.com: https://www.economist.com/leaders/2020/05/23/america-is-determined-to-sink-huawei.

Auchard, E., & Ingram, D. (2018, March 20). Cambridge Analytica CEO claims influence on US election, Facebook questioned. Retrieved from www.reuters. com: https://www.reuters.com/article/us-facebook-cambridge-analytica/cambridge-analytica-ceo-claims-influence-on-u-s-election-facebook-questioned-idUSKBN1GW1SG.

Bankable Frontier Associates LLC. (2008, March 24). Managing the Risk of Mobile Banking Technologies. Retrieved from www.ifc.org: https://www. ifc.org/wps/wcm/connect/d39fa663-96dd-4d91-8036-e9893b1ced89/7.2+M anaging+Mobile+Money+Risk.pdf?MOD=AJPERES&CVID=kbZlhJu.

Barakat, M. N. (2014, December 15). The Seven Operational Risk Types projected by Basel II. Retrieved from www.care-web.co.uk: http://www.care-web.co.uk/blog/seven-operational-risk-event-types-projected-basel-ii/.

Bell, C. G. (2015). *Supercomputers: The Amazing Race.* San Francisco: Microsoft Research.

Bitcoin is an innovative payment network and a new kind of money. (n.d.). Retrieved from www.bitcoin.org: https://bitcoin.org/en/#:~:text=Bitcoin% 20uses%20peer%2Dto%2Dpeer,and%20everyone%20can%20take% 20part.

Blank, S. (2020, June 11). The Chip Wars of the 21st Century. Retrieved from www.warontherocks.com: https://warontherocks.com/2020/06/the-chip-wars-of-the-21st-century/.

Carilllo, K. D., & Okoli, C. (2008). The open source movement: A revolution in software development. *Journal of Computer Information Systems*, 42(2), 1–9.

Cheng, T.-f., & Li, L. (2018, August 31). Huawei Unveils World's Most Advanced Chip to Counter Apple. Retrieved from www.asia.nikkei.com: https://asia.nikkei.com/Business/Business-trends/Huawei-unveils-world-s-most-advanced-chip-to-counter-Apple.

Chin, W. (2019). Technology, war and the state: past, present and future. *International Affairs,* 95(4), 765–783.

China: A Digital Payments Revolution. (2019, September). Retrieved from www.cgap.org: https://www.cgap.org/research/publication/china-digital-payments-revolution.

Collomb, A., Sok, K., & Leger, L. (2017). Distributed Ledger Technology. Retrieved from annales.org: http://annales.org/Financial_Regul_and_Gov/fintechs/2017-08-RI-CollombEtAl.pdf.

Consultation Paper — Technology Risk Management Guidelines. (2019, March). Retrieved from www.mas.gov.sg: https://www.mas.gov.sg/-/media/Consultation-Paper-on-Proposed-Revisions-to-Technology-Risk-Management-Guidelines.pdf.

Consultation Paper on Proposed Revisions to Business Continuity Management Guidelines. (2019, March 1). Retrieved from www.mas.gov.sg: https://www.mas.gov.sg/publications/consultations/2019/consultation-paper-on-proposed-revisions-to-business-continuity-management-guidelines.

Cudjoe, A. G., Anim, P. A., & Nyanyofio, J. G. (2015). Determinants of mobile banking adoption in the Ghanaian banking industry: A Case of Access Bank Ghana Limited. *Journal of Computer and Communications*, 3(2).

Davis, J. (2019, June 19). The TikTok Strategy: Using AI Platforms to Take Over the World. Retrieved from www.knowledge.insead.edu: https://knowledge.insead.edu/entrepreneurship/the-tiktok-strategy-using-ai-platforms-to-take-over-the-world-11776.

Dean, B. (2017, March 23). Privacy vs. Security. Retrieved from www.secureworks.com: https://www.secureworks.com/blog/privacy-vs-security#:~:text=We%20typically%20define%20security%20as,they%20can%20access%20specific%20data.

Econimides, N., & Katsamakas, E. (2006). Two-Sided Competition of Proprietary vs. Open Source Technology Platforms and the Implications for the Software Industry. *Management Science*.

Faggella, D. (2019, November 24). Smartphone AI Trends — Comparisons of Apple, Samsung, and More. Retrieved from www.emerj.com: https://emerj.com/ai-sector-overviews/smartphone-ai-trends-comparisons-apple-samsung/.

Gomez-Uribe, C. A., & Hunt, N. (2015). The Netflix Recommender System: Algorithms, Business Value. Retrieved from www.acm.org: https://dl.acm.org/doi/pdf/10.1145/2843948.

GovTech. (2018, Oct 3). ABCD: Not as Easy as You might Think. Retrieved from www.tech.gov.sg: https://www.tech.gov.sg/media/technews/stack-18-abcd-ot-as-easy-as-you-might-think.

Graham, F. (2010, November 22). M-Pesa: Kenya's Mobile Wallet Revolution. Retrieved from www.BBC.com: https://www.bbc.com/news/business-11793290.

Guidelines on Business Continutiy Management. (2003, June 1). Retrieved from www.mas.gov.sg: https://www.mas.gov.sg/regulation/guidelines/guidelines-on-business-continuity-management.

Guidelines on Outsourcing. (2018, October 5). Retrieved from www.mas.gov.sg: https://www.mas.gov.sg/regulation/guidelines/guidelines-on-outsourcing.

Guidelines on Risk Management Practices — Technology Risk. (2013, June 1). Retrieved from www.mas.gov.sg: https://www.mas.gov.sg/regulation/guidelines/technology-risk-management-guidelines.

Hardy, Q. (2018). How cloud computing is changing management. *Harvard Business Review*.

Heidmann, M. (2010). Overhauling banks' IT systems. *McKinsey Digital*.

History of Ecommerce. (2008). Retrieved from www.ecommerce-land.com: https://www.ecommerce-land.com/history_ecommerce.html#:~:text= History%20of%20ecommerce%20dates%20back,up%20residence%20 at%20web%20sites.

Hurtgen, H., & Mohr, N. (2018). *Achieving Business Impact with Data*. McKinsey & Company.

Io, R. (2019, October 3). Supervised vs. Unsupervised Learning: Key Differences. Retrieved from www.medium.com: https://medium.com/@recrosoft.io/supervised-vs-unsupervised-learning-key-differences-cdd46206cdcb.

Jackson, K., & Alering, A. (2020, June 23). The 5 Fastest Supercomputers in the World. Retrieved from www.sciencenode.org: https://sciencenode.org/feature/the-5-fastest-supercomputers-in-the-world.php.

Jackson, W. (2012, February 16). Mobile malware is on the march, and Android is target No. 1. Retrieved from www.gcn.com: https://gcn.com/articles/2012/02/16/mobile-malware-android-top-target.aspx.

Japanese supercomputer, crowned world's fastest, is fighting coronavirus. (2020, June 23). Retrieved from www.bbc.com: https://www.bbc.com/news/world-asia-53147684.

Japan's new supercomputer ranked fastest in world. (2020, June 23). Retrieved from www.english.kyodonews.net: https://english.kyodonews.net/news/2020/06/ebec3baa008c-japans-new-supercomputer-ranked-fastest-in-world.html.

Jarvis, S. (2010). *Supercomputer warfare: New research provides effective battle planning.* Warwick: University of Warwick.

Killing four myths about open source in financial services. (2019, June 28). Retrieved from Fintech Futures: https://www.fintechfutures.com/2019/06/killing-four-myths-about-open-source-in-financial-services/#:~:text=Major%20financial%20institutions%2C%20such%20as,like%20OpenPOWER%20and%20Linux%20Foundation.

Klein, A. (2020, April). China's Digital Payment Revolution. Retrieved from www.brookings.edu: https://www.brookings.edu/wp-content/uploads/2020/04/FP_20200427_china_digital_payments_klein.pdf.

Kleinman, Z. (2018, March 21). Cambridge Analytica: The story so far. Retrieved from www.bbc.com: https://www.bbc.com/news/technology-43465968.

Marr, B. (2018, August 20). 10 Amazing Examples of How Deep Learning AI is Used in Practice? Retrieved from www.forbes.com: https://www.forbes.com/sites/bernardmarr/2018/08/20/10-amazing-examples-of-how-deep-learning-ai-is-used-in-practice/#3299f08bf98a.

Martins, F. (2015, June 9). The History of the Mobile Payment Experience #INFOGRAPHIC. Retrieved from www.winthecustomer.com: http://winthecustomer.com/technology-changing-the-mobile-payment-customer-experience/.

MAS Consults on Proposed Enhancements to Technology Risk and Business Continuity Management Guidelines. (2019, March 7). Retrieved from www.mas.gov.sg: https://www.mas.gov.sg/news/media-releases/2019/mas-consults-on-proposed-enhancements-to-trm-and-bcm-guidelines.

MAS Issues New Rules to Strengthen Cyber Resilience of Financial Industry. (2019, August 6). Retrieved from www.mas.gov.sg: https://www.mas.gov.sg/news/media-releases/2019/mas-issues-new-rules-to-strengthen-cyber-resilience-of-financial-industry.

Matei, A. (2020, February 14). TikTok Slammed for being too Addictive in App's First "I quit" Essay. Retrieved from www.theguardian.com: https://www.theguardian.com/technology/2020/feb/14/first-quitting-tiktok-statement-shows-popular-app-has-come-of-age.

McLead, C. (2019, May 22). Top Rare Earth Reserves by Country. Retrieved from www.investingnews.com: https://investingnews.com/daily/resource-investing/critical-metals-investing/rare-earth-investing/rare-earth-reserves-country/.

McMillan. (n.d.). Is Supercomputing the New Space Race? Retrieved from www.wired.com: https://www.wired.com/insights/2012/10/is-supercomputing-the-new-space-race/.

Mellow, C. (2020, June 5). Taiwan Semi and Samsung are in the U.S.-China Crosshairs. Why Investors Shouldn't Worry. Retrieved from www.barrons.

com: https://www.barrons.com/articles/taiwan-semi-and-samsung-are-in-the-u-s-china-crosshairs-but-investors-shouldnt-worry-51591354800.

Mills *et al.* (2016). Distributed Ledger Technology in Payments, Clearing, and. Retrieved from papers.ssrn.com: https://papers.ssrn.com/sol3/papers.cfm?abstract_id=2881204.

Mitchell, A., & Diamond, L. (2018, February 2). China's Surveillance State Should Scare Everyone. Retrieved from www.theatlantic.com: https://www.theatlantic.com/international/archive/2018/02/china-surveillance/552203/.

Moore, K. (n.d.). Ecommerce 101 + The History of Online Shopping: What The Past Says About Tomorrow's Retail Challenges. Retrieved from www.bigcommerc.ecom: https://www.bigcommerce.com/blog/ecommerce/#what-is-ecommerce.

Moreno, J. P., & Sindhu, F. (2012, February 24). Rebuilding the Revenue Model: 5 Benefits of Core Systems Transformation. Retrieved from Information Week — Bank Systems & Technology: https://www.banktech.com/core-systems/rebuilding-the-revenue-model-5-benefits-of-core-systems-transformation/a/d-id/1295160.html.

Notice 644 Technology Risk Management. (2013, June 21). Retrieved from www.mas.gov.sg: https://www.mas.gov.sg/regulation/notices/notice-644.

Notice PSN05 Technology Risk Management. (2019, December 5). Retrieved from www.mas.gov.sg: https://www.mas.gov.sg/regulation/notices/psn05.

Olcott, J. (2019, September 15). Cybersecurity Vs. Information Security: Is There A Difference? Retrieved from www.bitsight.com: https://www.bitsight.com/blog/cybersecurity-vs-information-security.

Operational Risk Management. (1998, September 21). Retrieved from www.bis.org: https://www.bis.org/publ/bcbs42.htm.

Our history. (n.d.). Retrieved from www.ebay.com: https://www.ebayinc.com/company/our-history/.

Payment Services Act. (2019, February 20). Retrieved from sso.agc.gov.sg: https://sso.agc.gov.sg/Acts-Supp/2-2019/Published/20190220?DocDate=20190220#pr102-.

Pegueros, V. (2012, November 1). Security of Mobile Banking and Payments. Retrieved from www.sans.org: https://www.sans.org/reading-room/whitepapers/ecommerce/security-mobile-banking-payments-34062.

Principles of Operational Resilience. (2020, August 6). Retrieved from www.bis.org: https://www.bis.org/bcbs/publ/d509.htm.

Principles for the Sound Management of Operational Risk. (2021, May 16). Retrieved from www.bis.org: https://www.bis.org/publ/bcbs195.pdf.

Qualcomm Neural Processing SDK for AI. (n.d.). Retrieved from www.developer.qualcomm.com: https://developer.qualcomm.com/software/qualcomm-neural-processing-sdk.

Rapport, M. (2004, February 3). Stanford FCU Set to Mark 10-Year Anniversary as First Financial to Offer Online Banking. Retrieved from Credit Union Times: https://www.cutimes.com/2004/02/03/stanford-fcu-set-to-mark-10-year-anniversary-as-first-financial-to-offer-online-banking/?slret urn=20200820015729.

Response to feedback received — Consultation paper on the Technology Risk Management Guidelines. (n.d.). Retrieved from www.mas.gov.sg: https://www.mas.gov.sg/-/media/MAS/News-and-Publications/Consultation-Papers/Response-to-Consultation-Paper_TRM-Guidelines.pdf.

Schatsky, D., Muraskin, C., & Gurumurthy, R. (2015, January 27). Cognitive technologies: The real opportunities for business. *Deloitte Review* (16).

Silverstein, J. (2019, April 4). Hundreds of Millions of Facebook User Records were Exposed on Amazon Cloud Server. Retrieved from www.cbsnews.com: https://www.cbsnews.com/news/millions-facebook-user-records-exposed-amazon-cloud-server/.

Tao, L., & Perez, B. (2019, June 26). China has Decided not to Fan the Flames on Supercomputing Rivalry amid US Tensions. Retrieved from www.scmp.com: https://www.scmp.com/tech/policy/article/3015997/china-has-decided-not-fan-flames-super-computing-rivalry-amid-us.

The Basel Committee — overview. (n.d.). Retrieved from www.bis.org: https://www.bis.org/bcbs/.

Toh, T. (2020, June 28). Singapore GE2020: Ivan Lim incident 'regrettable', says Heng Swee Keat. Retrieved from www.straitstimes.com: https://www.straitstimes.com/politics/singapore-ge2020-ivan-lim-did-responsible-thing-by-withdrawing-says-lawrence-wong.

Torson, O. D. (2017, March 22). That Thing About Core Banking Platform. Retrieved from www.medium.com: https://medium.com/@odtorson/that-thing-about-core-banking-platforms-9e21610ea7ee.

Wang, C. (2020, June 7). Why TikTok made its user so obsessive? The AI Algorithm that got you hooked. Retrieved from www.towardsdatascience: https://towardsdatascience.com/why-tiktok-made-its-user-so-obsessive-the-ai-algorithm-that-got-you-hooked-7895bb1ab423.

Waterman, K., & Bruening, P. J. (2014). Big Data analytics: Risks and responsibilities. *International Data Privacy Law*, 4(2), 89–95.

Westerman, G., Bonnet, D., & McAfee, A. (2014). The nine elements of digital transformation. *MIT Sloan Management Review*.

What is blockchain for business? (n.d.). Retrieved from www.ibm.com: https://www.ibm.com/blockchain/for-business#:~:text=Applications%20of%20blockchain%20for%20business,government%2C%20retail%2C%20and%20more.

What is M-Pesa. (2007). Retrieved from www.vodafone.com: https://www.vodafone.com/what-we-do/services/m-pesa.

What is open source? (n.d.). Retrieved from www.opensource.com: https://opensource.com/resources/what-open-source.

Winder, D. (2020, April 19). Hacker Claims Popular Android App Store Breached: Publishes 20 Million User Credentials. Retrieved from www.forbes.com: https://www.forbes.com/sites/daveywinder/2020/04/19/hacker-claims-android-app-store-breach-publishes-20-million-user-credentials/#27a785da736d.

Wong, J., & Gallagher, D. (2020, June 4). Real Winner in U.S.-China Chip War Won't Be Either Side. Retrieved from www.wsj.com: https://www.wsj.com/articles/real-winner-in-u-s-china-chip-war-wont-be-either-side-11591265619.

World's Biggest Data Breaches & Hacks. (n.d.). Retrieved from www.informationisbeautiful.net: https://www.informationisbeautiful.net/visualizations/worlds-biggest-data-breaches-hacks/.

WTO. (2013). e-Commerce in developing countries. Retrieved from www.wto.org: https://www.wto.org/english/res_e/booksp_e/ecom_brochure_e.pdf.

www.diffen.com. (n.d.). Retrieved from Diffen: https://www.diffen.com/difference/Branch_Banking_vs_Unit_Banking.

4.3 Sample Questions

Question 1
Consider the following statements on the Core Banking System (CBS):
- When it was first introduced, the CBS led to a more customer-centric business strategy through the use of a single database.
- The CBS helped banks to overcome cybersecurity risk.
- The CBS revolutionized the banking industry along with the rise of the commercial internet in the 1990s.

How many of the statements are true of the CBS?

(a) 1
(b) 2
(c) 3

Question 2
Which of the following is the most appropriate aspect of technology risk management to which the setting up of firewalls belongs?

(a) Cybersecurity
(b) Data privacy
(c) Information security

Question 3

In the "war" on technology, the types of technologies that are contested are

(a) Supercomputer, operating systems, and cloud technology
(b) Crypto-currencies, open-source and distributed ledger technology
(c) Chips, supercomputer, and operating systems

Question 4

Which of the following is most appropriate for explaining the relatively stronger development in mobile payment in China and other developing countries than the United States?

(a) The wider embrace of open-source technologies
(b) The low usage of credit cards
(c) None of the above

Solutions

Question 1

Solution: Option **a** is correct.

Only the first point is correct.

Question 2

Solution: Option **a** is correct.

This is mentioned in the text.

Question 3

Solution: Option **c** is correct.

Cloud, distributed ledger, cryptocurrency, open-source are relatively new technology areas. States are not involved in active competition for these. On the other hand, chips, OS, and supercomputers are actively contested.

Question 4

Solution: Option **b** is correct.

Without credit cards, businesses had to find efficient payment means. The solution arose alongside the development of mobile technology.

Chapter 5

Decentralized Regulation and Governance

5.1 Overview

Learning Objectives
- Outline the issues of regulation and governance in the context of decentralization.

Main Takeaways

Main Points
- Regulation and governance are important notions regarding human social interaction and processes.
- Decentralization, brought to the fore by Fintech, is an important context to consider regulation and governance issues.

Main Terms
- **Regulation:** The aspect of governance related to the forward-steering of processes in an organization of a system.
- **Governance:** The aspects of control of an organization or a system towards desirable outcomes.
- **Decentralization:** The redistribution of functional tasks from a single entity in a system to multiple entities.

Decentralization is an emerging practical concept for regulation and governance. It is brought to the fore and general awareness by the rapid developments and innovative solutions in FinTech. As a notion, decentralization has been discussed and researched in governmental circles and academia, particularly in the social sciences and computer science (Decentralization, 2021). It is the stream of research from computer science that goes by the name of Byzantine Generals problems (Lamport *et al.*, 2019) that eventually led to the advent of cryptocurrency networks (Nakamoto, 2019) in which decentralization is a central notion.

The robust developments of FinTech, supported by the continual progress in ambient technologies, have made decentralization a practical possibility across all domains. Regulation and governance are general and consequential notions referring to processes at work in cementing the structures of human sociality (Enfield *et al.*, 2006), to which the study of financial interaction should rightfully belong. The consequence is the necessary accompaniment of regulatory and governance issues wherever coordinated social interaction shifts focus.

The present article is a survey of ideas on decentralized regulation and governance. Much has been written on decentralization, regulation, and governance, separately, as they are fundamental notions in the social sciences. While the composite picture is only an emerging issue, the intense focus on the area has produced much writing and research material.

The article begins with the section *Decentralization in Cryptocurrency Networks* surveying some cryptocurrency networks to reveal the ideas of decentralization, regulation, and governance. Then we will return to the basics in the sections *What is Decentralization?* and *Regulation and Governance* by examining the notions of decentralization, regulation, and governance. These notions used to be just theoretical for the general populace. With the proliferation of technologies and widespread internet usage, they have become concrete for many and a practical application possibility for corporations independent of size. In *Enabling Technologies*, we will survey some salient technological aspects that make inclusive decentralization on a big scale possible. Finally, in the section *Towards Decentralized Societies*, we explore facets of decentralized societies either enabled by or related to decentralized regulation and governance that are either already here or a future possibility.

5.2 Decentralization in Cryptocurrency Networks

5.2.1 *Bitcoin*

Learning Objectives
- Discuss the issues of regulation and governance for the Bitcoin system.

Main Takeaways

Main Points
- The Bitcoin system can function adequately due to its protocol designed to maintain consensus among distributed peers on the global state of bitcoin possessions.
- Regularity in system function is enabled by users who are willing to abide by the protocol and assume that most users are not malicious.
- The developer community behind the Bitcoin protocol is well organized through appropriate governance.
- Regulatory imposition on Bitcoin in incumbent financial regulatory agencies arises with the broader acceptance of Bitcoin as a stable piece of social technology to be reckoned with.

Main Terms
- **Protocol:** A system of rules governing how (software) components are to interact with each other.

Bitcoin is the first successful cryptocurrency project that spawned numerous other similar networks. They share the common characteristic that users can acquire, communicate and change their states on the Internet without relying on a central coordinator. Its success is also manifested through the high price of bitcoin against the US$ (which has risen from around 0.0008 and 0.08 in July 2010 (Bitcoin price history, n.d.) to 33,113 on January 4, 2021 (Bitcoin prices, n.d.)) and the opening up of a wealth of ideas associated to its underlying mechanisms. These ideas have been and are being dissected and reconstituted in the drive to create the next better network or the desire to comprehend what might be in store for society at large now that they are out in the open for anyone who is sufficiently keen and determined to tinker with and to create his or her system of interaction in the virtual world on the Internet or in the real tangible world.

The success of Bitcoin is contingent upon its proper functioning as a system (Meadows, 2008), which comprises users having to maintain a global state whose correctness is commonly agreed upon, as they incessantly send messages to each other to update their personal states.

A system that retains its holistic identity while it updates itself over time has to operate somewhere between the extremes of rigidity and arbitrariness. Too rigid, the system will barely be able to change internally. Too arbitrary, the constituent components will fall apart, causing the system to disintegrate. A physical system, such as a molecule, is held together by the mathematical laws that determine how the atoms making up the molecule interact with each other, insofar as we believe that the mathematical laws faithfully represent nature. An ecological system is a sustainable whole as the prey and predators rely on each other for food and keep competition in balance (Levin *et al.*, 2012). In the first case, the systems are regulated by the mathematical structure. In the second case, the feedback loops between the populations of prey and predators interact with each other.

Human interactional systems also require appropriate regulation to function, albeit in forms that differ from physical and biological systems. In place of mathematical laws, human regulation assumes the shape of man-made rules, laws, or protocols. Unlike living things and atoms, which are not scientifically imbued with a mental state of any sophistication or at all, human beings can cognize, have attitudes, carry in their preexisting value systems. They may cheat in their dealings with each other.

The most concretely visible aspect of Bitcoin is that there is a wallet software that needs to be downloaded and installed by users to be able to communicate with others in the network to be part of the community of bitcoin owners (Antonopoulos, 2014). The wallet software implements the Bitcoin protocol. It allows states in the form of the blockchain to be stored, and it also facilitates communication and transaction between peers on the Internet. Each user has the right to alter the ownership state of another user (and thereby his own) by sending him a number of bitcoins. This is achieved through the broadcasting of transactions in the network. The announced transactions potentially contribute to the global state of the system. To commit transactions to become the global state, an additional step is required whereby a special class of users, known as miners, put transactions into blocks, verifying that the transactions are mutually consistent before appending them to the end of the existing blockchain.

User behavior is thus regulated by the protocol underlying the wallet. State changes intended by the users, made through transactions, are regulated by miners, who are themselves regulated in behavior by the protocol. In large part, the protocol has been created by Satoshi Nakamoto (Nakamoto, 2019). Later developers continue to refine and add to it. Though the developers seem to come up on top in the hierarchy of decision making, their code developmental work is constrained by the need to keep the system on a path of positive growth and take into account voices from the user community.

Regulatory pressure is also imposed by agencies external to the Bitcoin network. By functioning as an observable system of transfers, exchanges of bitcoin with tangible goods and services can occur and be measured. Bitcoin thus functions operationally like money except that it has not been universally labeled as such. The impediment comes from the need to be recognized by the sovereign state, which is a prerequisite to conform to regulations as set by the national financial regulator. Primary concerns of financial regulation towards money-like instruments like Bitcoin are the potential use in criminal activities such as money laundering and tax evasion and the challenge they may pose to national currencies in functioning as legal tender and instrument for economic policies (De Filippi, 2014). National recognition has the effect of bringing the circulation of the instrument in question into mainstream institutions.

Before Bitcoin, attempts to create money-like instruments were stopped (Mullan, 2016) or restricted to local usage (Collom, 2005). These attempts were all organizationally centralized. On the other hand, the Internet, with its transnational nature, has fostered the growth and development of decentralized communities.

Among the remarkable ideas brought forth by the work of Satoshi Nakamoto, here we are concerned with the connections to issues of regulation and governance. A fascinating aspect is how regulation and governance can work out in a decentralized setting. This stands in stark contrast with the usual conception from a command-and-control perspective relative to a singular focal point.

The success of the Bitcoin network shows that decentralized regulation can work through (1) publicly available coded protocol spelling out clearly how interactions between agents should proceed, and (2) computational complexity to effectively ensure no once can cheat. Combined with an appropriate mix of social norms and motivations to provide implicit regulatory constraints, the network success will certainly be born from proper system functioning.

As Bitcoin and other cryptocurrencies gain wider acceptance by central banks worldwide (see (Legality of bitcoin by country or territory, n.d.) and references therein), financial regulators will have to start worrying about what regulation entails in a decentralized setting.

Conventional regulation targets individual entities to which actions and motives can be singularly ascribed. In peer-to-peer networks, which are often designed with the principle of a single point of failure avoidance, it is hard or even impossible to pinpoint individuals to which responsibilities can be attributed. Any well-described functionality may be dispersed among peers through appropriate protocol design to improve the system's robustness. A recent article considers just this problem and proposes to target the edicts and interdictions of regulation towards the middlemen that arise in the application layer above the network (Nabilou, 2019).

5.2.2 *Ethereum*

Learning Objectives
- Discuss the issues of regulation and governance for the Ethereum platform.

Main Takeaways

Main Points
- Ethereum is a cryptocurrency network built on the extension of a Bitcoin conceptual basis by the inclusion of smart contracts.
- In addition to similar regulatory and governance issues surrounding Bitcoin because they are both cryptocurrency networks, the decentralized organizations arising from the smart contracts that Ethereum enables, create a further level of regulatory and governance concerns.
- The use of code to regulate user behavior as smart contracts exemplify it is a manifestation of the concept of regulation by code.

Main Terms
- **Smart contract:** A computer program that runs on a cryptocurrency network that binds a number of users together, coordinating their interaction.
- **Regulation by code:** The notion that when users interact through binding to code, the underlying protocol serves to regulate their behavior.

While it is unknown who the inventor of Bitcoin is, the creator of the Ethereum network, second in value by market capitalization (All Cryptocurrencies, 2021), is well-known to be Vitalik Buterin. In the white paper for Ethereum (Buterin, 2013), Buterin outlined an extension to the Bitcoin protocol over its basic functionality of token transfer among users. Ethereum, known as a smart contract platform, also allows users to create contracts and engage themselves in contractual positions.

Ethereum started by modifying aspects of the Bitcoin architecture to suit its own needs while retaining others to rely on a cryptocurrency network's tried and tested foundation. Smart contracts and the programming language Solidity, invented to write the contracts, are comparable to transactional types and the Script language in Bitcoin, only more elaborate.

While Bitcoin employs a temporally hard Proof-of-Work (PoW) algorithm, Ethereum initially used a memory-hard hashing algorithm, known as Ethash, intended to avoid an energy-wasting mining competition similar to that found in the Bitcoin network.

Ethereum has, since the early stage of its development, been trying to move towards an alternative consensus algorithm called the Proof-of-Stake (PoS). It is believed that the PoS provides a lower barrier of entry into the network, strong resistance against centralization, and better support for shard chains that can support the up-scaling of the network (PoS, 2021).

One may interpret the PoW to be a regulatory protocol. A primary purpose of the algorithm in Bitcoin is to slow down the pace at which miners can complete the verification of their blocks and then broadcast the fact to the network to be accepted by the user community. Conflicts arise when two or more blocks are announced at about the same time. This can split the consensual view of the global state in the network. By adhering to the protocol, the forward flow of change in the network is constrained as there is a significant barrier of a computational nature to overcome for an acceptable change to be composed, thus reducing the chance of forking. This is an exemplary example of regulation by code as it has been discussed by De Filippi and Hassan (De Filippi *et al.*, 2018) since regulation may be understood to be the aspect of governance concerned with the steering of the flow of events and behavior (Braithwaite *et al.*, 2007).

In the Ethereum PoS protocol, the distinguished class of network users who create, check, and confirm blocks are called validators (rather than miners). According to the protocol, validators are chosen randomly from eligible users. One becomes an eligible user by staking, i.e., depositing 32 ETH to activate the validator software. The stake can be lost when validators attest to blocks that should not be so (Staking, 2021).

A primary application of smart contracts is to create a decentralized autonomous organization (DAOs). These are equivalent in concept to companies except that while companies are brought into existence in virtue of a national legal framework, DAOs owe their incarnation to the smart contracts that define them. These smart contracts, in turn, function on the foundation of the Ethereum network. As an analog of a company's board, employees and clients interact via smart contracts enacted over the Ethereum platform in the case of a DAO. Their actions, regulated by the code underlying the smart contract, are interpreted through the Ethereum network and are parsed into changes to the global state manifested by the blockchain.

Just as law operates to regulate the behavior of law-abiding citizens, code operates to regulate the behavior of protocol-abiding network users. Law undergoes gradual change through applications and amendments. But each time it is applied in the deliberation of a case, it is taken to be prescriptive. Similarly, the Ethereum protocol is implemented in code modified through an ongoing developmental process. On the other hand, the network protocol is taken to be correct and provides the bedrock for the creation and maintenance of smart contracts from the perspective of users. In the famous incident of the DAO Hack, it was pointed out that an error caused the incident in the smart contract behind the DAO rather than a bug in the Ethereum protocol (Siegel, 2020). This reinforces the normative strength of the underlying protocol to the users.

5.2.3 *Dfinity*

Learning Objectives
- Discuss the issues of regulation and governance for Dfinity.

Main Takeaways

Main Points
- In the Dfinity cryptocurrency system, governance tokens, known as "neurons," are used for voting to select proposals on project development for the community.

Main Terms
- **Internet Computer:** The system at the heart of Dfinity that can provide cloud computing to the global community in a decentralized manner.

Dfinity is a relatively new blockchain project initiated by Dominic Williams, who based it on a stiftung headquartered in Zug, Switzerland (Dfinity, 2021). Its stated purpose is to create an Internet Computer (IC) that provides cloud computing to the global community based on decentralization principles. Just as Bitcoin provides a decentralized alternative to remove the reliance on a middleman in token transactions, Dfinity aims to provide an alternative to cloud computing currently centered in the big technology firms such as Amazon and Google. Towards its goal, it has created the Internet Computer Protocol (ICP) to replace some existing internet protocols (What is the Internet Computer? 2021).

Financially, it is notable for having raised $102 million from Andreessen Horowitz and Polychain Capital in 2018 (Dfinity, 2021). Upon announcing its open algorithm governance system, its valuation soared to $9.5 billion and is expected to be one of the top cryptocurrency networks in terms of market capitalization when it is launched (Martin, 2020).

Token economics involves ICP tokens (Internet Computer's Token Economics, 2020). These can be transferred or converted into computational cycles for running applications on the IC. This allows the tokens to function as stable coins. In addition, they can also be locked within the Sodium Network — its governance system — to create "neurons" which can be used for voting in proposals on project development on Dfinity.

In this manner, coins, votes, and computational cycles are placed on the same platter, deriving value from one another, indicating a close connection between Finance, governance, and computation.

5.2.4 *Hedera*

Learning Objectives
- Discuss the issues of regulation and governance for Hedera.

Main Takeaways

Main Points
- Hedera is a decentralized cryptocurrency network that achieves consensus by using the Gossip-about-Gossip protocol and Virtual Voting.

- Instead of a blockchain, Hedera uses a data structure called a hashgraph to maintain the global state of the system.

Main Terms
- **Gossip-about-Gossip:** A protocol that ensures that nodes randomly gossip with other nodes regularly, during which differences in what the nodes know are leveled out through the exchange of the differences.
- **Hashgraph:** A data structure used by Hedera, in place of the blockchain, to maintain the consensual global state of its decentralized network system.
- **Virtual voting:** A way for each user to look at its own copy of the history of communication in the network to ultimately sequence the transactions in a way that is in consensus with everyone else in the system.

Unlike all the examples discussed thus far, Hedera Hashgraph does not operate based on a blockchain. The global state of the network is maintained in a distributed and decentralized manner, but instead of blocks and blockchain, the protocol uses a directed acyclic graph (DAG), called a hashgraph in this context, to sequence transactions as they arise over time across the network. Mining, as found in PoW algorithms, is not required. The system was first released in 2017 by Leemon Baird and is distinguished from Bitcoin and Ethereum by having a high throughput of over 10,000 transactions per second at a low transaction fee (Home Page, 2021).

Hedera's codebase is patented and not open source. This prevents its system from forking and also reduces the transparency of its protocols. Nonetheless, it has been proof-checked by Coq (the most established mathematical proof checker) that the hashgraph consensus algorithm is asynchronous Byzantine faulty tolerant (ABFT), thus theoretically affirming the security of the system.

Consensus in Hedera is achieved through its Gossip-about-Gossip protocol and Virtual Voting (Baird, 2017; Hedera Hashgraph, 2021). In place of blocks, Hedera has events. An event is created when a node communicates with another node. Each event contains transactions and some other data that can be used to trace back the entire communication history of the network. The protocol ensures that nodes randomly gossip with other nodes regularly, during which differences in what the nodes know are leveled out through exchanging the differences. In this way, information spreads through the network exponentially fast, explaining the high throughput of the system. Virtual voting is a way for each user to look at its own copy of the history of communication in the network to ultimately sequence the transactions in a way that is in consensus with everyone else in the system.

The nodes in the Hedera Hashgraph network are of two types: Consensus and Mirror. Consensus nodes receive transactions and contribute to consensus establishment in the network. The system rewards them. Mirror nodes store transactions and help optimize queries within the network. They do not send transactions or take part in consensus maintenance.

Hedera achieves decentralized regulation and governance at two levels — the interactional level within the network and the organizational level of the entire system.

The hashgraph consensus algorithm removes the need to crucially rely on any node or distinguished class of nodes (such as the miners in PoW systems) to achieve consensus.

The Gossip-about-Gossip protocol and Virtual Voting carried out by each node according to the protocol will ensure that transactions are duly transmitted and receive an ordering in time that is agreeable to all users. The Consensus nodes are unlike miners who require high-speed equipment to perform their function. Any node that carries the necessary software will contribute to consensus establishment. Hence, regulation at the interactional level is decentralized.

The governance at the organizational level is decentralized by developing the Hedera Hashgraph overseen by a governing council comprising 39 leading global organizations (Hedera Governing Council, 2021). Membership on the council is term-limited, and members do not receive profits from the network's operations. Members take partial ownership of the Hedera Hashgraph LLC in a publicly available agreement. Council members are responsible for making high-level decisions on software upgrades, treasury management, etc. The governing council members also operate the Consensus nodes for reaching consensus at the initial stage of the network's development. These operations are expected to be handed over to the community progressively over time.

5.3 What is Decentralization?

Learning Objectives
• Discuss the concept of decentralization.

Main Takeaways

Main Points
• The concept of decentralization can be traced back to the 18th century.

- Decentralization is commonly discussed in the context of government, economics, and technology.
- Decentralization can be discussed through system theory concepts.

Main Terms
- **Center:** An entity in a system that plays a crucial functional role for the system.
- **Peripheral:** The collection of entities in a system that is distant from the center.

While our concern with decentralization, as discussed in this article, is associated with the recent rise in the importance of Fintech as an academic area and industrial applications, decentralization is not a new idea. French writers used the term at the turn of the 18th century in France after the revolution, a period marked by efforts to redistribute government functions (Leroux, 2012). If one submits to those who observe the trends of civilizations through history, the alternation of decentralization and centralization may be a recurrent regularity in phases of development amidst the overall progress of humanity (Chase-Dunn, 2018; Sanderson, 1995).

Decentralization is commonly discussed in the context of government, economics, and technology. In governmental matters, the tendency to decentralize arises when centralization is perceived to be a bane with sufficient political traction. The result of decentralization is to diminish the decision-making power concentrated at the center, shifting that power to the peripheral. In economics, the idea of free markets (Doyle, 2005), where the interacting participants produce positive outcomes without explicit means of coordination, is directly translatable to decentralization. Technological decentralization is best represented by the Internet, which is now globally familiar. However, at best, this is an ideal that might have held initially.

For now, technological giants occupy the center-space in the Internet universe (De Filippi, 2019) either through the flow of internet traffic or through the use of cloud services.

Government, economics, and technology encompass such a wide range of human activities that it is fair to surmise that the dynamics of centralization and decentralization exist in every sphere of human social interaction. This perspective seems natural when attempting to understand the nature of the Fintech phenomenon precipitated by Bitcoin and is currently all the rage.

True to this view, developments in cryptocurrency networks under Fintech are not merely focused on Finance. Dfinity — one of the currently hottest cryptocurrency projects — has a plan to decentralize the Internet, which involves transforming tokens representing votes, economic value, and computational cycles from one form to another. It is anticipated that blockchain technology will bring about fundamental changes to society (Swan, 2015).

To gain insight into the nature of decentralization, it is helpful to adopt an abstract view with systems theory concepts (Meadows, 2008). Communication is the fabric of human social existence. Representing a human agent as a circle and edges connecting circles to be lines of communication between them, centralization and decentralization may be represented by Figures 5.1 and 5.2.

While centralization seems to be canonically represented by the diagram on the left, the one on the right is merely a schematic possibility out of infinitely many. Decentralization means removing a central node while maintaining the functional purpose of the system in question.

Reality is more complex than what these pictures suggest, as there may exist many different modes of connection amongst the entities. Thus, while cryptocurrency networks are decentralized, they are so for the specific purpose of storing records of transactions that make sense only in the

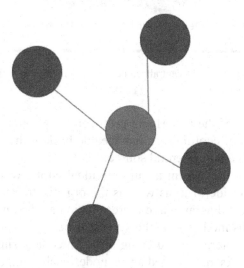

Figure 5.1:   Centralized communication topology.

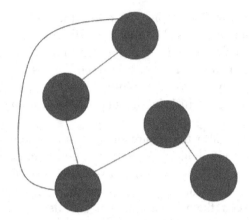

Figure 5.2:　Decentralized communication topology.

Firm

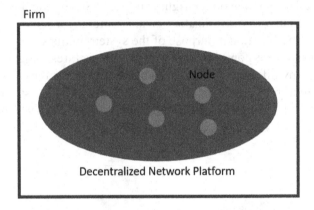

Figure 5.3:　Decentralized network maintained by a firm.

common context of the underlying protocol. This commonly shared and accepted system of coordination is traceable back to the originator of the project, which is again a central source.

Representing the system as an individual entity, which contains the network nodes inside of it, as well as the organization that launches the system, we have a diagrammatic representation as shown in Figure 5.3.

This view distinctly shows the system as being composed of interacting components internally and being represented as a single entity when seen externally. As represented by a node, each component has some degree of autonomy in carrying out its own actions. At the same time, it has to contend with co-existential issues within the system.

As we will discuss next, regulation and governance must proceed along with such an appreciation of the underlying structure (Hsieh *et al.*, 2017).

5.4 Regulation and Governance

5.4.1 *Definitions and Related Notions*

Learning Objectives
- Present definitions of regulation and governance and discuss related notions.

Main Takeaways

Main Points
- In critical analyses of the notions of regulation and governance, it is found that there exists a variety of interpretations surrounding common conceptions.
- A common conception is that governance refers to aspects of control of a system or an organization. At the same time, regulation is a subset of it that refers to the forward-steering of the flow of the organization or system towards intended goals.
- Commonly related notions are control, management, law, compliance, accounting, reporting, and risk.

Main Terms
- **Accounting:** May refer to the activity associated with the discipline of Accountancy or the social concept of responsible recording and tracking.
- **Compliance:** The notion, dual to regulation, that concerns the circumstances around how agents may respond to regulation.
- **Control:** The power to affect the state of a system.
- **Law:** Is the basis on which regulation in a sovereign state can be rightfully carried out.
- **Management:** All activities involved in running an organization.
- **Reporting:** The transmission of data, recorded in some media form, to inform others of a situation.
- **Risk:** The negative aspects of uncertainty.

We do not attempt to define regulation and governance but only to provide a survey of definitions from the literature to indicate the variety of interpretations that can be attached to them on the one hand and to obtain some clarity about the notions for critical analyses on the other.

In a reflection on regulation (Black, 2002), Julia Black, in working towards a suitable conceptualization of regulation in a decentered context, discusses numerous definitions of and perspectives on the term found in the literature. The primary understanding of the term comes from the command-and-control perspective, where a central source of power exercises control over constituents through the use of rules that are enforced through sanctions. A government-centric elaboration results in the following three textbook definitions (Black, 2002, Sect. 2):

- Regulation is the promulgation of rules by the government accompanied by mechanisms for monitoring and enforcement, usually assumed to be performed through a specialist public agency.
- Regulation is any form of direct state intervention in the economy, whatever form that intervention might take.
- Regulation is all mechanisms of social control or influence affecting all aspects of behavior from whatever source, whether they are intentional or not.

These definitions are taken as a reference point against which definitions from other contexts are contrasted. The following key dimensions underlying the notion are also picked out (Black, 2002, Sect. 2):

- What is regulation?
- Who or what does it?
- What form does it take?
- With respect to what actors or area of life?
- How is it done, via what instruments/techniques?

As well as a proposed definition that applies to decentered settings (Black, 2002, Sect. 3):

> *Regulation is the sustained and focused attempt to alter the behavior of others according to defined standards or purposes to produce a broadly identified outcome or outcomes, which may involve mechanisms of standard-setting, information-gathering, and behavior modification.*

This definition is inspired by cybernetics (Ashby, 1961; Novikov, 2015), namely the study of control within general systems theory (Von Bertalanffy, 1972; Meadows, 2008). It includes elements of intentionality and goal-setting, the broad generality of systems (e.g., not merely confined to governments), and a specification of tasks required to bring about the outcomes. Apart from its internal semantics, which establishes its status as a definition, it harbors an empirical angle that enables it to be applied to and tested on social activities in the real world on which the regulatory standards constrain.

Governance and regulation are often mentioned alongside each other. In loose usage, as alluded to before, the terms are interchangeable as both connote control towards achieving desirable outcomes. However, each term has been formed into common phrases or is associated with other terms which provide additional distinctive depth to them, e.g., corporate governance, governance and government, regulation, and regulatory bodies According to the introduction to the journal Regulation and Governance (Braithwaite *et al.*, 2007), governance is about providing, distributing, and regulating in the context of governments.

Regulation is seen to be a narrower term than governance, relating to the steering of the flow of events and behavior. In general, we may take governance to refer to all aspects of control of an organization or a system towards desirable outcomes. Between regulation and governance, governance refers to all visible aspects of control that also include regulation. Hence, governance is a more encompassing term, while regulation is more closely associated with a process of forward steering.

Several notions are often related to regulation and governance, namely, Control, Management, Law, Compliance, Accounting, Reporting, and Risk. It is apt to mention them here for the record and to briefly clarify the relationships as analysis of issues of regulation and governance may readily invoke one or another. It is to note that the clarity is meant only to pivot and steer the present discussion as it has been noted, for instance, by Julia Black in (Black, 2002), that terms only gain their meanings from other terms. The accurate picture is vague, and what we can cognize are semantical shades for each term from a web of concepts.

- Control — Control is a basis notion of cybernetics (Ashby, 1961; Novikov, 2015), coming in at an abstract level where systems theory (Von Bertalanffy, 1972; Meadows, 2008) is meant to address. The power of abstraction is general applicability. In virtue of this, we have explained regulation and governance in terms of control of systems above.

- Management — Management refers to all activities involved in running an organization (Robbins *et al.*, 2018). Standards and purposes are presupposed. Hence, management occurs within the constraints set out by governance and regulation.
- Law — The relationship between law and regulation is conceptually analyzed (Black, 2002). It is admitted that definitions of law and regulation are redescriptions of one another in the broad view. With this as a caveat, we may make do with the common shade of meaning from the description that regulation is the part of the law that is *instrumentalist in orientation and contained in the mass of technical statutes, statutory instruments, and other secondary and tertiary rules that set out, often in intimidating detail, standards of conduct to be followed* (Black, 2002, Sect. 4).
- Compliance — Compliance occupies the opposite side of a coin to regulation. If an agent regulates another, the other is said to be in compliance if he submits to be regulated. This connection brings out the relational nature of regulation. It is meaningless to discuss regulation in a vacuum without also seeking to understand the driving forces behind those who comply. Theoretical analyses of compliance, or responses to regulation, may be found in (Etienne, 2011; Mitchell, 2007).
- Accounting — Accounting can refer to the discipline of Accountancy or its more general meaning as it is used in the phrase *social accounting* or *to account for*. Its essential aspects seem to be (1) reporting to others the internal state of an entity and (2) committing to being consistent or compliant with stipulations. Point (2) ensures that what is reported in Point (1) is relevant and trustworthy to those in the community from which the stipulations arise. In this light, accounting is a social concept.
- Reporting — Reporting refers to the transmission (either explicitly or implicitly) of data recorded in some media form to inform others of a situation.
- Risk — Risk refers to the negative aspects of uncertainty. Uncertainties may bring about positive outcomes, in which case, the appropriate term/phrase to use is *potential, potential reward*, or just *reward* in short. In Finance, this is usually referred to by the term *return*. Risk is an inseparable aspect of regulation and governance as the control of the system occurs through time. There is always an element of

failure to achieve the intended goal or maintain the trajectory on a good path.

5.5 Enabling Technologies

5.5.1 *The Internet*

Learning Objectives
- Outline the evolution of the Internet as an enabling technology for the decentralization of social processes.

Main Takeaways

Main Points
- The Internet has made possible near-instantaneous communication across the globe at affordable costs.
- The liveness of the Internet has fostered the growth of communities constituted by members who share common interests and unrestricted by geographical distances or cultural differences.
- Open-source software communities are a distinguished class of Internet communities that have precipitated the vibrant FinTech developments since Bitcoin appeared on the scene in c. 2009.

Main Terms
- **Open source:** An internet movement that requires software to be published together with its source code so that others may learn from the underlying ideas.

Just as the ancient Silk Road connected the East to the West across the Asian continent between 114 BCE and 1450 CE made possible trade and cultural exchange where it had not been possible before (Silk Road, 2021), the Internet of the 20th century connected the world into an informational web that made possible the near-instantaneous transmission of data on the globe, allowing not just numbers to be sent, but complex software as well, fostering the growth of communities that are engaged in various forms of interactions.

The open nature of the Internet allowed for widespread participation. The invention of HTML and the Internet browsers in the 1990s enabled media forms with rich semantical content to be transmitted (A history of HTML, 2021). Informational forms that are most meaningful to man are writings, images, and motion. Thus, text alone is insufficient as a medium of informational exchange if the Internet were meant for everyone. Images and videos are necessary.

The Internet enabled collaboration beyond one-off projects. It became possible to store large amounts of data with cheap storage devices to be later retrieved. This allowed activities to be recorded and gave rise to communities in which members come together for some shared purpose. The stored memory will enable identities to be formed in a virtual world, which may or may not be closely associated with any in the real world. Each identity maps to the agent that operates that identity in the community and is associated with its deeds in there.

A most distinguished class of these are the open-source software development communities. These peer production communities have been well studied (Benkler, 2016) as they epitomize a novel form of economic production. The target of their production is software. The most remarkable ones are complex software systems comparable to or even better than those produced by conventional corporations that regard software as private property and protect them with secrecy and intellectual property law. On the contrary, open-source software is served with open source licenses (Rosen, 2005) that generally prevent anyone down the line of usage from hoarding the software for personal use. This ensures the persistence of a common reference point from which construction may progress without the risk of disruption.

Interestingly, many cryptocurrency network communities, including the original one, are built upon such open-source software communities. Real-world communities that persist must be structured and well embedded into their ambient social and physical environment. However, numbing familiarity with and assumptions about the background in the real world often hide away the structure beneath. In contrast, the evolution of communities and interactions on the Internet lay bare the underlying structure and processes.

5.5.2 *RegTech and Other Techs*

Learning Objectives
- Review the development of technologies in regulation and related domains.

Main Takeaways

Main Points

- The development of regulatory technologies may be distinguished into three phases: RegTech 1.0, RegTech 2.0, and RegTech 3.0.
- The middle phase RegTech 2.0 is associated with the rise of Fintech during the fallout from the Global Financial Crisis of 2008, while RegTech 1.0 and RegTech 3.0 span the periods before and after it, respectively.
- RegTech arises alongside FinTech as regulators need to keep up with the appropriate technological means to carry out their tasks in light of technological changes to how financial interactions are carried out.

Main Terms

- **GovTech:** The technological ecosystem that arises alongside FinTech to serve the functions of governmental services.
- **LegalTech:** The technological ecosystem that arises alongside FinTech to serve the functions of legal services.
- **RegTech:** The technological ecosystem that arises alongside FinTech to serve the functions of regulation.

RegTech may be understood to stand for regulatory technology or as a buzzword. According to (Weber, 2017), the latter first arose in the United Kingdom in 2015 when it was mentioned alongside FinTech by the Government Office for Science and the British Finance Ministry. RegTech is sometimes regarded as a part of Fintech.

This takes the view that regulation is a part of Finance. Any system with an identifiable regulatory component may have RegTech as a subset of the technologies applied to the system. Thus, GovTech (Desmond *et al.*, 2017) and LegalTech may justifiably claim RegTech as a component. Note that the "Gov" in GovTech is more commonly aligned to "Government" than "Governance."

The landscape of RegTech is given a detailed analysis by Arner *et al.* (2016).

The evolution of regulatory technology is segmented into RegTech 1.0, RegTech 2.0, and RegTech 3.0. RegTech 2.0 is the phase associated with the rise of FinTech that occurs after the Global Financial Crisis of 2008 and the advent of the cryptocurrency networks starting with Bitcoin from 2009. RegTech 1.0 is before that, and RegTech 3.0 refers to the impending future. RegTech 2.0 is characterized by the massive data requirements due to post-crisis regulation changes, progress in data science, economic incentives for companies to enter the space with innovative solutions to lower the cost of regulation, and the pressure to improve supervisory tools regulators given their mandate to uphold financial stability.

RegTech comprises technologies for improving regulatory processes as well as complementary compliance. Monitoring, reporting, risk management, fraud, market manipulation detection, complex transactions analysis, and stress testing are conventional concerns. The continual development and widespread adoption of technology can produce an abundance of data for analysis. This is matched by the development of technological tools for analytics and big data analysis. The traditional regulatory concern of Know-Your-Customer (KYC) is transforming into the more encompassing goal of Know-Your-Data (KYD) (Weber, 2017).

FinTech ushers in many new players into the space of financial service providers, with the Internet constituting the medium of communication and exchange. This is indeed a shift at the infrastructural level as traditional financial communication is focused on networks that serve the heavyweights of financial institutions, namely the banks and the exchanges, such as SWIFT, CHIPS, and Fedwire. With the Internet as a medium, cybersecurity emerges more prominently as a financial regulatory issue. RegTech is also causing a reconsideration of regulatory frameworks.

A recent new dimension is a regulatory sandbox in which FinTech systems are created and tested in a closed environment for the suitability, efficiency, and risk assessments (Arner *et al.*, 2016).

5.6 From Decentralized Communities to Decentralized Societies

5.6.1 *Internet Governance and ICANN*

Learning Objectives
- Recognize the decentralized nature of internet governance and the dual centralized, decentralized nature of ICANN.

Main Takeaways

Main Points
- The governance structure of today's Internet is decentralized and follows a multi-stakeholder model.
- The ICANN is a U.S-based global organization. It is decentralized in virtue of its global nature. It is centralized as it is the sole organizational entity that maintains a register of internet addresses cum domain names.

Main Terms
- **ICANN:** Internet Corporation for Assigned Names and Numbers.

It is apt to begin an account of decentralized societies with the Internet. The Internet enables many of the possibilities for decentralized regulation and governance, and the Internet itself is a model of decentralized governance, albeit an imperfect one.

The Internet grew into the shape it takes today by a complex amalgamation of smaller networks over time. The earliest network in the story is the ARPANET, created in the 1960s and was under the purview of the Department of Defense of the United States. The CSNET started operating in 1981 to connect computer science departments at academic and research institutions. The NSFNET was created by the U.S. National Science Foundation (NSF) in 1985, which eventually played the role of bridging the ARPANET and CSNET into today's Internet. Participation in these networks was initially restricted to the military and the academic in the United States. The advent of the NSFNET brought involvement of academic institutions across the world through the 1980s. Commercial networks began to interconnect in 1991.

The critical issue in enabling such a vast network to operate soundly and provide global communication services to the global community for social good is coordination. This is provided by appropriate governance. The governance structure of today's Internet is decentralized and follows a multi-stakeholder model. The stakeholders are drawn from the government and private sectors, academic and research communities, and various organizations internationally. In such a model, global actors are convened to contribute to or vote on proposals. Those proposals which achieve appropriate consensus become tasks for construction works on the Internet. This can be a laborious process.

While the governance of the Internet is basically decentralized, there is an aspect of the Internet that is centralized in one organization. The

Internet Corporation for Assigned Names and Numbers (ICANN) maintains the Domain Name System (DNS) root zone of the Internet. The DNS is how entities on the Internet can locate each other by names as names associated with IP addresses in the hierarchical DNS. As this is a crucial and fundamental service, ICANN may be seen as a critical internet infrastructural organization.

The ICANN is a U.S.-based non-profit organization. It had been contracted to the National Telecommunications and Information Administration (NTIA) of the United States Department of Commerce to provide the Internet Assigned Numbers Authority (IANA) stewardship functions and was under the oversight of the Department of Commerce. It transited into a global multi-stakeholder organization from October 2016, when the contract with the Department of Commerce ended.

Due to its association with the United States government and its power to decide on domain names and issuance prices, ICANN has been the subject of criticisms. The European Commission has, in the past, called for the reduction of U.S. authority over ICANN (Internet governance too US-centric, 2014). Opponents argue that ICANN's position allows it to censor websites unilaterally, to which ICANN has been obliged to explain that it is not the Internet Content Police (ICANN, 2015).

Blockchain domain names are an application of blockchain technology to create a decentralized DNS. Having the records of internet addresses and names stored in a network of peers ensures that no one entity can exercise absolute control over the usage of domain names in the network. The Interplanetary File System (IPFS) is a protocol for storing and sharing data in a peer-to-peer network that can perform this function. Attempts have been made to use the IPFS to create blockchain domain names to circumvent the restrictions set by ICANN (Unstoppable Domains Partners, 2020).

Thus conveyed, the overall picture is the necessity of some form of decentralized governance in a distributed setting with multiple stakeholders such as the Internet. At the same time, centralization and decentralization forces act in a constant tug-of-war in ongoing developmental processes.

5.6.2 *Decentralized Finance (DeFi)*

Learning Objectives
- Present Decentralized Finance (DeFi) as a range of financial applications that have arisen over cryptocurrency networks and, in particular, smart contract platforms.

Main Takeaways

Main Points

- DeFi is the notion that borrowing, lending, trading, asset management, insurance, and other familiar financial operations are carried out in a decentralized setting.
- Centers that are dispersed through decentralization may gather again in different forms somewhere in the DeFi value chain.
- Regulation may be built into the design of DeFi in the form of embedded regulation.

Main Terms

- **Compound:** A prime example of a DeFi platform.
- **cToken:** The token in exchange for a deposit in other cryptocurrencies into the Compound platform.
- **DeFi:** Decentralized finance.
- **Embedded regulation:** The notion that regulation of a decentralized network is performed by entities that are found within the network.

DeFi is the notion that borrowing, lending, trading, asset management, insurance, and other familiar financial operations are carried out in a decentralized setting, in contrast to the reliance on middlemen as it has conventionally been the norm (Hertig, 2020). The scope of issues around DeFi ranges from specific arrangements of how each type of financial operation is to be carried out decentralized to the global consideration of the impact on the financial system if the role of middlemen is replaced by smart contracts. Just as the finance industry is subject to strict regulation, DeFi will also come under the same scrutiny for systemic risk. Decentralized regulation will thus become a significant concern.

Without waiting for conventional Finance to figure out how to transform operations to work in a decentralized setting to reap the potential benefits such as lower transactional costs, the world of cryptocurrency networks has begun experimenting with DeFi. Smart contract platforms such as Ethereum are particularly fertile grounds for such experimentations as financial operations can be implemented through smart contracts. The ecosystem of decentralized applications (dApps) and DAOs on these platforms provide an environment where financial services may thrive, and DeFi take root. The blockchain software technology company ConsenSys even compiles and publishes the state of DeFi development on the Ethereum platform every quarter. Among the DeFi applications that have sprung up are decentralized exchanges, lending platforms, stable coins, and prediction markets.

A leading example of a DeFi platform is Compound (https:// compound.finance/) which comprises at its core, a protocol together with the ecosystem of dApps that are written with it. Compound is primarily concerned with the borrowing and lending of a set of cryptocurrencies which, at one Point, comprises Dai, Ether, USD Coin, 0x, Tether, Wrapped BTC, Basic Attention Token, Augur, and Sai. A user may lend to Compound any of these tokens and receive Compound tokens, also known as cTokens, in exchange. cTokens are equivalent to bank deposits, and they represent the amount of assets held in Compound. Just like ordinary tokens, they can be transferred to other users. When borrowing one token, a user needs to submit and lock in another type of token as collateral with Compound. If the collateral falls in value below that of the borrowing, the user loses his collateral but gets to keep the borrowing.

Interest is earned by the user in the case of lending to Compound, while it is charged in the case of borrowing. Interest rates are calculated by the protocol and are commensurate with the pool of tokens that are held — the bigger the size of the pool, the lower the rates tend to be. Compound also has a governance token, known as COMP, issued to borrowers and lenders in proportion to the interest yielded from the assets lent or borrowed. Governance tokens are created by the protocol each time an Ethereum block is mined. Any user can vote to change the interest rates with the governance token in his possession. If a proposal garners at least 1% of the total COMP supply, it is accepted, and code change is effectuated over the next several days. In this manner, Compound is a decentralized, self-governing system, regulated and coordinated through its protocol.

The cTokens of Compound can be put into service in the Compound ecosystem to earn yield, giving rise to yield farming or liquidity mining activity. For instance, cTokens may be parked at trading venues for token pairs known as liquidity pools. Each pool corresponds to a pair of tokens. These pools are maintained by automated market makers, much like in the real world of currency exchanges. Market makers hedge their risks by maintaining these liquidity pools. The larger the size of a pool, the less risk there is for the pool to dry up in the face of impending requests for exchange. The quantities of the two tokens in the pool also determine the exchange rate. Pools compete with each other for liquidity through the offer of attractive yields.

In conventional Finance, regulation plays a necessary function to control risk at the systemic level and protect consumers of financial products. DeFi challenges conventional regulation because it has always been targeted at identifiable entities focusing on key individuals in the financial ecosystem. In DeFi, these players are either dispersed into a much larger pool with distributed roles and responsibilities, replaced by roles with no fixed identity, or substituted by protocols and codes. This is at the heart of the challenge to regulation brought about by decentralization. Just as FinTech arises with decentralization, it is expected that RegTech will also evolve accordingly to acquire the technological capabilities for decentralized regulation. In the article (Zetzsche *et al.*, 2020), which examines DeFi from the perspective of regulation, the authors consider the potential of DeFi to dilute the effectiveness of traditional methods of regulation and enforcement.

A stance of resolution is achieved by two interesting ideas that are put across in the paper: (1) that centers that are dispersed through decentralization will gather again in different forms somewhere in the DeFi value chain, and (2) regulation may be built into the design of DeFi in the form of embedded regulation. Point (1) is a consolation to conventional regulation as traditional means may still be applied to the new centers that arise in the DeFi value chain. For instance, (Nabilou, 2019) considers the possibility to refocus regulation on the applications that arise from the decentralized systems as an indirect way to regulate since the existence of the decentralized infrastructure is inseparable from the downstream value chain that it creates. Point (2) is the ultimate expression of how decentralized regulation may take shape with developments in RegTech.

5.6.3 *Governance of Common Goods*

Learning Objectives
- Sketch how the governance of common goods can be carried out with blockchain technology.

Main Takeaways

Main Points
- Using blockchain technology, decentralized governance, and coordinated usage of common-pool resources in a community can be achieved through ex-ante automation and ex-post verification.

Main Terms
- **Common-pool resources:** Natural or informational resources that are commonly shared by users from a community.
- **Ex-ante automation:** The creation of rules, algorithms, and processes based on forecasts of activities.
- **Ex-post verification:** The verification of adherence to the protocol after the occurrence of intended activities.

"Goods" here is taken in the general sense to mean "common-pool resources" (CPR). Thus, goods may refer to natural resources or informational common resources, such as open-source software.

The governance of CPR is a traditional topic of investigation by the economist cum Nobel Laureate Elinor Ostrom. The central issue of a CPR is that without suitable coordination, the CPR is likely to be either under- or over-utilized. On the contrary, if the community can monitor its members behaviorally and sanction offenders, then it is possible to improve the usage of the CPR towards optimality. A special unit will have to be designated for surveillance and policing to maintain coordination within the community in a centralized setting. Without the appropriate technology, this is difficult to achieve in a decentralized setting (Ostrom, 2000).

Using blockchain technology, (Poux *et al.*, 2020) argues that coordinated usage of CPR in a community through decentralized governance can be achieved through *ex-ante* automation and *ex-post* verification. Through the use of smart contracts, the former permits cooperation without having to rely on a trusted middleman. The latter helps establish confidence and trust in the means of coordination achieved through software. These measures reduce the need to have centralized surveillance and policing.

An actual example of a blockchain system used in the tracking of goods is Provenance (Baker *et al.*, 2015). The system records the state of goods to be transported on the blockchain so that agents dealing with the goods along the supply chain can interact off the data without the need for a central and trusted third party. This may also be a boon to sustainability efforts since the origin of the goods is typically also written into the blockchain.

References/Further Readings

A history of HTML (2021, January 19). Retrieved from https://www.w3.org/People/Raggett/book4/ch02.html.

All Cryptocurrencies. (2021, January 7). Retrieved from https://coinmarketcap.com/all/views/all/.

Antonopoulos, A. M. (2014). *Mastering Bitcoin: Unlocking Digital Cryptocurrencies*. O'Reilly Media, Inc.

Arner, D. W., Barberis, J. N., & Buckley, R. P. (2016). The emergence of RegTech 2.0: From know your customer to know your data.

Ashby, W. R. (1961). *An Introduction to Cybernetics*. Chapman & Hall Ltd.

Baird, L. (2017, September 14). How Hashgraph Works — A Simple Explanation w/ Pictures [Video]. YouTube. https://www.youtube.com/watch?v=wgwYU1Zr9Tg.

Baker, J., & Steiner, J. (2015). Provenance Blockchain: The Solution for Transparency in Product. Provenance.org.

Benkler, Y. (2016). Peer production and cooperation. In *Handbook on the Economics of the Internet*. Edward Elgar Publishing.

Von Bertalanffy, L. (1972). The history and status of general systems theory. *Academy of Management Journal*, 15(4), 407–426.

Bitcoin price history. (n.d.). Retrieved from https://www.investopedia.com/articles/forex/121815/bitcoins-price-history.asp.

Bitcoin prices. (n.d.). Retrieved from https://www.coinbase.com/price/bitcoin.

Black, J. (2002). Critical reflections on regulation. *Australian Journal of Legal Philosophy*, 27, 1.

Braithwaite, J., Coglianese, C., & Levi-Faur, D. (2007). Can regulation and governance make a difference? *Regulation & Governance*, 1(1), 1–7.

Buterin, V. (2013). A Next Generation Smart Contract & Decentralized Application Platform. Whitepaper. Ethereum Foundation.

Chase-Dunn, C. (2018). *Rise and Demise: Comparing World Systems*. Routledge.

Collom, E. (2005). Community currency in the United States: The social environments in which it emerges and survives. *Environment and Planning A*, 37(9), 1565–1587.

Decentralization. (2021, January 20). Wikipedia. https://en.wikipedia.org/wiki/Decentralization.

Desmond, J., & Kotecha, B. (2017). State of the UK GovTech Market. Retrieved from public.io.

Dfinity. (2021, January 12). Wikipedia. https://en.wikipedia.org/wiki/Dfinity.

Doyle, E. (2005). *The Economic System*. John Wiley & Sons.

Enfield, N. J., & Levinson, S. C. (2006). Human sociality as a new interdisciplinary field.

Etienne, J. (2011). Compliance theory: A goal framing approach. *Law & Policy*, 33(3), 305–333.

De Filippi, P. (2014). Bitcoin: A regulatory nightmare to a libertarian dream. *Internet Policy Review*, 3(2).

De Filippi, P. (2019). Blockchain Technology and Decentralized Governance: The Pitfalls of a Trustless Dream. Decentralized Thriving: Governance and Community on the Web, 3.

Harper, C. (2020, December 23). What is XRP, and How is it Related to Ripple? CoinDesk. https://www.coindesk.com/what-is-ripple-what-is-xrp.

Hedera Governing Council (2021, January 12). Retrieved from https://hedera. com/council.

Hedera Hashgraph (2021, January 12). Retrieved from https://en.bitcoinwiki.org/ wiki/Hedera_Hashgraph.

Hertig, A. (2020, September 19). What is DeFi? CoinDesk. https://www. coindesk.com/what-is-defi.

Home Page (2021, January 12). Hedera Hashgraph. https://hedera.com/.

Hsieh, Y. Y., Vergne, J. P. J., & Wang, S. (2017). The internal and external governance of blockchain-basedorganizations: Evidence from cryptocurrencies. In *Bitcoin and Beyond* (Open Access) (pp. 48–68). Routledge.

ICANN is Not the Internet Content Police (2015, June 12). ICANN. https://www. icann.org/news/blog/icann-is-not-the-internet-content-police.

Internet governance too US-centric, says European commission (2014, February 12). *The Guardian*. https://www.theguardian.com/technology/2014/feb/12/ internet-governance-us-european-commission.

Lamport, L., Shostak, R., & Pease, M. (2019). The Byzantine generals problem. In *Concurrency: The Works of Leslie Lamport* (pp. 203–226).

Leroux, R. (Ed.). (2012). *French Liberalism in the 19th Century: An Anthology*. Routledge.

Legality of bitcoin by country or territory (n.d.). In Wikipedia. Retrieved from 2021, January 6, https://en.wikipedia.org/wiki/Legality_of_bitcoin_by_ country_or_territory.

Levin, S. A., Carpenter, S. R., Godfray, H. C. J., Kinzig, A. P., Loreau, M., Losos, J. B., ... & Wilcove, D. S. (Eds.). (2012). *The Princeton Guide to Ecology*. Princeton University Press.

Martin, J. (2020, September 30). Dfinity poised to launch straight into Top 5 crypto tokens by market cap. Cointelegraph. https://cointelegraph.com/news/ dfinity-poised-to-launch-straight-into-top-5-crypto-tokens-by-market-cap.

Meadows, D. H. (2008). *Thinking in Systems: A Primer*. Chelsea Green Publishing.

Mitchell, R. B. (2007). Compliance Theory. In *The Oxford Handbook of International Environmental Law*.

Mullan, P. C. (2016). The Liberty Dollar and Bernard von NotHaus. In *A History of Digital Currency in the United States* (pp. 87–109). Palgrave Macmillan, New York.

Nabilou, H. (2019). How to regulate bitcoin? Decentralized regulation for a decentralized cryptocurrency. *International Journal of Law and Information Technology*, 27(3), 266–291.

Nakamoto, S. (2019). *Bitcoin: A Peer-To-Peer Electronic Cash System*. Manubot.

Novikov, D. A. (2015). *Cybernetics: From Past to Future* (Vol. 47). Springer.

Ostrom, E. (2000). Collective action and the evolution of social norms. *Journal of Economic Perspectives*, 14(3), 137–158.

Poux, P., de Filippi, P., & Ramos, S. (2020, December). Blockchains for the governance of common goods. In *Proceedings of the 1st International Workshop on Distributed Infrastructure for Common Good* (pp. 7–12).

Proof-of-Stake (POS) (2021, January 12). Retrieved from https://ethereum.org/en/developers/docs/consensus-mechanisms/pos/.

Robbins, S. P., & Coulter, M. A. (2018). *Management* (14th Edition). Pearson Education.

Rosen, L. (2005). *Open Source Licensing* (Vol. 692). Prentice Hall.

Sanderson, S. K. (1995). *Civilizations and World Systems: Studying World-Historical Change*. Rowman Altamira.

Siegel, D. (2020, December 18). Understanding the DAO Attack. CoinDesk. https://www.coindesk.com/understanding-dao-hack-journalists.

Silk Road. (2021, January 19). Wikipedia. https://en.wikipedia.org/wiki/Silk_Road.

Staking (2021, January 12). Retrieved from https://ethereum.org/en/eth2/staking/.

Swan, M. (2015). *Blockchain: Blueprint for a New Economy*. "O'Reilly Media, Inc."

The Internet Computer's Token Economics: An Overview. (2020, October 7). Medium.https://medium.com/dfinity/the-internet-computers-token-economics-an-overview-29e238bd1d83.

Third-Party Relationships: Risk Management Guidance. (2013, October 30). Office of the Comptroller of the Currency (OCC). https://www.occ.gov/news-issuances/bulletins/2013/bulletin-2013-29.html.

Unstoppable Domains Partners With Opera Browser to Integrate Decentralized Websites. (2020, March 20). Business Wire. https://www.businesswire.com/news/home/20200330005064/en/Unstoppable-Domains-Partners-With-Opera-Browser-to-Integrate-Decentralized-Websites.

Weber, R. H. (2017). Regtech as a new legal challenge. *Journal of Financial Transformation*, 46, 10–17.

What is the Internet Computer? (2021, January 12). Dfinity. https://dfinity.org/faq/what-is-the-internet-computer.

Zetzsche, D. A., Arner, D. W., & Buckley, R. P. (2020). Decentralized Finance. *Journal of Financial Regulation*, 6(2), 172–203.

5.7 Sample Questions

Question 1
Which of the following is associated with a consensus protocol?

(a) Proof-of-Work
(b) Gossip-about-Gossip
(c) All of the above

Question 2
Select the incorrect response to the following statement:
Regulation conventionally proceeds by imposing compliance on individual entities. Thus, regulation will break down in the context of DeFi.

(a) True. There are too many entities over which functions are dispersed, making it impossible to assign responsibility properly
(b) False. A strategy is to impose regulation on business entities that arise from the decentralized network and to prioritize regulation of measures of significance such as size
(c) False. Innovations in RegTech may lead to embedded regulation in decentralized networks

Question 3
Which of the following functions of governance is most closely associated with regulation?

(a) Distributing
(b) Providing
(c) Steering

Question 4
What does regulation by code mean?

(a) It refers collectively to the mechanisms of software developed by RegTech companies
(b) It refers to the imposition of desired behavior by expressing the required stipulations through computer programs and having users interact through these conduits
(c) It refers to having robots to ensure that members of a regulated community conform to stipulations through automated monitoring

Question 5
Which of the following came latest in the organized forward steering of Bitcoin network and community?

(a) Bitcoin protocol
(b) Developer community leadership processes
(c) Regulation by national financial regulators

Solutions

Question 1

Solution: Option **c** is correct.

Proof-of-Work is the consensus protocol of Bitcoin. Gossip-about-Gossip is an algorithm that is used in Hedera.

Question 2

Solution: Option **a** is correct.

The reasons in Options b and c are given in the text to point out how regulation may proceed in the context of decentralized networks.

Question 3

Solution: Option **c** is correct.

Fundamental governance functions distributing, providing, and regulating. Regulating refers to the steering of the flow of events and behavior.

Question 4

Solution: Option **b** is correct.

The text explains "regulation by code" like this: users interact through binding to code, the underlying protocol serves to regulate their behavior.

Question 5

Solution: Option **c** is correct.

Bitcoin protocol came first as it has been the invention of Satoshi Nakamoto. Leadership processes in the developer community come after that. Bitcoin is not under the regulatory purview of financial regulators.

Part C: Global Fintech Trends

Chapter 6

Global Fintech Trends

Learning Objectives
- Review the history and development of financial technology, Fintech regulation, and crises.
- Describe the different Fintech development paths of the developed and emerging markets.
- Summarize the landscape and market structure in six different countries.
- Review the digital disruption from China and responses in ASEAN.
- Discuss the relationship between China and the US in Fintech investment, education, and development.

Main Takeaways

Main Points
- Both US and China are major actors in Fintech.
- Regulation plays an important role in shaping the landscape.
- Fintech is disruptive to the banking sector.
- Student loans play an important role in finance and talents development.
- China has a large number of students outside China and an impact on the US universities.
- China is taking the lead in Fintech with more investment and a national strategy.
- The US is slowing down in investment in Fintech.
- AI, Blockchain, Cloud, and Data Technology are essential for Fintech.
- Data collection is done via IoT and cloud services.

- Singapore, Australia, and India are catching up on Fintech.
- China is dominating and will continue to dominate Fintech with a holistic and comprehensive development in financial services and technology.

Main Terms

- **Fintech Hub:** A region that hosts many Fintech associations contributing to the rapid growth of the sector and several incubators.
- **Global Financial Crisis:** A financial crisis in 2008 when global financial markets and global banking systems were under extreme stress and economies faced a downturn.
- **InsurTech:** A combination of technological innovations and the current insurance industry model to improve efficiency.
- **Near-Field Communication (NFC):** A short-range wireless technology used to transfer information between devices like smartphones quickly and easily.
- **Millennial:** The generation born between 1981 and 1996.
- **Student Loan:** Loan with a competitive rate to support students.
- **Phone-based Wallet:** E-Wallet technology deployed in a phone.
- **Ant Financial:** Formerly known as Alipay and now known as Ant Technology Group. It is China's largest digital payment platform.
- **Financial Technology 1.0:** Technologies focused on infrastructure construction and financial market globalization.
- **Financial Technology 2.0:** Technologies focused on traditional financial institutions and digitization of financial markets.
- **Financial Technology 3.0 or Fintech:** Use of nascent and Mobile Internet technology in the financial sector to create new business models and serve new customers.
- **Big Data Technology:** Various techniques used to extract large information sets and analyze complex data.
- **Artificial intelligence:** Various technologies used to simulate human intelligence with the aid of computation software and hardware.
- **Cloud Computing:** General computer resources like data cloud storage and computing power are not directly managed by individual users or nodes.
- **Blockchain:** A decentralized and distributed ledger that maintains digital records with the aid of cryptography.
- **Internet Finance:** New financing arrangements such as crowdfunding and P2P lending.
- **Fintech Unicorn:** A private company or start-up in Fintech with a high valuation (usually over $1 billion).

- **Evolutionary Algorithm:** This is a subset of evolutionary computation, a generic population-based metaheuristic optimization algorithm.

6.1 Regional Trends and Fintech Future

An introduction to Fintech is given in the Preface and the first chapter of the book by Lee and Linda (2018). This chapter covers the definition of Fintech, the history, the motivation, the problems, the solutions, the types, and the challenges faced by Fintech companies and start-ups. In particular, the LASIC model outlines Fintech unicorn's characteristics and describes the necessary but not sufficient conditions for Fintech start-ups to grow exponentially.

The following reference is selected to provide a comprehensive overview of this topic. You are required to read the listed study materials.

Reference/Further Reading

Lee, D., & Low, L. (2018). *Inclusive Fintech: Blockchain, Cryptocurrency and ICO*. World Scientific, Chapter 10, pp. 437–448.

6.2 Global Fintech Development

6.2.1 *History of Financial Technology and Fintech*

The development of modern Fintech can be traced back 150 years. It can be divided into three stages based on different development foci and features. Financial Technology 1.0 began with the developed countries focusing on infrastructure construction and financial market globalization. Financial Technology 2.0 is about introducing technology to traditional financial institutions and the digitization of financial markets. The emergence and development of Internet technology companies laid the foundation for Financial Technology 3.0 or Fintech, which introduced new and mobile Internet technology. Start-ups and technology companies began to provide financial services. The first three stages of development occurred mainly in developed countries. However, the Financial Technology revolution and rapid development in Asia and Africa can be considered Inclusive Fintech.

(a) Financial Technology 1.0 (1866–1967): Financial Globalization
The beginning of financial globalization was marked by the successful laying of the world's first trans-Atlantic submarine cable in 1866, which

enabled major markets in Europe and the United States to communicate instantaneously, connecting the world economy and finance as a whole.

World War II disrupted the globalization of finance. However, the technology developed in communication encryption and password cracking systems was subsequently used by corporations like IBM (International Business Machines Corporation) and incorporated into early computers. The rapid development of computer technology during the War laid a foundation for the future development of artificial intelligence (AI) and technologies used in the credit card system.

(b) Financial Technology 2.0 (1967–2008): Financial Digitization

In 1967, Barclays Bank in the UK introduced the world's first automated teller machine or ATM, marking the beginning of Financial Technology 2.0. In the same year, Texas Instruments produced the handheld financial calculator, which made the operations of the financial industry more efficient and convenient and improved the efficiency of the financial work.

In the field of payments, Bank Automatic Clearing System (BACS), New York Clearing Houses Inter-Bank Payment System (CHIPS), and Society for Worldwide Interbank Financial Telecommunication (SWIFT) have been successively established to facilitate the settlement of international financial transactions. Also, in terms of securities trading, Nasdaq (NASDAQ), established in 1971, introduced electronic trading for stocks, reducing bid-ask spreads and increasing liquidity in the over-the-counter market.

With the rise of the Internet in the 1990s, Wells Fargo Bank of the United States provided an online account verification service to customers through the World Wide Web in 1995. This development introduced the Internet application in the field of finance and laid the foundation for Financial Technology 3.0, or what is commonly known as Fintech.

(c) Financial Technology 3.0 and Fintech (2008–present): Financial Mobilization

This development of Fintech was followed by the global financial crisis (GFC) in 2008. While traditional finance suffered a setback, Fintech developed rapidly during this period, perhaps as it was seen as a solution to some of the problems plaguing traditional finance despite the rapid development in financial technology. Public mistrust of traditional financial institutions, represented by Banks, provided an opening for Fintech companies to create new business models and serve new customers. In the aftermath of the GFC, financial institutions attempted to improve their profitability with technology.

We also witnessed the evolution of the smartphone during the post-GFC period. The acceleration of mobile data transmission speed provided an opportunity for Financial Technology 3.0 to exploit the field of financial applications on mobile phones and other nascent technologies such as AI, Blockchain, Cloud, and Data Analytics.

6.2.2 The Macro-Development of Technology and the Policy Environment

During Financial Technology 3.0, Fintech business models and technology advanced beyond the Internet. Driven by the technological core of AI, blockchain, cloud computing, and data analytics, the Fintech industry is now involved in payment and settlement, wealth management, loan financing, retail banking, and insurance.

(a) Artificial Intelligence (AI)

The core breakthroughs in applying AI in the financial field lie in deep learning, intelligent analysis, and final intelligent decision making. Big data, cloud computing, intelligent hardware, and subsequent blockchain technologies are all the foundations for supporting the upper layers of AI. From the perspective of the current trend of AI applications in the financial field, the application of computing intelligence combined with big data technology has enabled the employment of such technology in marketing, risk control, payment, investment consulting, investment research, and customer service.

In January 2019, the World Intellectual Property Organization (WIPO), a body under the auspices of the United Nations, released a research report saying that China and the United States are leading the global competition in AI. Besides China and the US, the UK, France, and Japan are all making comprehensive investments in AI. In October 2016, the National Science and Technology Council in the US published two important strategy documents: "Prepare for the Future of Artificial Intelligence" and "National Artificial Intelligence Research and Development of Strategic Planning." It raised AI to the level of national strategy and made grand plans and blueprints for AI development in America. In December 2016, the U.S. again issued its report, "Artificial intelligence, Automation and Economics," which focused on the expected economic impact of AI-driven automation and described broad strategies that could increase the benefits of AI and reduce its costs.

The UK has the highest number of AI companies in Europe, followed by Germany and France. Since 2005, the UK has been adding AI companies every year at twice the rate of the other two countries combined. In recent years, the UK has invested many resources in the field of AI. First, in terms of scientific research, the British government, through the EPSRC, has invested 17 million pounds in the research and development of AI technology in British universities. One thousand government-funded AI Ph.D. programs have been set up to develop AI research vigorously. By April 2019, more than 30 universities were offering graduate courses in AI. Second, the UK supports global capital investment in the AI industry in the UK and grants tax exemption to AI enterprises. As a result, the UK attracted £12 billion of investment globally in 2017, and there are now more than 220 AI start-ups in the UK.

In Asia, China's AI development stands out, accounting for 68.67% of the total number of AI companies in Asia. Beijing and Shanghai alone have as many AI companies as the rest of Asia combined.

(b) Blockchain
Countries around the world are generally supportive of blockchain technology. Many actively promote the application of blockchain technology in daily life. Except for Singapore and the Philippines, which have recognized the legality of encrypted digital currency such as Bitcoin, other countries have said they will forbid Bitcoin transactions. Concerning ICO (Initial Coin Offering), although not explicitly banned by various countries, these offerings come with various restrictions, rigorous supervision and examination, and the highlighting of risks. A survey of the enterprises involved in ICOs revealed that compliance risk and stringent application requirements are the most pressing issues regarding blockchain application in Finance. At present, China's blockchain technology is in the initial stages of development, and some related applications, such as Bitcoin and ICO, have been explicitly banned. Nevertheless, the compliance risks of blockchain applications in the future are still the financial industry's focus.

Theoretically, blockchain can reduce the cost of the financial industry infrastructure as the technology is malleable to many application areas. However, obstacles to extensive deployment of the technology arise from the relatively immature technology. Issues such as high-frequency calibration, disaster recovery, technical standards, laws, and regulations remain unresolved. As a result, most enterprises are cautious about blockchain technology, and there are few mass adoption use cases in the global financial industry.

An example of the uptake in this industry is Singapore which recognizes the legality of ICOs. Most ICOs raise small amounts of money, roughly between $1.5 million and $15 million. However, Singapore is the third-largest ICO hub in the world. The Singapore government has been supportive of this industry. It has recognized the legitimate use of Bitcoin in transactions. It has issued favorable tax policies, believing that Bitcoin transactions are commercial activities that will not interfere too much with normal business. With an open and inclusive attitude, Singapore is expected to become the blockchain center in Asia to implement blockchain projects launched by enterprises, the Monetary Authority (MAS), and others.

Furthermore, blockchain is a bridge to Fintech 3.0 with innovations such as Decentralized Finance (DeFi), Tokenization (including Non-Fungible Tokens and Security Tokens), Smart Contracts, and Central Bank Digital Currencies. All these developments and the emphasis on interoperability among blockchains, together with other technologies, augur well for mass adoption and the development of Web3.0.

(c) Cloud Computing

The global cloud computing market is growing and deepening the transformation of the industry. It enables more and more enterprises to see innovation opportunities and capitalize on them. Cloud computing is regarded as the third IT wave after the PC and Internet waves. It has become an important pillar to support the development of the information industry. Cloud computing is the main driving force for enterprise transformation. It has brought about fundamental changes in consumption and business, and triggers the transformation of the entire industry. The development of cloud computing technology has entered a mature stage, and its application is increasingly focused on security, stability, and risk prevention and control.

In 2017, Amazon AWS, Microsoft Azure, Ali Cloud, Google, and IBM were ranked the top five in the global market share for the public cloud storage, with Amazon having the highest share at 51.8%. Patent filings in the cloud computing industry have more than doubled in the past

5 years. IBM, Microsoft, and Google, all headquartered in the United States, ranked as the top three, with Intel, Amazon, and HP included in the top ten companies possessing cloud computing patents. This means that six of the top 10 cloud computing patent owners are in the US, demonstrating the US dominance in this area. Huawei, a Chinese company, ranked eighth globally, ahead of HP in the United States and SAP of Germany. The rest of the world has some ways to catch up with the US in this area.

(d) Big Data or Data Analytics

After years of development and experience with various types of data and the availability of increasing amounts of data, big data analysis of data and the speed at which it takes place has made great strides. The rise of smart hardware, such as wearable devices and smart home systems, added a new dimension of offline applicability.

Big data can overcome traditional data analysis limitations such as multi-dimensional and multi-form data. With big data and machine learning, financial data computing and analysis now encompass areas such as personal credit investigation, credit extension, risk control and insurance pricing.

The 2017 World Digital Competitiveness Ranking by IMD showed that countries' digital competitiveness is highly correlated with their overall competitiveness. Countries with strong digital competitiveness are also highly competitive and more likely to generate disruptive innovation. The application of big data analysis in the financial industry is still in its infancy. The global financial big data lacks a unified storage management standard and sharing platform, and the protection of personal privacy has not yet evolved into a credible security mechanism. Developed countries, such as the United States, Britain, South Korea, and Japan, have always attached great importance to big data in promoting economic development and social change and improving overall competitiveness. Big data helps countries improve their ability to acquire knowledge from their vast and complex data resources, to help promote innovation and accelerate developments in the science and engineering fields. Such actions help them maintain their position and even aim to lead the digital economy era.

The United States is the first country to turn big data from a business concept to a national strategy. In 2012, the White House Office of Science and Technology Policy released the Big Data Research and Development Initiative. Now, it regards big data as an important strategic resource and vigorously defends its first-mover advantage of big data technology and industrial development. In 2014, the United States released the white paper "Big Data: Seizing Opportunities and Protecting Values," which reaffirmed the importance of seizing the major opportunities that big data can bring to economic and social development. In 2016, the United States released the Federal Big Data Research and Development Strategic Plan, forming the top-level design of the system covering seven dimensions of technology research and development. These areas include data credibility, infrastructure, data openness and sharing, privacy security and ethics, talent training, and multi-agent collaboration, to create a future-oriented big data innovation ecosystem.

In 2012, the UK ranked big data as the first of eight forward-looking technology fields. In November 2017, it released a white paper, "Industrial Strategy: Building a Britain Fit for the Future," for the whole society. This white paper focused on AI and big data economy, putting the country at the forefront of the AI and big data revolution. At the end of April 2018, the UK released the report "Industrial Strategy: Artificial Intelligence," putting forth a series of concrete measures in five dimensions, namely, encouraging innovation, cultivating and pooling talents, upgrading infrastructure, improving the business environment, and promoting balanced regional development.

Regarding the trend of big data in Asia, developed countries and regions such as Japan and South Korea view the development of big data as an important national strategy, while countries such as India regard the development of big data industry as a golden opportunity to catch up in development. Take South Korea, for example. At the end of 2016, South Korea released "the Medium and Long-term Comprehensive Countermeasures for Intelligent Information Society" based on big data and other technologies to respond to the challenges of Fourth Industrial Revolution. South Korea has defined the big data industry as one of its nine strategic industries. Its goal is to become one of the world's top three big data powerhouses by 2019. The Japanese government also took the lead in using big data by releasing massive data such as national statistics and maps on general websites to unify the expression, the form, and the file format of data.

6.2.3 *Major Global Market Structure*

In the global development of Fintech, it is generally agreed that there are two paths. One path is the Chinese model, which grows explosively and develops through market demand and technology innovation. It is a model that has been used in India, Kenya, and other less developed countries. The main characteristics are the ability of the new business model to reach the underserved and other new customers. The other path is the American model, which develops progressively and relies on technology to promote innovation that is somewhat constrained by regulation. However, as the market demand is not strong enough and market size remains relatively the same, consumers' experience and support are relatively less pervasive.

(a) The United Kingdom (UK)

Since 2008, the UK has developed into a global Fintech hub. In recent years, the UK Fintech industry has developed rapidly. According to the Fintech database of Ernst & Young, more than half of UK Fintech companies are focused on bank payments, and 20% are concentrated in the credit and lending spheres.

London is the Fintech hub in the UK and also the most successful one in Europe. London has a long history of venture capital investing. Angel investors and venture capitalists have attached great importance to funding Fintech. New financing instruments such as crowdfunding and P2P lending are important sources of working capital for the early stages of such Fintech companies. In recent years, some cities outside London have attracted a growing number of Fintech companies and talents thanks to national policies, the maturing business environment and lower operating and living costs.

The UK's advantages mainly come from three sources. First, its long history of colonialization and mercantilism laid a solid foundation for its global division of labor and cooperation. After the 16th century, Britain started its global expansion. "The Wealth of Nations" mentioned that Britain's wealth was mainly derived from its division of labor and trading globally. The legacy of its colonial heritage has also brought substantial advantages to the development of Britain's Fintech industry. On the one hand, British companies have little resistance to foreign investment, merger and acquisition, culture, or ideology. As the Fintech sector matures, we see Fintech companies acquiring other Fintech companies domestically and globally. On the other hand, The UK also has a strong ability to attract international capital to promote the development of its Fintech industry. Second, the British government has done a better job than other western developed countries in securing foreign investments. Third, the UK's sound education and training system provides a source and strong support for talent transfer in the Fintech industry.

In summary, the UK has emerged as a global center of Internet finance due to the following factors: a well-supported and well-run ecosystem; abundant reserves of talent, capital, and demand in the Fintech industry; and supportive government policies, which include the pioneering of the sandbox regulatory model, facilitating regulatory innovation, and promoting the balanced development of Fintech.

(b) The United States (US)

The Fintech market in the US is very mature, with a balanced distribution of corporate financing for the various segments. Among them, financing in the payment segment accounts for the highest proportion, amounting to 30%. The payment industry has been innovative, followed by the lending market. Remarkably, the emergence of the Fintech industry came about spontaneously without government intervention.

After more than one hundred years of development, the financial market of the US can provide relatively complete and comprehensive products and services. Traditional banking and financial institutions have been very active in using the Internet and other technologies for financial service innovation. The finance industry in the United States can only grow in new areas not covered by traditional big financial firms. For example, the current development of the credit card market has inhibited the growth of online payment. According to KPMG, in 2018, Fintech investment in the US reached US $52.5 billion, more than double the US $24 billion in 2017, with a record 1,061 transactions.

Fintech development in the US is relatively concentrated, the most representative of Silicon Valley and New York. They originate from Silicon Valley, which has relatively mature professionals. The well-established interconnection structure within the Fintech ecosystem enables start-ups to benefit from large venture capital funds with investment experience. New York is a global financial center, and several Fintech institutions have sprung up here to tap on Wall Street's vast capital base and existing financial market expertise. The biggest advantage of Silicon Valley is technological innovation, numerous Fintech unicorns are hatched here, and GAFA (Google, Apple, Facebook, Amazon), four major enterprises, will continue to expand investment in the field of Fintech.

America's strength comes from two sources. First, its research and development capabilities in basic science are the best in the world. The government has recently increased investment in basic research through the STEM (Science, Technology, Engineering, and Mathematics) program and actively developed the design and implementation of the interdisciplinary system. This will have far-reaching significance for the development of the US Fintech industry. On the one hand, the US is a pioneer in technological innovation. For example, its big data research is world-class because it was the first-mover in scientific and technological research and development. On the other hand, the cultivation and accumulation of scientific and technological talents is also crucial. Second is the strength of the business and strategic planning capabilities of American companies.

This is reflected in the rapid transformation of basic research (inventions) into commercial applications by American enterprises. The power of strategic planning is reflected in the fact that the US companies can envision future trends, focus and optimize their resources to make their vision a reality. For example, many new trends in business (e.g., smartphones, business intelligence services, etc.) emerged in the US first.

While regulations are changing rapidly, the challenge is still posed by tighter regulation as compared to many other jurisdictions.

(c) Singapore

The financial industry in North America is relatively mature, with the needs of a high proportion of financial service users satisfactorily met. Fintech focuses on providing consumers with more convenient financial services, and its role is more similar to the "icing on the cake." By contrast, in the Asia-Pacific region, as represented by China and the Southeast Asian countries, the level of financial services is relatively backward. There are still a large number of unserved needs and untapped markets. In this region, Fintech serves more than a supporting role. In fact, for some countries, Fintech enables financial services to reach many long-tail users by providing "timely help." On the whole, the Asia-Pacific region presents a huge market opportunity for Fintech applications and large development potential.

Singapore is a leading financial center in the world and a leading competitor in the field of Fintech. Singapore has done an excellent job of providing government support, funding, building innovation centers, and setting up regulatory sandboxes. Singapore has a high degree of ease of doing business. English as the language of business makes it the preferred gateway for global financial capital to enter the Asian market. As the most favorable region for Fintech development globally, Singapore has a relatively loose "regulatory sandbox" system, a series of cross-regional cooperation agreements, and more than 80% Internet coverage.

More than 300 Fintech start-ups have been set up in Singapore. More than 20 multinational financial institutions and technology companies have set up innovation laboratories and research centers in Singapore, including LATTICE80, the world's largest Fintech center. Singapore has many top Fintech companies, such as Bluzelle, DragonWealth, and Fastacash.

In Singapore, the electronic wallet has difficulty dislodging the dominant position of traditional credit cards at present. P2P operation is subject to unprecedented strict regulation, while blockchain finance faces much less regulation.

(d) Australia

Australia's Fintech industry is developing rapidly and is a "rising star" of Fintech. According to the KPMG report, Australia has advanced Internet banking and mobile terminal industries, making it an ideal entry point for global financial markets into the Asian eco-economic zone. In the past five years, from the Fintech financing of only 51 million US dollars in 2012 to over 600 million US dollars in 2016, Australia has created a healthy and active Fintech industry.

Australia is home to many of the world's top Fintech companies. However, if the National Innovation and Scientific Development plan, beginning in December 2015, is fully implemented, it may help the Australian economy head towards higher development and innovation. The plan will help to bridge some gaps, especially the availability of venture capital (ranked 40th globally), and through the information and communication technologies, create new business models (41st) around the world. At the beginning of 2019, Australia's emerging Fintech ecosystem has attracted the government's attention, with the Federal government investing more than 500 million dollars in innovation-related industries.

(e) China

Currently, there are seven global Fintech hubs and 23 regional Fintech hubs in the world. The seven global Fintech hubs are Beijing, San Francisco, New York, London, Shanghai, Hangzhou, and Shenzhen. According to the data, of the 23 regional Fintech hubs, 15 are from Asia and the Americas, while seven are from Europe. The development trend of regional Fintech hubs generally shows that Asia and America are at the forefront, while Europe is developing a little slower.

Beijing is home to the regulatory authorities of the Fintech industry. It has many of the world's top universities in science, technology, and information engineering and a large number of Fintech companies. As a domestic financial center and a relatively developed Internet economy, Shanghai has a good foundation for the development of Fintech. Shanghai is a competitive place for Fintech enterprises. Shenzhen is a magnet for financial institutions and has a favorable environment for Internet entrepreneurship, laying a foundation for the development of Fintech. Shenzhen has the added advantage of having both hardware and software development capabilities. According to KPMG, 21 Fintech companies from Beijing, 15 from Shanghai, and seven from Shenzhen made the top 50.

The Hong Kong Special Administrative Region of China (HKSAR) has several advantages for developing Fintech. It has a sound legal system, abundant talent, well-developed information and information, and multiple capital channels for investing in start-ups. China's Taiwan region is actively developing the Fintech industry with the advantages of a sound financial system, a sound credit system, a solid information foundation, and users' willingness to try new technologies. Recently, The Financial Regulatory Commission of the Taiwan region of China has been promoting the development of the Fintech industry in the Taiwan region of China by significantly relaxing restrictions on the financial industry to invest in Fintech-related industries.

(f) India

In 2018, India's GDP ranked sixth in the world. It is the second-most populous country globally, and its economic growth that exceeded 7% made It the fastest-growing major economy in the world. It is also a member of THE BRICS and G20 countries. In 2016, Mr. Modi's government proposed the "Start-Up India, Stand Up India" slogan. It has launched a series of Fintech-friendly policies, including the unified payment system (UPI) and Adhaar identity system. Indian Fintech has many bright spots and potential in blockchain, payment, P2P lending, intelligent investment management, inclusive finance, technology-driven integrated banking services, Internet financial security, and biometrics.

Over the past few years, India has experimented with several guidelines and reforms, such as issuing new banking policies and licensing microfinance banks and payment banks. It introduced a unified payment interface, included India's unbanked population in the official financial services directory, and strengthened the payment ecosystem.

India's financial services industry is grappling with some of its long-standing challenges, such as falling profit margins and rising non-performing assets. The industry also has many challenges due to the entry of non-traditional financial players. Several initiatives by the government and regulators have led to a shift towards a platform-driven economy. For India to embrace an open banking architecture and unleash the true potential of a shared ecosystem, it must be built on four foundations: government, regulators, traditional institutions, and Fintech.

AI is growing at more than 400% in India, with AI-related start-ups attracting $150m in investment over the past five years.

According to S&P estimates, India's technological development in blockchain can create as much as $5 billion in commercial value over the next five years. The development of blockchain in India's financial services sector is in line with its global peers. Many industry-specific associations are building blockchain prototypes for many use cases. Trade finance, cross-border payments, note discounting, digital identity, and supply chain finance have been the preferred application areas for India's blockchain.

To establish a digital economy, the government, with the support of regulators, actively works to create a progressive digital ecosystem. The government is accelerating its move towards a "paperless and cashless delivery of services" system, often referred to as an "India Stack." In the past few years, some digital platforms have been set up under the Digital India Initiative.

The development of the Fintech industry for emerging markets and Asia tends to be more inclusive as the regulation, or the lack of it has allowed new business models to develop and align the interest of policymakers in serving the underserved. On the other hand, the well-regulated and developed markets focus more on serving existing customers faster, better, and cheaper. The former emphasizes inclusive Fintech and social scalability, while the latter focuses more on bank-tech or technical scalability, thus differentiating the priorities and approaches of the markets. However, as the Fintech industry matures and crosses borders and interoperability becomes more pervasive, there will be fewer opportunities for regulatory arbitrage and the differences between the markets will narrow.

Reference/Further Reading

Xin, D. (2019). 金融科技：模式变革与业务创新 [Financial Technology: Model Revolution and Business Innovation], Chapter 1. Shanghai University of Finance & Economics Press.

6.3 Case Study: US versus PRC in Banking and Fintech

6.3.1 *Introduction*

In 1956, John McCarthy invited researchers from different disciplines such as language simulation, neuron nets, complexity theory, and others to a summer workshop called the Dartmouth Summer Research Project on Artificial Intelligence (AI) to discuss what would ultimately become the field of AI.[1] The term "AI" was chosen at that time to differentiate it from "thinking machines," a field that included cybernetics, automata theory, and complex information processing.

There are several definitions for AI, and the following are some:

AI refers to the study and use of intelligent machines to mimic human action and thought. With the availability of Big Data, advances in computing, and the invention of new algorithms, AI has risen as a disruptive technology in recent years.[2]

AI is a branch of computer science dealing with the simulation of intelligent behavior in the computer and the capability of a machine to imitate intelligent human behavior.[3]

AI refers to the theory and development of computer systems able to perform tasks normally requiring human intelligence, such as visual perception, speech recognition, decision-making, and translation between languages.[4]

Generally, most people think of AI as a system that thinks like a human or a system that works like a human without figuring out how human reasoning works or how a human reasoning model performs tasks. For those who are interested in more detailed discussions, there are several textbooks worth consulting.[5]

---

[1] https://www.forbes.com/sites/bernardmarr/2018/02/14/the-key-definitions-of-artificial-intelligence-ai-that-explain-its-importance/#601f57bb4f5d.

[2] https://www.imda.gov.sg/sgdigital/tech-pillars/artificial-intelligence.

[3] https://www.merriam-webster.com/dictionary/artificial%20intelligence.

[4] https://en.oxforddictionaries.com/definition/artificialintelligence.

[5] https://courses.csail.mit.edu/6.034f/ai3/rest.pdf, Russel, S.; Norvig, P. (2010). *Artificial Intelligence: A Modern Approach*, 3rd ed. Prentice Hall. Neapolitan, R.E.; Jiang, X. (2018). *Artificial Intelligence: With an Introduction to Machine Learning*, 2nd ed. CRC Press.

According to Neapolitan and Jiang (2018), AI approaches can be classified as follows: (i) Logical Intelligence (LI), (ii) Probabilistic Intelligence (PI), (iii) Emergent Intelligence (EI), (iv) Neural Intelligence (NI) and (v) Language Understanding (LU). The last three are the most interesting as evolution computation and swarm intelligence under EI are drawing attention. These researches are inspired by the biological evolution of decentralized and self-organized systems. NI is modeled loosely after the human brain using Neural networks and deep learning, while LU deals with machine reading comprehension.

Another classification is to split the approaches into (i) Symbolic, (ii) Deep Learning, (iii) Bayesian Networks, and (iv) Evolutionary Algorithms. Symbolic AI's are based on high-level "symbolic" (human-readable) representations of problems, logic, and search.[6] Deep learning (also known as deep structured learning or hierarchical learning) is part of a broader family of machine learning methods based on learning data representations instead of task-specific algorithms. Learning can be supervised, semi-supervised or unsupervised. Bayesian networks are a type of probabilistic graphical model that uses Bayesian inference for probability computations. An evolutionary algorithm (EA) is a subset of evolutionary computation, a generic population-based metaheuristic optimization algorithm. An EA uses mechanisms inspired by biological evolution, such as reproduction, mutation, recombination, and selection. In this chapter, we go beyond what is being described in traditional textbooks and look at applications. To illustrate the use in practice and the issues of interest to practitioners and investors, we look at specific issues analytically using a two-country study. We will focus on the issue of "Who is Winning the Artificial Intelligence Race between PRC and US: Alibaba, Tencent, Ping An, Baidu and Zhong An versus Alphabet, Amazon, Apple, Facebook, and Microsoft." Figure 6.1 presents the race among the technology giants.

(a) Summary

(1) **PRC:** The ecosystem of firms in China has a more complete suite of "finance to lifestyle" AI products than US firms. Alibaba launched the Platform for AI or PAI 2.0, and it has become a market leader in AI and Cloud, setting a new standard. There is a lack of understanding of Chinese Fintech companies, their business models, and risk

---

[6]https://en.wikipedia.org/wiki/Symbolicartificialintelligence.

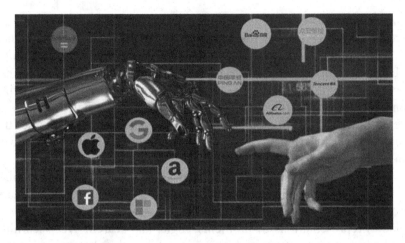

Figure 6.1: Who's winning the artificial intelligence race between PRC and US: Alibaba, Tencent, Ping An, Baidu and Zhong An vs. Alphabet, Amazon, Apple, Facebook and Microsoft.

management practices. Most business models and risk assessment methods via the Internet and digital devices are unique in China and not found elsewhere. Ping An seems to be less recognized by analysts but is the leader in technology in China for many financial, consumer, health, and insurance businesses. Tencent is another very interesting company that is not widely acknowledged in the English-speaking world. It has some innovative services that will be described in this chapter. Paying close attention to developments in the Chinese regulatory framework, business models, and risk management methods can bear fruits for investors.

(2) **US:** Amazon is considered to be the undisputed leader for technology in the world. Facebook, Microsoft, Apple, and Google are leaders in technology with excellent operation capabilities. While these companies are well researched, the regulatory framework and changes remain a major risk factor.

(3) Both US and PRC firms face regulatory issues and are the core of the debate on the future of workers. Most of all, these technology firms wish to operate without government intervention. However, most of them have benefited from either government funding or lax regulation

and are unlikely to be outside the influence of their governments in the future. Beginning 2020, the Chinese regulators have begun to tighten their grip on Chinese fintech companies, especially regarding how loans are disbursed and the quantum of interest charged. While understanding technology is essential, monitoring the business environment, business innovations, risk management methods, and regulatory changes are significant determinants of the performance of Fintech stocks and projects.

6.3.2 *AI and Finance: China Gets It while the US is Years Behind*

AI integrates finance with data from unintentioned (text, chat, images) and intentioned (merchandise receipts) sources to offer suggested choices of goods and services to people in lifestyle, business, investment, cognitive services, and SME activity. For such applications that use data and the cloud, China has decidedly pulled ahead of the US in general.

With its launch of PAI, Alibaba has pulled ahead of Tencent in combining finance with intentioned and unintentioned data. Combining finance data and cloud requires a horizontal conglomerate style where new rings of businesses surround a center dominated by data analysis instead of a vertical pyramid structure.

The following summary is based on the research data of the reference given at the end of this chapter. With PAI, Alibaba is the new global leader. Ping An deserves rerating as it grows into a diversified financial healthcare conglomerate. Tencent has excellent technology. Baidu has lost its edge and seems to be trying to get back by jettisoning old businesses while jumping into AI through acquisitions. Both strategies have serious risks. Moreover, Baidu's credit has been systemically deteriorating.

A. US companies — China has also pulled ahead because US companies have had to deal with the following:
   (1) entrenched lobbyists (in DC) who are protecting cartels and vice versa;
   (2) state/federal regulators on the warpath after GFC ($360 billion in fines);
   (3) a laundry list of state/federal regulations which curtail the flexibility of the US Big 5 in Fintech;

(4) difficulties of the conglomerate structure as evidenced by the collapse of GE financial services;

(5) weakening of relationships between Big 5 and DC military complex and universities;

(6) an absence of any national strategy.

B. Chinese firms adapt quickly after failure and keep on trying anew. Our rankings for the US companies, which consider the suite of AI products, multiple valuations, and several operational and credit criteria, show Apple as the best and Amazon as the worst. Amazon and Google have the best AI platforms, but it is a myth that these are superior to China.

C. If we combine operational metrics and valuations to the AI mix, Amazon is the least attractive. Microsoft has failed to do anything meaningful after a 15-year head start. Facebook also fails to impress. Apple is the best overall, but Huawei's new technology is at least as good as Apple's.

(a) Gaping Holes in the Landscape

AI has been commoditized. China's overall AI push is as good as that of the US — arguably better. All of the companies in this report can now translate thousands of Bibles per second. Moreover, they can all process hundreds of thousands of photos per second. They all have talking personal butlers, staggering video offerings, dazzling facial recognition statistics, and the ability to anticipate our wants, needs, and desires for food, travel, health, education, books, news, wellness, and even lifemates.

Only Alibaba and Ping An offer these AI tools and a full suite of services in payments, insurance, loans, credit ratings, money market, wealth management, crowdfunding, and FX. The US firms all have a gaping hole in this regard.

Alibaba's gaping hole is in entertainment/content. The gaping hole in Amazon is financial services, as is almost all of the US firms. Why the gaping hole in financial services? Aside from the seven reasons mentioned above, a prime reason is that financial services are highly regulated in the US. The financial products introduced by US tech companies have to skirt around banking regulations. Consequently, many of the financial products introduced were not successful. Few have heard of Microsoft Wallet, Google Hangout, and Facebook Messenger Pay. Even Apple Pay is 80% smaller than Alipay.

Amazon has a small SME loan book, but the other services in wealth management, crowdfunding, ratings, insurance, and any financial products are virtually absent. Under different circumstances, Amazon could have been the largest bank in the world. Facebook and Google have remained in their niches, making most of their revenues from advertising.

Lastly, the other gaping hole in the landscape is the absence of other global players outside the two countries of China and the US. Europe has none. Japan has none (SoftBank is a holding company). Korea has none. There is no dominant regional player in India, Brazil, Indonesia, Eastern Europe, Scandinavia, or Russia. This leads us to conclude that what Tencent, Ping An, and Alibaba have done is a remarkable accomplishment. Few other companies globally have managed to accomplish anything close to them.

(b) Other Issues: Politics, Policy, and Regulation

   (i) US companies face similar risks as those in China. The dominance of the US companies in advertising will have eventual political consequences and force a political anti-trust showdown at some point. The influence of these companies is in the spotlight, and regulators and legislators are looking into addressing the power of these "unelected" arbiters of what content can or cannot be carried on their platforms.

  (ii) In China, the government has tried to foster competition between Alibaba and Tencent. With Baidu not gaining as much ground as its two rivals since the day Google left China in 2010, it is a two-horse race. With PAI 2.0, Alibaba has arguably pulled ahead of Tencent. The competition has consequences as upcoming players need to "pick sides." Only regulation can stop the first movers in China, as well as in the US, from becoming monopolies. Currently, Alibaba, Tencent, Google, and Amazon are well entrenched in their respective spheres.

 (iii) China aggressively supports the internet economy, which is one foundation of their 5-year plan. The foundation of the current 5 year plan is the "internet Plus economy." Alibaba is likely in the center of this. Furthermore, it is entirely conceivable that Alibaba's new platform PAI 2.0 can be a cornerstone of SOE reform, tax reform, and a conduit for millions of jobs in the SME sector. Companies everywhere are expected to play a political and social stability role in the US and China. Alibaba portrays itself as a company for the "small potato." All these firms are political creatures, and this affects their valuations. So far, Alibaba is playing its cards right. So is Ping An.

(c) Master Summary: AI Analysis

AI is an essential component to analyze data from the Internet of Things (IoT) system (Figure 6.2). In practice, IoT collects the physical data from sensors, mobile, and other digital devices, which is then sent to the Neural Network with Machine Learning where it is combined with data stored in the cloud platform from financial services, cognitive services, lifestyle, health, autonomous vehicles, robotics, and advertising, and then is processed and analyzed using AI.

The AI financial services (Figure 6.3) are in the area of payments, insurance, personal loans, small and medium enterprise (SME) loans, credit rating, money market securities, wealth management, crowdfunding, and currency exchanges. We can compare ATPA (Alibaba, Tencent, Ping An, Baidu) and AMGAF (Amazon, Microsoft, Google, Apple, Facebook). These financial services are dominated by Chinese technology companies, such as Alibaba, Tencent, Ping An, and to a lesser extent Baidu. The US Technology firms, Amazon, Microsoft, Google, Apple, Facebook are missing out on most of these opportunities.

It is interesting to note that eight out of the nine companies (Figure 6.4) have their own cloud for the storage of data in the form of Intentional,

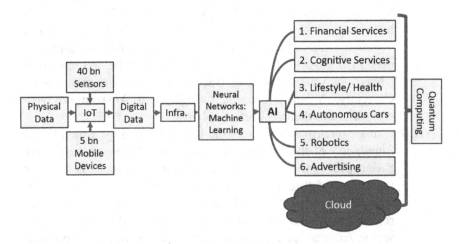

Figure 6.2: Artificial intelligence described on a single chart.

Source: Schulte Research Estimates.

Company	Payment	Insurance	Personal Loans	SME Loans	Credit Rating	Money Market	Wealth Mgmt	Crowd-funding	Currency Exchange
Alibaba	AliPay (400 mn) (51.8% ms)	Ant Zhong An	Personal loans - Ant	SME loans – Ant SME Service	Zhima Credit	Yue'bao (CNY1.2tn)	Ant Financial, AliPay	ANTSDAQ	AliPay
Tencent	WePay (300 mn) (38.3% ms)	Zhong An	Weilidai	Weilidai	WeBank	/	WeBank	JD.com	/
Ping An	Ping An Bank	Ping An Insurance	Ping An Bank	Ping An Bank	Ping An Insurance	Ping An Asset Mgmt	Ping An Asset Mgmt	/	Ping An Bank
Baidu	Baidu Wallet (100 mn)	/	/	/	Yes	/	Yes	/	/
Amazon	/	Electronic Damage Insurance (UK)	/	USD$3bn SME loans (Amazon Lending)	/	/	/	/	/
Microsoft	MSFT Wallet	/	/	/	/	/	/	/	/
Google	Google Wallet, Android Pay	/	/	/	/	/	/	/	/
Apple	Apply Pay (85 mn, 450% YOY)	/	/	/	/	/	/	/	/
Facebook	Messenger Pay	/	/	/	/	/	/	/	/

MISSED OPPORTUNITY

Figure 6.3: AI financial services comparison.

Note: Alibaba way ahead. Ping An and Tencent also dominate.
Source: Schulte Research Estimates, Zenith.

Unintentional, IoT/Car, and Cognitive Services data. The data collection capabilities of most of the companies are very strong, and one success factor is the prevalence of weak privacy protection. Until recently, such data usage and purchase of data have few constraints in China.[7] In May 2018, China quietly released the final version of a new data privacy standard that goes even further than the European General Data Protection Regulation (GDPR). This places EU and Chinese data legislation on a far more level footing than American data law.[8] Chinese law addresses privacy protection with standards on the collection and usage of personal information. The China National Information Security Standards Technical Committee (SAC/TC260) has developed more than 240 national

---

[7] https://www.networksasia.net/article/chinas-data-privacy-law-came-effect-may-and-it-was-inspired-gdpr.1529296999.
[8] https://assets.kpmg.com/content/dam/kpmg/cn/pdf/en/2017/02/overview-of-cyber security-law.pdf.

Company	Intentional Data	Un-intentional Data	IoT/Car	Cognitive Service	Cloud
Alibaba	AliPay, Taobao, Tmall, Alibaba.com, Alibaba Express, Yue'bao, Tmall, Alibaba Cloud (750 mn)	Youku, Weibo, UCWeb, Cainiao Logistics, Yahoo! China, SCMP, AliWangWang, LaiWang, PAI, Ding Talk	"Connected Car" with SAIC, AutoNavi, Ali Health, KFC	Platform for Artificial Intelligence (PAI 2.0), Tmall Genie	Ali Cloud
Tencent	WeChat Pay, 3rd Party Providers (JD.com, Didi, etc.)	WeChat (938 mn), QQ (700 mn), Qzone, WeChat Ecosystem, Gaming	Didi, Dianping review site	WeChat Voice/ Image, Tencent Video	Tencent Cloud
Ping An	Ping An Bank, Ping An Insurance, Ping An Asset Mgmt (350 mn)	Ping An Health, Ping An Securities	Ping An Auto Owner, Wanjia Clinics	Facial recognition, Voice print	Ping An Health Cloud
Baidu	Baidu Search, Baidu Wallet	Baidu Search	Food Delivery Service, Project Apollo	Little Fish	Baidu Cloud
Amazon	E-commerce (B2C, C2C)	Shopping search	Echo, Kindle, Whole Foods, Amazon Books, Logistics	Alexa, Rekognition, Polly, Lex, Amazon Video	AWS
Google	Google Play Store, Google Search	Google Search, Android OS, G-mail, Maps, Chrome, Snapchat (166 mn MAU), Youtube, Waymo	Android OS, Waymo	Health, Translation, Google Assistant, Google Face, Deep Mind	Google Cloud
Apple	iTunes (800 mn), Apple Music, Apple Pay (85 mn)	iOS, Safari	iPhone (1 bn), iPad, iPod, Mac, Apple Watch	Siri, Face Recognition	iCloud
Microsoft	Xbox, Microsoft Wallet (small)	LinkedIn, Office, Skype, Bing, IE	Kinect, Microsoft Surface, Windows Phone	Zo, Computer vision/ Speech/ Language API	Azure
Facebook	Messenger Pay	Facebook, Facebook Messenger (1.96 bn), Whatsapp(1.3 bn)	Oculus, Project Titan	Deep face, Deep text, Translation	/

(left margin label: same technology)

Figure 6.4: AI data source comparison.

Note: Alibaba may leapfrog all with PAI, Ding Talk, and Tmall Genie. This puts Alibaba in its own league with Tencent very close.

Source: Schulte Research Estimates.

standards related to cybersecurity (i.e., Cloud, Industrial Control Systems, and Big Data) since 2010. The Cybersecurity Law requires personal data collected or generated in China to be stored domestically. Enterprises and organizations that violate the Cybersecurity Law may be penalized up to RMB 1,000,000. Since the law presents clear obligations of network operators and security requirements, it is not surprising that most large financial institutions and technology companies will or have already become network operators.

As of 2018, Amazon is leading U.S. and Alibaba is leading Asia in the AI cloud space and AI cloud services in China are developing rapidly (Figure 6.5). According to the Synergy Research Group, in 4Q 2020, the global leader in cloud services is Amazon with 32% of the global market share, followed by Azure (Microsoft subsidiary) with 20%, Google Cloud with 9%, Alibaba Cloud with 6%, IBM Cloud with 5%, Salesforce with 3%, Tencent Cloud with 2% and Oracle Cloud with 2%. In China, Alibaba leads, with Meituan and Tencent ranking second and third, respectively. Baidu is ranked 10th in China. Alibaba is leading the Asia market. Alibaba Cloud's international operations are registered and headquartered in

Company	Market Share (in respective markets)	Comments
Alibaba	41%	Leader in Asia, >100 newly developed AI services Services in storage, networking, healthcare, logistics, lifestyle, media, business enhancements, and etc.
Tencent	7%	#3 in Chinese Market, services in public/private storage for personal/business use
Baidu	1%	Small cloud service
Amazon	47%	Amazon AWS: Global & US leader
Microsoft	10%	Fastest Growth Rate, 97% YOY Azure & Office 365
Google	4%	Fast growing, 45 teraflops of data (45 trillion bytes/second) Services include AI APIs', storage, search history, e-mail, etc. 71,000 searches/second New quantum computer
Apple	1%	Small cloud service, primarily strong in private data collection Services in location, storage, and security

(same technology)

Figure 6.5: AI cloud comparison: Amazon big winner.

Note: Alibaba leader in Asia.

Source: Schulte Research Estimates, HostUCan, Skyhighnetworks.

Singapore. It is expanding its service into countries and regions involving the Belt and Road Initiative. Alibaba Cloud will have an integrated cloud technology and innovation platform for the Winter Olympics in 2022. In March, it opened its first data center in Indonesia. In 2017, it launched 316 products and features; 60 were focused on high-value fields, including AI.[9] Its reported revenue was 4.39 billion yuan (US$664.96 million) in 2018Q1, up 103% from the same period last year. Total revenue for the 2017 fiscal year reached 13.39 billion yuan, up 101%.[10]

AI Cognitive Services is a set of machine learning initially developed by Microsoft to solve the problems in AI (Figure 6.6). The goal was to democratize AI by packaging it into discrete components that are easy for developers to use in their apps. These services include image, facial, and voice recognition, as well as natural language learning. So, it is not surprising to note that Microsoft leads in this field, allowing Web and Universal Windows Platform developers to use their algorithms. While Microsoft has made a wide and deep mark, Alibaba PAI has made even more progress than Microsoft.

---

[9]https://technode.com/2018/05/10/alibaba-cloud-q1-2018-results/.

[10]http://www.chinadaily.com.cn/a/201806/27/WS5b3337f5a3103349141df403.html.

Company	Image Recognition	Facial Recognition	Voice	Natural Language Understanding	Video
Alibaba	Document recognition, image search+, PAI	Identity authentication, Alipay	Customer service AI, voice->text service, etc., PAI	Real-time translation services, PAI	Video analysis, broadcast service, PAI
Tencent	Fashion trend analysis	Identity authentication	WeChat Voice/Image	Translation	Tencent Video
Baidu	xPerception, Pixlab API, WICG Shape Detection API	Baidu Facial Recognition (99.7% accuracy)	Voice Search, Text-Speech Converter, Deep Voice (97% accuracy)	Translation, Speech Recog., Kitt.AI, RavenTech	/
Amazon	Amazon Rekognition	Emotion recog., Face Comparison	Alexa, Lex	Alexa, Echo, Polly	Amazon Video
Microsoft	Image understanding, Celebrities/Landmark recog.	Face API, Emotion, Verification, Detection	Speech Verification, Text-Speech Converter	Translation, Text analytics, LUIS	Video analysis, Video Indexer
Google	Image searching	Google Face	Google assistant	Translation AI, Text analytics	YouTube
Apple	Classification/ Detection/ Checking	Facial Rec.	Siri	Siri	/
Facebook	Text recognition, translation	Deep Face	Oculus VR Voice Recog.	Translation, Deep Text	/

Figure 6.6:   AI cognitive services comparison: Microsoft winner.

Note: There is a "me too" attitude. Microsoft has made a wide and deep mark. But, Alibaba PAI is deeper and broader than anyone else.
Source: Schulte Research Estimates, Zenith.

As for AI Lifestyle such as media, food, travel, entertainment, interaction, search, education, and health, the Chinese technology companies are ahead, with Tencent and Alibaba taking the lead (Figure 6.7). The Chinese Ministry of Science and Technology has identified BAT (Baidu, Alibaba Group Holding, Tencent Holdings) as the champions to partner with the government to spur China's AI strategy to accelerate the country towards global technology leadership. "Baidu's focus will be on autonomous driving; the cloud computing division of Alibaba is tasked with a project called 'city brains,' a set of AI solutions to improve urban life, including smart transport; Tencent will focus on computer vision for medical diagnosis; while Shenzhen-listed iFlytek, a dominant player in voice recognition, will specialize in voice intelligence."

(d) Master Summary: How the Ecosystems are Evolving
Alibaba has expanded its e-commerce business Taobao and Tmall to Finance (Ant Financial) and Tech Service Provider (Alibaba Cloud).

Company	Media	Food	Travel	Entertainment	Interaction	Search	Education	Health
Alibaba	Live media, news production, media interaction, etc.	KFC China, Koubei, Ele.me	Air/train tickets, hotel booking	Audio/video solutions, video game services, e-commerce, Youku, AGTech	Online shopping support	Personalized search, direct marketing service, big data analytics	Media education services	Utilities payment, Hospital-patient comm., smart diagnosis
Tencent	QQ music, Joox, Tencent Video/ News	Meituan Dianping	LY.com	E-commerce, video games	WeChat	WeChat Search, Sogou	Koo Learn, Ke.qq	WeChat Intelligent Hospital
Baidu	Book recomm.	/	Ctrip	/	/	Search engine (76% market share), personalized search, data marketing	Baidu Education (Jiaoyu)	Health Search
Amazon	Books, music, TV streaming	Whole Foods, Amazon Fresh	/	TV streaming, Amazon Studio	/	Search recomm.	Amazon Inspire	/
Microsoft	/	/	/	X-box/gaming	Skype, LinkedIn	Bing	MSFT Education	MSFT Health
Google	Google Videos	/	Google Flights	YouTube	Snapchat, Gmail, Google+	Search engine, personalized search, data marketing	Google for Education	Google Health, Google Fit
Apple	ITunes	/	/	Apps, App Store, Game development kits	Messages	/	/	Health apps
Facebook	Facebook newsfeed	/	/	Facebook games	Facebook, Whatsapp, Instagram	Internal Search Function	/	/

China is way ahead

Figure 6.7: AI lifestyle comparison.

Note: Tencent + Alibaba winner. Microsoft + Baidu falling behind.
Source: Schulte Research Estimates, Zenith.

Figure 6.8 shows the most comprehensive AI ecosystem that is unmatched by any other company. It has achieved all these innovations while being the most profitable of any tech company. Alibaba will produce its own AI chip as well as develop quantum processors and expand into the semiconductor business in 2019Q2. AliNPU, the new AI chip, has the potential to support technologies used in autonomous driving, smart cities, and smart logistics and driven by its R&D arm Damo Academy. Pingtouge, a new semiconductor subsidiary, will focus on customized AI chips and embedded processors. Alibaba acquired IC (Integrated Design) vendor Hangzhou C-Sky Microsystems in April 2018.[11]

With data from Banking Services, Government Services, Lifestyle Services and Business Services using AI, Alibaba is able to access a large pool of data in China (see Figure 6.9). Figures 6.10–6.12 show the different types of deep tech for various Chinese tech giants.

---

[11] https://www.zdnet.com/article/alibaba-to-launch-own-ai-chip-next-year/.

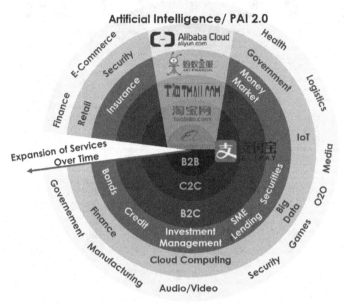

Figure 6.8: Alibaba: e-commerce + the fullest AI ecosystem of any company on earth.

Note: It has achieved this while being the most profitable of any company.

Source: Alibaba Website, Schulte Research.

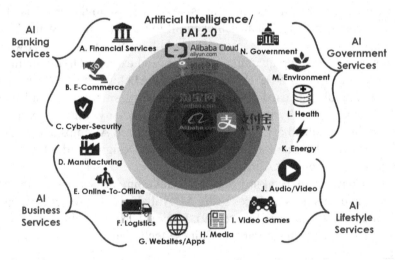

Figure 6.9: Alibaba AI: A truly common man's bible — access to virtually any and all data dumps of all of China.

Source: Alibaba Cloud Website, Schulte Research.

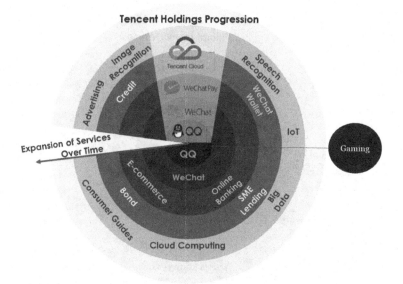

Figure 6.10: Tencent: From social media network to the use of unintentional data to create a full ecosystem.

Source: WeChat, Schulte Research.

Tencent also has access to social media data generated by QQ, Wechat, and Wechat Pay stored in Tencent Cloud, amounting to possibly a billion people's postings, chats, file transfers, photos, locations, and other personal information. Tencent is China's largest social network company with 1 billion users on its app WeChat and 632 million monthly user accounts on social networking platform Qzone. Tencent has extended beyond instant messaging using QQ and social networking to gaming, digital assistants, mobile payments, cloud storage, education, live streaming, sports, movies, and AI.[12] Tencent AI Lab was set up in 2016 with the mission to "Make AI Everywhere." It focuses on fundamental research in machine learning, computer vision, speech recognition, natural language processing, and Game, Social, Content, and Platform AI applications.

Ping An is also providing Health, Real Estate, Transport, Smart City, Government, and Finance services, besides insurance. Thus, it has a huge database at its disposal via its cloud services. Ping An Technology is set

---

[12] https://www.forbes.com/sites/bernardmarr/2018/06/04/artificial-intelligence-ai-in-china-the-amazing-ways-tencent-is-driving-its-adoption/#151b245f479a.

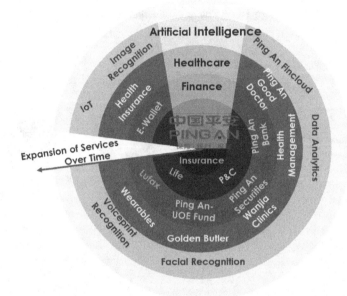

Figure 6.11: Ping An has made greater strides into becoming an autonomous financial ecosystem than any other company.

up to focus on AI, Intelligent Cognition, Blockchain, and Cloud. "AI is one of the core technologies of Ping An Technology and has been used in a series of solutions, including predictive AI, cognitive AI, and decision-making AI. Based on the disease prediction model, predictive AI has been applied to predicting influenza, diabetes, and other diseases. In particular, in the field of cognitive AI, technologies such as facial recognition technology and voiceprint recognition technology have reached the world-leading level; Ping An Brain smart engine integrating AI technologies such as deep learning, data mining, and biometrics can provide six integrated modules including decision making."[13]

With Tencent, Alibaba, and Ping An as its largest shareholders, Zhong An provides pure online insurance services and has slowly expanded into many areas beyond e-commerce insurance that started with the Singles' Day online sales of Alibaba. ZhongAn Technology AI research service covers image recognition, NLP, complex transaction processing, and

---

[13] https://tech.pingan.com/en/.

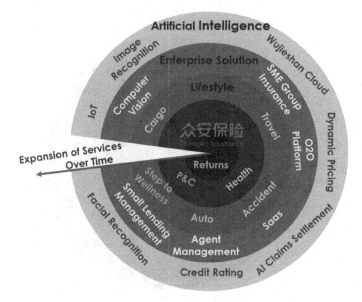

Figure 6.12: Zhong An: Only 3 years old, the largest pure online, cloud-based insurance company globally.

others to (i) help customers understand the users through data analysis and (ii) to set up intelligent applications in less time with mature AI technology and rich experience.[14] It focuses on Natural Language Processing, Image Processing, Complex Transaction Processing, and Machine Learning. Its cloud service platform, Anlink, provides blockchain-based BaaS and AI-based AIaaS and platform security to offer new solutions under different business scenarios such as finance, medical and health care, supply chain, shared R&D, culture, government affairs, and public welfare.[15]

Baidu is another company to watch as they transform its search engine to AI services, regaining its expansion momentum after a wides-cale management shakeup (Figure 6.13). It is now pursuing a riskier strategy of acquisition and expanding its Baidu Cloud business. Baidu has recently launched China's first cloud-to-edge AI chip — Kunlun. With Kunlun, Baidu offers an AI platform to help enterprises deploy AI-infused

---

[14]https://www.zhongan.io/en/technology.html.
[15]https://www.zhongan.io/en/anlink.

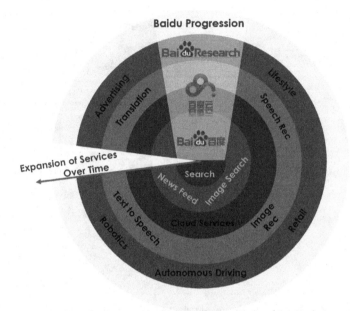

Figure 6.13   Baidu: Stumbled in its transition from search engine to AI, regaining momentum after a widescale management shakeup and pursuing the risky acquisition strategy.

Source: Baidu Website, Schulte Research.

solutions and have their own hardware to maximize AI processing. The chip can accommodate the high-performance requirements of a wide variety of AI applications. It can provide AI capabilities such as speech and text analytics, natural language processing, and visual recognition.[16] Baidu's program, Apollo, aims to make Baidu's AI technologies available to car makers for free as a "brain" for their cars in exchange for access to data. DuerOS is Baidu's voice assistant, and Baidu has teamed up with more than 130 DuerOS partners. Its voice assistant is in more than 100 brands of appliances, such as refrigerators, TVs, and speakers. Baidu is also partnering with Huawei to develop an open mobile AI platform to support the development of AI-powered smartphones, and with Qualcomm

---

[16]https://cio.economictimes.indiatimes.com/news/business-analytics/will-baidus-cloud-to-edge-ai-chip-kunlun-change-the-face-of-ai-market-beyond-china/650 66114.

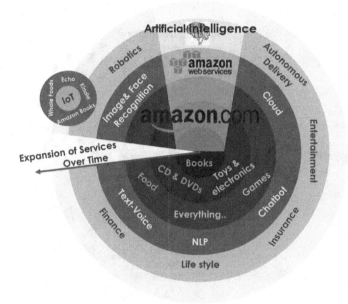

Figure 6.14: Amazon: Online bookstore for 3 years to #1 global player in almost everything, including Cloud, enviable execution + impressive global ambition.

to optimize its DuerOS for IoT devices and smartphones using Qualcomm's Snapdragon Mobile Platform.[17]

Meanwhile, in the US, the tech giants are transforming fast too. Originally an online bookstore, Amazon has transformed itself into the number one AI player in almost everything, including cloud and machine learning. Efforts have been spent building the capabilities in robotics, data center business such as the Amazon Web Services (AWS), health and pharmacy with the acquisition of PillPack, voice technology such as Alexa, and voice-based home appliance business as the Echo[18] (Figure 6.14). The acquisition and expansion of Whole Foods, physical bookstores, and AI-powered cashless Go Stores are signaling that they are

---

[17] https://www.forbes.com/sites/bernardmarr/2018/07/06/how-chinese-internet-giant-baidu-uses-artificial-intelligence-and-machine-learning/#6a5d71f2d557.
[18] https://www.wired.com/story/amazon-artificial-intelligence-flywheel/.

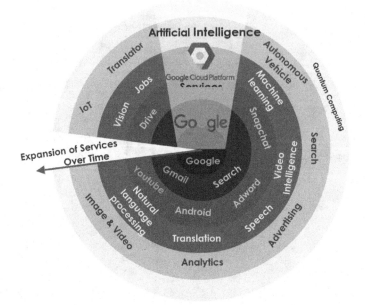

Figure 6.15: Google: From #16 in a search engine, Google has used AI to become an advertising behemoth. But, it is not on the radar screen in finance.

combining online and offline businesses using AI.[19] Four major AI products are (i) Amazon Lex — a service for building conversational interfaces into any application using voice and text; (ii) Amazon Polly — a service that turns text into lifelike speech; (iii) Amazon Rekognition — a service that makes it easy to add image analysis to applications; and (iv) Amazon Machine Learning — a service that makes it easy for developers of all skill levels to use machine learning technology.[20]

Google's advertising revenue grew from a mere US$70 million in 2001 to a staggering US$95.38 billion in 2017. The recent results showed that Google accounted for 86% of its parent Alphabet's 2018Q2 revenue of US$26.24 billion. Google's other revenues, including cloud services, hardware, and app sales, grew 37% to US$4.4 billion over the same

---

[19] https://www.cnbc.com/2018/09/04/inside-amazons-big-plans-to-get-to-2-trillion-club-health-ai-retail--more.html.

[20] https://docs.aws.amazon.com/aws-technical-content/latest/aws-overview/artificial-intelligence-services.html.

quarter a year earlier. However, Alphabet's other investments, such as the self-driving car business Waymo and health-tech company Verily, continued to lose money, accounting for an operating loss of US$732 million in the second quarter.[21] Google AI, formerly known as Google Research, is Google's AI research and development branch for its AI applications. Google products are interesting and include (i) Google Auto ML vision — a machine learning model builder for image recognition; (ii) Google Assistant — a voice assistant AI for Android devices; (iii) TensorFlow — an open-source framework used to run machine learning and deep learning, including AI accelerators; and (iv) DeepMind — a division responsible for developing deep learning and artificial general intelligence (AGI) technology.[22] Google Search, Street View, Google Photos, and Google Translate all use Google's Tensor Processing Unit, or TPU, to accelerate their neural network computations behind the scenes[23] (Figure 6.15). The chip has been specifically designed for Google's TensorFlow framework, a symbolic math library that is used for machine learning applications such as neural networks.[24] The third-generation TPU was announced on May 8, 2018 and Google "would allow other companies to buy access to those chips through its cloud-computing service."[25]

Microsoft's recent growth has been spurred by its cloud services that include Azure, which has grown in excess of 70% over the previous year (Figure 6.16). Microsoft's focus on fast-growing cloud applications and platforms is helping it beat the slowing demand for personal computers that has hurt sales of its popular Windows operating system.[26] Its AI applications are exciting, and most important of all, it is designing AI to be trustworthy, creating solutions reflecting ethical principles, such as Fairness, Reliability and Safety, Privacy and Security, Inclusiveness, Transparency, and Accountability. The commercialization of some of the

---

[21] https://qz.com/1334369/alphabet-q2-2018-earnings-google-is-more-than-just-advertising-now/.

[22] https://whatis.techtarget.com/definition/Google-AI.

[23] https://cloud.google.com/blog/products/gcp/an-in-depth-look-at-googles-first-tensor-processing-unit-tpu.

[24] https://en.wikipedia.org/wiki/Tensorprocessingunit.

[25] https://www.nytimes.com/2018/02/12/technology/google-artificial-intelligence-chips.html.

[26] https://www.reuters.com/article/us-microsoft-results/microsoft-sales-and-profit-beat-estimates-on-cloud-growth-idUSKCN1MY2T8.

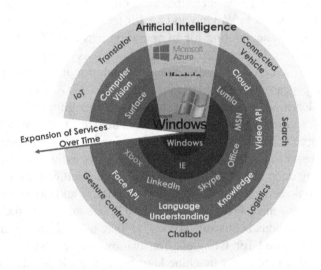

Figure 6.16: Microsoft: Started as dominant PC operating system but failed in the all-important transition to mobile, trying to recover by its Azure Cloud. Why is Microsoft not a dominant leader in SME lending?

projects on mobile devices, such as improving crop yields, has yet to contribute directly or significantly to revenue.

Unlike Microsoft, Apple's AI strategy continues to focus on running workloads locally on devices, rather than relying heavily on cloud-based resources, as competitors like Google, Amazon, and Microsoft do (Figure 6.17). With more privacy protection going forward, the company's emphasis is on user privacy and selling devices incorporating these features. The Create ML framework is the app maker to train AI models on Mac. Xcode is Apple's own app for coding programs for its devices. Swift, rather than Python, is Apple's programming language, and the advantage is the drag and drop features used to train models. The updated Core ML software is also a sparser model that takes up less space on devices once they are embedded into apps.[27]

Facebook created Facebook AI Research (FAIR) group in 2013 to advance the understanding of intelligence's nature to create intelligent machines (Figure 6.18). The research code, data sets, and tools like

---

[27]https://www.cnbc.com/2018/06/13/apples-ai-strategy-devices-not-cloud.html.

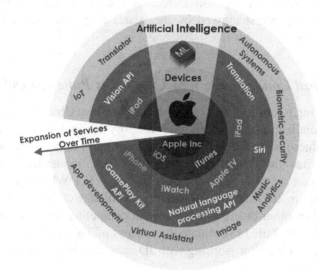

Figure 6.17: Apple: This is a hardware company with excellent marketing, unimpressive AI and seems to have stumbled in the progression. Too late to the game?

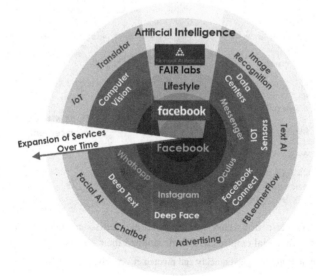

Figure 6.18: Facebook: The most incredible one-trick pony ever. They control the social network plus people think this is important — but for its own sake? One of the worst scores.

PyTorch, fastText, FAISS, and Detectron are open source.[28] However, their efforts are overshadowed by the issues of privacy intrusions and misuse of data.

6.3.3　*Project Conclusions: Why China Has Pulled Ahead*

It is interesting to observe that few countries can beat China when it comes to commercialization, especially one done by technological companies. When a Chinese project or initiative fails to impress or is otherwise unsatisfactory or has low market acceptance, successful replacements in a different direction are created to take over (Figure 6.19). When Alibaba's Lai Wang, started in 2011, failed to counter the challenge of Tencent's Wechat, it refocused on other businesses rather than competing head-on. Similarly, Tencent's Pai Pai failed to emulate the success of Taobao. It was closed in April 2016, 2 years after working with JD.com, in which it acquired 15%,

Company	Duds	Successful Replacements
Alibaba	Lai Wang, Alibaba.com (HK)	Ant Financial, AliPay, Taobao, Tmall, Alibaba Cloud, PAI 2.0, Zhima Credit, ANTSDAQ, Yue'bao, Youku, Weibo, etc.
Tencent	Pai Pai, E-commerce	WePay, Weilidai, WeBank, JD.com, WeChat, Didi, Tencent Cloud, etc.
Ping An	Ping An Good Car	Ping An Bank, Ping An Insurance, Ping An Asset Mgmt, Ping An Health, etc.
Baidu	O2O Wai Mai	Baidu Wallet
Microsoft	Microsoft Wallet	Skype
Google	Google Hangout	Android Pay
Facebook	Messenger Pay	/
Apple	Apple Pay	/
Amazon	Amazon Lending Amazon Insurance	/

Duds with no replacement

Figure 6.19:　Chinese firms have implemented and jettisoned quicker. China dropped duds and created financial empires. US firms stopped their efforts.

Note: China had duds but morphed quickly and pivoted effectively.

---

[28] https://code.fb.com/ai-research/fair-fifth-anniversary/.

Table 6.1: Project conclusions (1).

General Conclusions
1. The Cloud is the foundation of AI strategy. Alibaba dominates in Asia. Amazon dominates in US.
2. Cognitive services are the foundation of AI development — voice, image, face, video, language. However, there is a 'me too' and, surprisingly, a feeling that AI is already commoditized.
3. SMEs and corporates can access cheap AI tools which allow them to access new forms of credit and offer new products. This is the age of the SME.
4. Firms, especially in China plus other GEMS, are leapfogging banks rapidly. They are using AI to analyze vast amounts of integrated data in order to offer new financial services to billions of unbanked people and millions of unbanked SMEs.

and 11 years after Pai Pai was set up.[29] On the other hand, US firms are not as adept at pivoting to new areas or applications.

The conclusions are that while manufacturing chips is important, the cloud is the foundation of AI strategy at this stage of the competition (Table 6.1). Alibaba dominates in Asia while Amazon dominates in the US. Cognitive services are the foundation of AI development, especially regarding voice, image, face, video, language recognition, and learning. While there is differentiation in the deepness of the AI technologies, the "me too" development strategy seems to have created a feeling that AI services are already commoditized. Small and Medium Enterprises (SMEs) and corporates have access to cheap AI tools that allow them to access new forms of credit and offer new products. This new age of the SME will empower the smaller enterprises to level the playing field, as long as the incumbents do not exert pressure on the regulators via their power of sheer employment numbers.

Given that regulators are wary of job losses, the incumbents have a certain influence over the policymakers and legislators in implementing anti-competition rules in the current climate. In China, firms are leap-frogging banks because of the failure of the banks to serve the under-served. Furthermore, with weak privacy protection in the earlier years, data technology combined with AI allowed firms to offer new financial services to millions of unbanked or underbanked population and SMEs.

---

[29] https://walkthechat.com/tencents-product-failure-history/.

Table 6.2:   Project conclusions (2).

Chinese Firms Conclusions
1. PRC firms are better at monetizing technology for mass use.
2. PRC has a long-term, coherent plan for AI while the US has no plan.
3. Chinese are more willing to share data with vendors.
4. Alibaba and Ping An are much further into new territory than anyone else.
5. Integration of finance and lifestyle is welcomed and encouraged by PRC.
6. PRC has a clear national policy of increasing access to credit for individuals and SMEs.

Table 6.3:   Project conclusions (3).

Reasons for China's Success over US
1. US heavily entrenched incumbents and lobbying groups have impeded progress to protect cartels.
2. Multiple regulators who launched investigations after the devastation of the GFC and imposed fines of US$300 billion on financial firms discouraged new consumers credit products.
3. Many of the Chinese companies learned though bitter experience. They were toughened by a highly competitive environment.
4. China succeeded since there are no entrenched incumbents and lobbying groups and financial innovation starts from scratch.

The observations point to the fact that Chinese firms are better at monetizing technology for mass adoption. With President Xi emphasizing technology transformation with AI as a leading technology, China has a long-term, coherent plan. The US is still struggling to come to grips with how AI can be commercialized for mass adoption, besides military uses. It is also known that even with tighter privacy protection laws in China, the Chinese are more willing to share their private data with vendors. While we focus on Alibaba's achievements, Ping An has moved further than other competitors into new territory. The Chinese government encourages the integration of finance and lifestyle with a clear national policy of providing access to credit for individuals and SMEs (see Table 6.2).

There are good reasons why the Chinese firms have more successes than the US firms (Table 6.3). First, the incumbents and lobbying groups in the US have impeded progress by their sheer determination to protect their own turfs. Second, multiple regulators who launched investigations

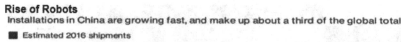

Rise of Robots
Installations in China are growing fast, and make up about a third of the global total

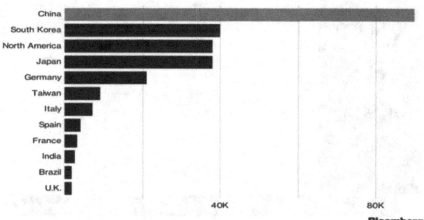

Figure 6.20: Robot installations in China are 1/3 of the global rise of robots.

Source: International Federation of Robotics, National Robot associations, Bloomberg Intelligence.

on the devastation of the GFC imposed US$300 billion of fines, thus discouraging new consumer credit products. Third, many Chinese companies learned from bitter experience and were toughened by a highly competitive environment. QR codes were banned for a short period due to the lobby by the incumbents, but the ban was eventually lifted on the grounds of social benefits. Finally, China succeeded since there were few legacy issues with the only path to success being "new–new." Banking and regulatory structures were absent and the monetary infrastructure was very immature, resulting in regulation not being able to keep up with innovation. Financial innovation can be likened to manufacturing innovation where the Chinese lead in robot installations (Table 6.3 and Figure 6.20).

(a) Master Summary: Ranking for AI, Financials, and Valuations

The following tables show a few rankings based on specific metrics. These analyses should not be used for investment purposes as one of the authors is an independent director of Lu International, a subsidiary of Ping An. The analyses are based on financial, operational, and AI performance. Figures 6.21–6.25 show the summary and various rankings.

		First	Second	Third	Laggard
Business Per	Operational Health	Facebook	Alibaba	Tencent	Amazon
	Revenue Diversification	Microsoft	Alibaba	Tencent	Facebook
	Valuation	Ping An	Apple	Google	Tencent
	Credit Health	Google	Apple	Tencent	Baidu
Artificial Intelligence	Fintech	Alibaba	Ping An	Tencent	Facebook
	Insurtech	Ping An	Alibaba	Tencent	Facebook
	Healthtech	Ping An	Alibaba	Amazon	Baidu
	Cloud	Amazon	Microsoft	Alibaba	Facebook
	Data Source	Alibaba	Ping An	Tencent	Baidu
	Cog Services	Google	Alibaba	Microsoft	Facebook
	Lifestyle	Tencent	Alibaba	Amazon	Baidu
	Securities	Ping An	Alibaba	Tencent	Microsoft
Overall Winners/Losers		Ping An	Alibaba	Tencent	Baidu/Facebook

Figure 6.21: Master summary: Financial, operational, artificial intelligence analysis.

	AI Scorecard	Financials	Valuation	Average
1. Ping An	2	4	1	2.3
2. Alibaba	1	2	7	3.3
3. Google	5	4	3	4.0
4. Apple	6	5	2	4.3
5. Tencent	3	3	8	4.7
6. Facebook	8	1	6	5.0
7. Microsoft	7	6	4	5.7
8. Baidu	9	7	5	7.0
9. Amazon	4	8	9	7.0

Figure 6.22: Overall rankings: Ping An and Alibaba dominate in all categories.

Note: Ranking of each company's performance across all three areas: Artificial Intelligence Services, Financials, and Valuation. "1" is best, "9" is worst.

	1 Alibaba	2 Ping An	3 Tencent	4 Amazon	5 Google	6 Apple	7 Microsoft	8 Facebook	9 Baidu
FinTech	10	10	9	7	6	7	4	4	5
InsureTech	9	10	9	6	4	4	4	4	4
HealthTech	9	10	8	8	7	7	7	5	4
Cloud	8	5	7	10	8	6	9	4	5
Data source	9	8	9	8	8	8	7	7	6
Cognitive Services	9	8	7	8	10	7	9	7	8
Lifestyle	9	8	10	9	9	9	7	9	6
Securities	9	10	9	4	5	6	4	5	5
Average	9.0	8.6	8.5	7.5	7.1	6.8	6.4	5.6	5.4

Figure 6.23: Artificial intelligence scorecard.

Notes: Chinese firms have diversity and consist of a full menu. US firms tend to specialize through one brand. This age of AI requires a diversified ecosystem. Specialist firms lose out. *Scoring from 1 (worst) to 10 (best).
Source: Schulte Research Estimates.

	1 Facebook	2 Alibaba	3 Tencent	4 Alphabet	5 Apple	6 Microso	7 Baidu	8 Amazon
Retained Earnings (US$mn)	3	5	4	1	2	8	6	7
Gross Margin (%)	1	2	5	4	7	3	6	8
Net Margin (%)	1	2	3	6	5	4	7	8
Revenue CAGR (5yrs) (%)	2	1	3	6	7	8	4	5
Cash/Total Asset	4	1	3	5	6	8	7	2
Tangible Leverage	1	3	5	2	6	8	4	7
ROE (%)	2	5	3	6	1	4	7	8
ROC (%)	3	6	2	5	1	4	7	8
ROA (%)	3	2	1	4	5	6	7	8
Average	2.3	3.1	3.3	4.6	4.6	6.2	6.3	7.2

Figure 6.24: Financial rankings.

Notes: Facebook/Alibaba best in operations; Baidu/Amazon worst. Microsoft also mediocre. *Ranking from 1st (best) to 9th (worst). *ROE/ROC/ROA are next 4Q estimates.

	1 Ping An	2 Apple	3 Alphabet	4 Microso	5 Baidu	6 Facebook	7 Alibaba	8 Tencent	9 Amazon
P/E	1	2	4	3	5	6	7	8	9
P/B	1	4	2	6	3	5	7	8	9
PEG	2	7	6	8	3	1	4	5	9
Price/ Free Cash Flow	1	2	4	3	5	7	6	8	9
EV/EBITDA	NA	1	2	3	5	4	7	8	6
EV/EBIT	NA	1	2	3	5	4	6	7	8
Average	2.4	2.8	3.3	4.3	4.3	4.5	6.2	7.5	8.5

Figure 6.25: Valuation rankings.

Notes: Ping An cheapest; Amazon most expensive. *Ranking from 1st (best) to 9th (worst).

(b) Master Summary: Strategic Direction

Successful technology companies tend to focus on building the ecosystem. This means that they build the capabilities of the entire spectrum of technologies by integrating the high Price to Earning (PE) rather than those with low PE. A combination of IOT plus AI with an integrated ecosystem presents excellent business opportunities. The Chinese firms are more diversified in revenue than the US firms. In terms of advertising as a revenue ratio, US firms such as Facebook and Alphabet/Google have a higher ratio. Data-rich firms have the opportunity to increase their revenue in this area (Figures 6.26–6.30).

(c) Master Summary: Research and Development — Strategic Development

Most US technology companies have a similar vision for the future based on AI, Big Data, and Language Processing (Figure 6.31). However, each has its niche, with Facebook focusing on Virtual Reality, Microsoft on Human-Computer Interaction, Apple on Chips, Amazon on Drones and Robotics, and Google on Quantum Computing. Chinese firms are similar but more diversified.

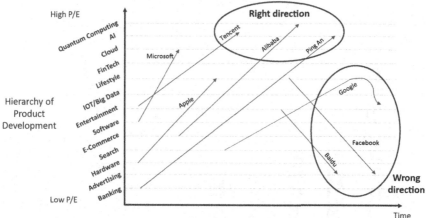

Alibaba, Tencent, and Ping An have IOT/AI *plus* fully integrated systems. Baidu dropped the ball.

Figure 6.26: Strategy directions: The key is integrated ecosystems.

Note: Specialization in IOT + AI is a liability. Google/Facebook have thrown away spectacular opportunities.

Source: Schulte Research.

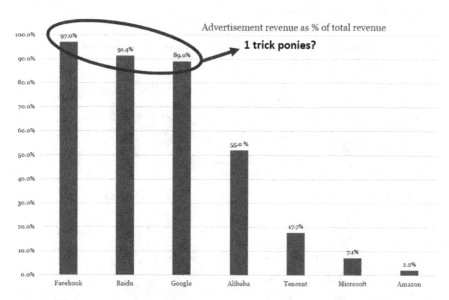

Figure 6.27: Advertisement: Facebook is leading. Other data-rich firms have the potential to expand revenue source.

Source: Schulte Research Estimates, Bloomberg.

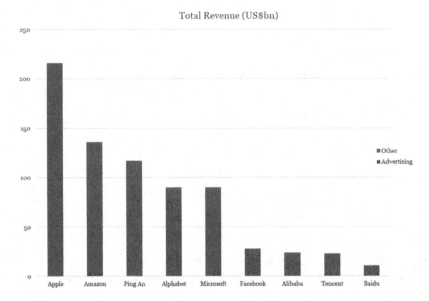

Figure 6.28:　Total Revenue: Apple is leading. Other data-rich firms have the potential to expand revenue sources.

Source: Schulte Research Estimates, Bloomberg.

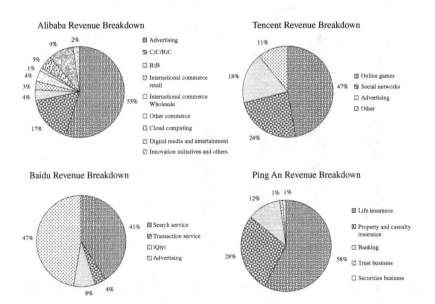

Figure 6.29:　Chinese companies' revenue breakdown.

Note: China is much more diversified than the US: PRC has a deeper, more integrated ecosystem.
Source: Schulte Research Estimates, Bloomberg, Company filings.

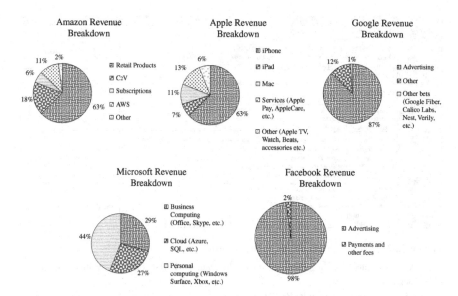

Figure 6.30: US companies' revenue breakdown.

Note: These five companies are essentially specializing. I think the US companies have moved away from the conglomerate model at the wrong time?

Source: Schulte Research Estimates, Bloomberg, Company filings.

Companies	Research Direction	Unique Selling Point
Facebook	1.Facebook AI Research (FAIR) – semantic analysis, sentient analysis, etc. 2.Natural Language Processing and Speech – translation services, word sense disambiguation, etc. 3.Applied Machine Learning – streamline content delivery, connect users with desired content 4.Data Science – human interaction analysis, market intelligence, etc. 5.Virtual Reality – augmented reality experiences	Virtual Reality
Microsoft	1.Artificial Intelligence 2.Computer Vision 3.Human – Computer Interaction 4.Human Language Technologies 5.Search and Information Retrieval	Human – Computer Interaction
Apple	1.Apple Car/Autonomous Driving 2.Augmented Reality 3.HealthTech – Health Functions within Apple Watch 4.Chips – Hardware improvement	Chips
Amazon	1.Image/Face Recognition 2.Voice Recognition 3.ChatBot AI 4.Drone Delivery 5.Warehouse Robotics	Drone, Robotics
Google	1.Machine Translation System 2.Deep Learning Algorithms – Detection of Diabetic Retinopathy 3.Quantum Computing 4.Big Data Analytics 5.Machine Intelligence/Perception	Quantum Computing

Figure 6.31: Research directions: US firms.

Note: All companies have a similar vision of the future: AI, Big Data, and Language!

Source: Schulte Research.

Companies	Research Direction	Unique Selling Point
Alibaba	1.Financial Securities Exchange Core 2.Customer Service AI 3.Intelligent Manufacturing – Cloud computing/big data analytics 4.Health Data Platform – Integration of patient data, image analysis, diagnosis 5.Commercial Vehicle Networks – logistics enhancement and optimization	Securities Exchange, Intelligent Manufacturing
Tencent	1.Artificial Intelligence 2.Machine Learning – Stock Picking, HFT, Portfolio Management 3.Big Data – Trend Analysis 4.Cloud Computing	Portfolio Management
Ping An	1.Data Mining – Social Media User Behavior, Engagement Rates 2.Computational Algorithms 3.Big Data Analytics – Purchasing Patterns, WMPs	WMPs
Zhong An	1.Financial Platforms/Cores – E-commerce Platforms, Insurance Cores, Finance Cores 2.Data Analytics/ Risk Management Modelling 3.AI – Transaction Decision-making 4.Blockchain – Digitalize Off-chain assets, Data Storage, Secure ID 5.AI – Customer Service ChatBot	Blockchain
Baidu	1.Artificial Intelligence – image/speech recognition 2.High-Performance Computing/Big Data Analytics 3.Natural Language Processing 4.Deep Learning 5.Augmented Reality	High-performance computing

Figure 6.32: Research directions: Chinese firms.

Note: All companies have a similar vision of the future. Chinese firms show higher degree of diversification.

Source: Synergy Research, Schulte Research.

Alibaba's unique selling point (USP) is Securities Exchange and Intelligent Manufacturing. Tencent's USP is portfolio management as its unique point, while Ping An has focused on Wealth Management Products (WMPs) as its USP, among many other initiatives. The USP of Zhong An is blockchain, and that of Baidu is high-performance computing (Figure 6.32). However, given the dynamic market, this unique focus point may change with time and market trends. Acquisitions reveal the directions of the companies, and Figures 6.33 and 6.34 show the trend of acquisitions by these companies.

(d) Master Summary: Cash Flow, M&A, and Capex

It is interesting to observe that tech companies invest in building their ecosystem, given their high market capitalization and cash position. Banks are pursuing new technology but not doing enough in this space, partly due to the lower market capitalization, lower cash flow, lower cash reserves, high capital requirement, regulatory constraints, board composition with less tech expertise, fiduciary duties, and other reasons that have been well documented. Figures 6.35 to 6.38 show the financials.

Reference/Further Reading

Lee, D., & Schulte, P. (2018). *AI & Quantum Computing for Finance & Insurance: Fortunes and Challenges for China and America* [Chapter 2]. World Scientific, pp. 27–72.

Company	Acquisition	Amount (US$)	Year	Description	Comment
Facebook	WhatsApp	19bn	2014	Messaging	Consolidation of social network industry
	Oculus	2bn	2014	VR	
	Instagram	1.01bn	2012	Social Network	
	LiveRail	500mn	2014	Video ad.	
Microsoft	LinkedIn	26.2bn	2016	Social Network	Failed hardware attempt on Nokia. LinkedIn is the new bet on professional network.
	Nokia	8bn	2013	Phone	
	Skype	8.5bn	2011	Messaging	
	Mojang	2.5bn	2014	Game developer	
	Yammer	1.2bn	2012	Corp communication	
Apple	Beats Electronics	3bn	2014	Headphone	Lifestyle + Health
	HopStop.com	1bn	2013	Transit guide	
	Lattice	200mn	2017	AI	
	Gliimpse	200mn	2016	Health	
Amazon	Whole Foods Market	13.7bn	2017	Supermarket	O2O bet on Whole Foods
	Twitch	970mn	2014	Game streaming	
	Souq.com	580mn	2017	E-commerce	
	Elemental Technologies	500mn	2015	Mobile video	
	Annapurna Labs	37mn	2015	Chip maker	
Google	Motorola Mobility	12.5bn	2012	Phone	Another failed case of acquiring phone company
	Waze	1.3bn	2013	Map	
	Apigee	625mn	2016	API platform	
	DeepMind	500mn	2014	AI	

Figure 6.33: Major acquisitions: US firms.

Note: US firms invest heavily in acquiring smaller firms that do not necessarily operate in their industry.
Source: Synergy Research, Schulte Research.

Companies	Acquisition	Amount (US$)	Year	Description	Comment
Alibaba	UCWeb	4.7bn	2014	Mobile browser	Contents + data
	Youku	3.5bn	2015	Chinese Youtube	
	AGTech Holdings	2.39bn	2016	Lottery	
	SCMP	262mn	2015	Media	
	Wandoujia	200mn	2016	Android app store	
Tencent	Supercell	8.6bn	2016	Game developer	Consolidation of game industry
	China Music Corp	2.7bn	2016	Music	
	Riot Games	400mn	2011	Game developer	
	Miniclip SA	na	2015	Game developer	
	Sanook	na	2016	Thai web portal	
Baidu	91 Boyuan Wireless	1.9bn	2013	Android app store	Diverse
	Beijing Huanxiang Zongheng Chinese Literature	31.3mn	2013	Online publisher	
	TrustGo	30mn	2013	Mobile security	
Ping An	Autohome	1.6bn	2016	Auto website	Auto insurance

Figure 6.34: Major acquisitions: Chinese firms.

Note: All companies have a similar vision of the future. Chinese firms show higher degree of diversification.
Source: Synergy Research, Schulte Research.

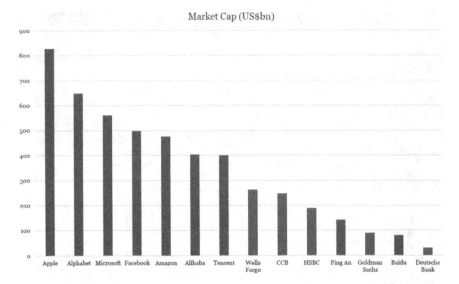

Figure 6.35: Market cap.

Note: Tech companies are a gathering force in market cap. They dominate capital markets now. Banks can't hold a candle to tech spending.

Source: Schulte Research Estimates, Bloomberg.

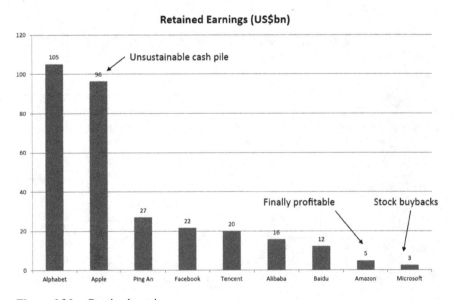

Figure 6.36: Retained earnings.

Note: Alphabet and Apple are sitting on mountains of cash, much of it as untaxed offshore cash.

Source: Schulte Research Estimates, Bloomberg.

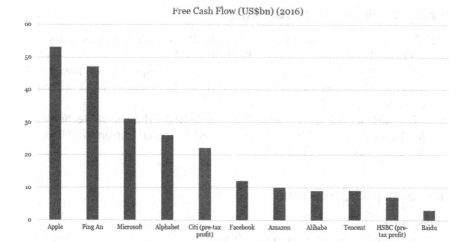

Figure 6.37: Free cash flow.

Note: Cash flows from operations — investment in operating capital (mostly fixed assets).

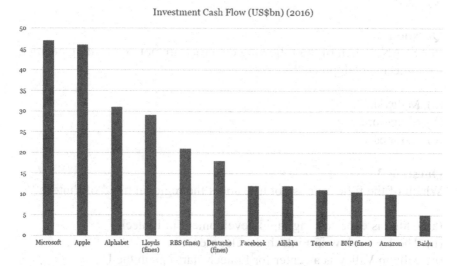

Figure 6.38: Investment cash flow (net spending in PP&E, Capex, M&A).

Source: Bloomberg.

References/Further Readings

Lee, D., & Low, L. (2018). Inclusive Fintech: Blockchain, Cryptocurrency and ICO. World Scientific, Chapter 10, pp. 437–448.

Lee, D., & Schulte, P. (2018). AI & Quantum Computing for Finance & Insurance: Fortunes and Challenges for China and America. World Scientific, Chapter 2; pp. 27–72.

Xin, D. (2019). 金融科技：模式变革与业务创新 [Financial Technology: Model Revolution and Business Innovation]. Shanghai University of Finance & Economics Press. Chapter 1.

6.4 Sample Questions

Question 1
_____ is not a big actor in the Fintech area

(a) US
(b) China
(c) Japan

Question 2
In ASEAN, which of the following countries are not in a leading position for Fintech development?

(a) Malaysia
(b) Singapore
(c) Indonesia

Question 3
Which of the following is not true about the regional trend of Fintech?

(a) China is experiencing rapid development in Fintech
(b) The US is slow in Fintech development
(c) Silicon Valley is a center for Fintech start-ups in the US

Question 4
Which of the following is related to Mobile Internet technology?

(a) Financial Technology 1.0
(b) Financial Technology 2.0
(c) Financial Technology 3.0

Question 5

Which of the following belongs to the technical core of Financial Technology 3.0.

(a) Mimicking human behavior
(b) Extracting information from the Internet of Things
(c) All of above

Question 6

Which of the following is incorrect?

(a) The US develops Fintech according to strong market demand and technology innovation
(b) Singapore has a language advantage for global financial capital entering the Asian market
(c) India's Fintech industry is not in a mature stage

Question 7

Which of the following statement is true?

(a) The ecosystem of firms in China has a less complete suite of "finance to lifestyle" AI products than US firms
(b) AI is an essential component to analyze data from the Internet of Things (IoT) system
(c) When it comes to commercialization, many countries can beat China

Question 8

Which of the following is why the Chinese tech firms are having more successes over the US tech firms?

(a) The incumbents and lobbying groups in the US have impeded progress by their sheer determination to protect their turfs
(b) Multiple regulators who were on the warpath after the devastation of the GFC imposed US$300 billion of fines, thus discouraging new consumer credit products
(c) Both of above

Question 9

According to the ranking of each company's performance across all three areas: Artificial Intelligence Services, Financials, and Valuation, which company has the highest score?

(a) Ping An
(b) Alibaba
(c) Google

Solutions

Question 1

Solution: Option **c** is correct.

Generally and globally, the big actors are the US and China.

Question 2

Solution: Option **c** is correct.

Refer to the reading of Section 6.1.

Question 3

Solution: Option **b** is correct.

US is a developing fast in Fintech.

Question 4

Solution: Option **c** is correct.

Financial Technology 3.0 exploits the field of financial applications on mobile phones and other nascent technologies such as AI, Blockchain, Cloud, and Data Analytics.

Question 5

Solution: Option **c** is correct.

Financial Technology 3.0 exploits the field of financial applications on mobile phones and other nascent technologies such as AI, Blockchain, Cloud, and Data Analytics.

Question 6

Solution: Option **a** is correct.

Market demand is not enough in the US model.

Question 7

Solution: Option **b** is correct.

(a) The ecosystem of firms in China has a more complete suite of "finance to lifestyle" AI products than US firms. (c) China is good at commercialization.

Question 8

Solution: Option **c** is correct.

Refer to the reading of Section 6.3.

Question 9

Solution: Option **a** is correct.

Refer to Figure 6.22.

Chapter 7

Unicorns and China Tech

Learning Objectives
- Review four Fintech unicorns in China.
- Review new online financial instruments such as P2P loans and crowd-funding for Internet finance in the Chinese market.
- Review e-commerce and digital finance development in China and their implications on rural villages using Alibaba as a successful case.
- Explore the evolution of Fintech and its regulation in China.

Main Takeaways

Main Points
- Alibaba, Tencent, Ping An, and Huawei are four Fintech unicorns in China.
- P2P lending in China in recent years is developing rapidly.
- The size of the Chinese crowdfunding market is huge, encompassing movie products, Fintech firms, and financial products.
- The rise of new technology is the most important factor in enabling access to financial services for rural residents and micro businesses.
- China's regulatory framework on digital finance after 2015 provided detailed rules on different types of DFS.

Main Terms
- **P2P loan:** Lending between one individual and another individual without a financial institution as the middleman.
- **O2O:** Online to offline.

- **Bancassurance:** An arrangement between a bank and an insurance company that increases the insurance company's client base by using the bank's client base.
- **Enterprise Intelligence (EI):** The technology of extracting relevant information from an enterprise and analyzing the data to extract real value.
- **The fourth industrial revolution:** The application of modern smart technologies to industrial practices.
- **P2B:** Peer to Business: A concept in which individuals lend to established businesses.
- **Crowdfunding:** A new business financing method in which funds are raised from a large group of people.
- **Hollowed Villages:** The abandoned villages due to depopulation and housing modernization.
- **"Left-Behind" Children:** Children left behind in a rural area by parents working in the urban areas, to be brought up by grandparents or other relatives.
- **Alipay:** The world's leading third-party payment platform initiated by Ant Financial Services Group.
- **MYBank:** A private bank, initiated by Ant Financial, with licenses granted by the banking regulator.
- **WeBank:** The first private bank, initiated by Tencent Holdings Ltd, with licenses granted by the banking regulator.
- **WePay:** A competing payment platform initiated by Tencent Holdings Ltd.
- **DFS:** Digital Financial Services, which includes a broad range of financial services delivered through digital channels.
- **LBP:** Lending Business Permit, which is a business license to operate a lending company legally.
- **PBOC:** People's Bank of China, the central bank of China, carries out monetary policy and regulation of financial institutions.
- **CBRC:** The China Banking Regulatory Commission, an agency authorized by the State Council to regulate the banking sector in mainland China.

7.1 Unicorns in China: Ping An, Tencent, Huawei, Alibaba

The following reference is selected to provide a comprehensive overview of this topic. You are required to read the listed study materials.

Reference/Further Reading

Lee, D., & Schulte, P. (2018). *AI & Quantum Computing for Finance & Insurance: Fortunes and Challenges for China and America*. World Scientific, Chapters 7–9, pp. 163–243.

7.2 Rise of Chinese Finance

The following references are selected to provide a comprehensive overview of this topic. You are required to read the listed study materials.

References/Further Readings

Lee, D., & Deng, R. (2018a). *Handbook of Blockchain, Digital Finance, and Inclusion* (Vol. 2, Sections 1.3–1.4, pp. 15–25). Elsevier.

Lee, D., & Teo, E. (2015). *The Game of Dian Fu*. Retrieved on August 18, 2015, from http://www.smu.edu.sg/sites/default/files/skbife/pdf/The%20Rise%20of%20Chinese%20Finance%20颠覆.pdf.

7.3 Fintech Changing Social Inclusion in China

The following reference is selected to provide a comprehensive overview of this topic. You are required to read the listed study materials.

Reference/Further Reading

Lee, D., & Deng, R. (2018b). *Handbook of Blockchain, Digital Finance, and Inclusion* (Vol. 1, Chapter 2, pp. 19–35). Elsevier.

7.4 Regulating Fintech in China

The following reference is selected to provide a comprehensive overview of this topic. You are required to read the listed study materials.

Reference/Further Reading

Lee, D., & Deng, R. (2018c). *Handbook of Blockchain, Digital Finance, and Inclusion* (Vol. 2, Chapter 3, pp. 45–64). Elsevier.

7.5 Sample Questions

Question 1
Which of the following statement is true?

(a) Tencent mainly focuses on foreign markets
(b) Tencent relies on Wechat only
(c) Both Alibaba and Tencent have extended their business to many countries in Asia either via investment, acquisition, joint venture, or collaboration

Question 2
Which of the following is not true about the regional trend of Fintech?

(a) China has rapid development in the Fintech area
(b) The US is slow in Fintech development
(c) Huawei as a listed company leads in 5G technology

Question 3
Which of the following company is not a leading company for payments platforms in China?

(a) Alibaba
(b) Tencent
(c) Huawei

Question 4
Internet finance is developing many new online financial instruments, including

(a) P2P loans
(b) Online crowdfunding
(c) both of above

Question 5
In recent years, P2Ps have developed due to____

(a) The low barriers of entry
(b) Strong liquidity and convenient procedures
(c) Both of above

Question 6
The different types of crowdfunding can be categorized into the ___ main groups?

(a) 2
(b) 4
(c) 5

Question 7
In rural areas, Alibaba Group released the "1,000 counties and 10,000 villages" program in October 2014 to___

(a) Better serve the rural residents
(b) Support agricultural innovation and economic development
(c) Both of above

Question 8
Which of the following statement is not true?

(a) Both Alibaba and Tencent have expanded their business to Asia
(b) Fintech has substantially increased customer experience at Ping An
(c) The poor income level and education shortage are two main issues in rural areas of China

Question 9
Which of the following is the most important factor to enable access to financial services for the rural residents and micro businesses?

(a) The rise of new technology
(b) The local government supports
(c) Increase in rural population

Question 10
While the Chinese government has been aware of the risks associated with DFS and the need for regulation for almost a decade, the regulatory work has progressed ____.

(a) Slowly
(b) Very fast
(c) Same as the US

Question 11
What is considered a landmark regulatory achievement for China in 2015?

(a) Guideline on the Promotion of the Healthy Development of Internet Finance
(b) Provisional Rules on the Administration of the Business Activities of Online Lending Intermediaries
(c) Regulation on Non-Depositing Loan Institutions

Question 12
Which of the following is not true?

(a) DFS in China developed much earlier than elsewhere
(b) China's regulatory framework on digital finance before 2015 was very preliminary
(c) Internet banking was first introduced in China by traditional financial institutions

Solutions

Question 1

Solution: Option **c** is correct.

Tencent focuses more on Chinese market, and it has many other products/businesses besides Wechat.

Question 2

Solution: Option **c** is correct.

Huawei is a private company.

Question 3

Solution: Option **c** is correct.

Huawei does not have payment-platform product.

Question 4

Solution: Option **c** is correct. Refer to the reading of Section 7.2.

Question 5

Solution: Option **c** is correct.

Refer to the reading of Section 7.2.

Question 6

Solution: Option **b** is correct.

The categories of crowdfunding can be four main groups: debt-based, equity-based, reward-based and donation-based.

Question 7

Solution: Option **c** is correct.

Refer to the reading of Section 7.3.

Question 8

Solution: Option **c** is correct.

The rural hollowing and left-behind Children are two main issues in rural areas of China.

Question 9

Solution: Option **a** is correct.

According to the reading about the fast growth of Taobao Villages in China, rise of new technology is the key factor.

Question 10

Solution: Option **a** is correct.

While the Chinese government has been aware of the risks associated with DFS and the need for regulation for almost a decade, the regulatory work has progressed slowly to leave room for the growth of DFS.

Question 11

Solution: Option **a** is correct.

A landmark regulatory achievement was the joint promulgation of the Guideline on the Promotion of the Health Development of Internet Finance ("Guideline") by ten central government ministries and commissions on 18 July 2015.

Question 12

Solution: Option **a** is correct.

In China, DFS developed much later than elsewhere, with major development only beginning in the late 1990s as the financial services sector modernized and developed in the context of the overall process of economic liberalization.

Chapter 8

Technology Convergence

Learning Objectives
- Identify the driver of evolutionary system change.
- Review six types of technology convergences.

Main Takeaways

Main Points
- Evolutionary systems, including technologies, tend to increase exponentially with the force of technological convergence.
- Exponential innovation is described by converging technologies.
- The future trend in technology is about the integration of different technologies.
- Technology convergence could maximize the benefit of each technology and minimize its limitations.
- AI, blockchain, and IoT combine machine learning systems, decentralized frameworks, and billions of objects in life.
- AI and blockchain provide decentralized storage solutions and machine learning in mitigating cyber threats.
- AI boosts virtual experience while blockchain enables scaling capability for AR and VR.
- AI and blockchain converge in autonomous robots, 3D printing, and quantum computing to accelerate the revolution of many industries.

Main Terms
- **Technological convergence:** Digital convergence, which is the tendency for integrating multiple unrelated technologies.
- **End to End solution:** A concept that describes a complete functional solution from a system or service from beginning to end without an intermediating party.
- **IOTA:** A blockchain-based data exchange layer for IoT.
- **Cyber defense:** Secure information infrastructure to defend against threats in the cyber domain.
- **Data integrity:** Refers to the accuracy, completeness, and consistency of data.
- **Virtual eCommerce:** A part of e-commerce that utilizes VR devices.

8.1 Law of Accelerating Returns and Technological Convergence

The following reference is selected to provide a comprehensive overview of this topic. You are required to read the listed study materials.

Reference/Further Reading

Lee, K. C. D., Chong, G., & Ding, D. (2020). Convergence of AI, data and blockchain [Chapter 3], in *Artificial Intelligence, Data and Blockchain in a Digital Economy*, World Scientific, pp. 107–125.

8.2 Convergence of Different Technologies

The following references are selected to provide a comprehensive overview of this topic. You are required to read the listed study materials.

Reference/Further Reading

IMDA, edited by Lee, K. C. D. (2020). *Artificial Intelligence, Data and Blockchain in a Digital Economy*, World Scientific.

8.3 Sample Questions

Question 1

Focusing on only one technology or sector can

(a) Miss the broader impacts and opportunities driven by converging technologies
(b) Make the technology more advanced
(c) Develop the technology more efficiently

Question 2

According to "The Latest Exponential and Combinatorial Illustration of What the Future Will Bring," which of the following does not belong to the technology foundation?

(a) Cloud
(b) Internet
(c) Smart cities

Question 3

According to "The Latest Exponential and Combinatorial Illustration of What the Future Will Bring," cyberwar is most closely associated with

___.

(a) Technology
(b) Innovation accelerators
(c) Future scenarios

Question 4

Which of the following is not a benefit of integrating blockchain with IoT?

(a) Security
(b) Speed
(c) Legal and compliance

Question 5
Which one of the following statements is not true?

(a) AI can help scan fingerprints, or retina for biometric logins
(b) Blockchain could be used in natural language processing for information selection
(c) Blockchain uses the Merkle tree structure for data integrity to boost cybersecurity

Question 6
Which one of the following is an example to show integration of blockchain and VR?

(a) Live entertainment
(b) Virtual eCommerce
(c) Both of (a) and (b)

Question 7
Which technology represents the next stage of automated manufacturing?

(a) 3D printing
(b) Blockchain
(c) Quantum computing

Solutions

Question 1

Solution: Option **a** is correct.

According to Deloitte's report, focusing on only one technology or sector can miss the broader impacts and opportunities driven by these converging technologies.

Question 2

Solution: Option **c** is correct.

Refer to the reading of Section 8.1.

Question 3

Solution: Option **c** is correct.

Refer to the reading of Section 8.1.

Question 4

Solution: Option **c** is correct.

Refer to the reading of Section 8.2.

Question 5

Solution: Option **b** is correct.

It is AI rather than Blockchain to be applied for information selection.

Question 6

Solution: Option **c** is correct.

Refer to the reading of Section 8.2.

Question 7

Solution: Option **a** is correct.

The question is about automated manufacturing. Only 3D technology is closely related. Now with the help of 3D printers, companies can develop personalized items with increasing precision and efficiency, saving both time and money.

Chapter 9

Computational Law

Learning Objectives

Review the developments from legal informatics to computational law:

- Recognize the scope of the discipline of legal informatics.
- Outline the developments in legal informatics.
- Summarize key concerns in computational law.
- Summarize the technological landscapes in and around the legal space.

Discuss aspects of computational law:

- Outline legal text analysis.
- Outline computational models in the legal domain.
- Outline computational contracts.

Main Takeaways

Main Points

- Legal informatics is concerned with legal information, legal information processing, information law, and ICT law.
- Legal informatics encompasses the following topics: computational law, jurimetrics, lawbots, legal expert systems, and legal information retrieval.
- Key notions in the developments of legal informatics are jurimetrics, cybernetics, computation, the internet, smart contract, natural language processing, and AI.
- Computational law is concerned with the codification of legal documents into computational forms that humans and/or machines can interpret.
- Computational law is also concerned with computational contracts.

- LegalTech, RegTech, and ComplianceTech are the three main technological landscapes in and around the legal space.
- Legal texts may be analyzed by means of a legal ontology as the latter provides the concepts for framing the underlying semantics in the texts.
- A legal ontology supports meaningful interaction between humans and machines in the legal domain.
- A legal ontology may be applied to statutory reasoning and legal argumentation.
- A computational model in the legal domain is a computer algorithm, program, or app that captures certain key aspects of legal data. Analyses may be performed to eventually produce relevant legal information downstream.
- The notion of a computational contract underlies the varied notions of contract across disciplines by focusing on the computational aspect.
- A computational contract may be expressed in a suitable language that facilitates both human understanding and machine processing.
- A computational contract may be a record of legal code or be itself a source of law.
- By including operational aspects into the code that defines a computational contract, transaction costs due to the monitoring and enforcing aspects of contracting may be reduced.

Main Terms
- **Legal informatics:** The discipline that is concerned with legal information.
- **Jurimetrics:** A discipline that applies quantitative analysis methods to law.
- **Cybernetics:** A discipline that studies control and feedback in systems.
- **Computation:** The activity underlying devices during information processing.
- **The internet:** The global medium of information exchange that arose in the later part of the 20th century.
- **Smart contract:** A rule of engagement for a number of users that is written in computer code and operates on a decentralized network.
- **Natural language processing:** A subfield of computer science that studies methods of handling and making sense of human languages.
- **AI:** Acronym standing for Artificial Intelligence.
- **Computational contract:** A contract that is written in computer code for computational processing and comprehension.

- **Cognitive computing:** A discipline that is concerned with facilitating the platform-based interaction between humans and machines.
- **LegalTech:** The landscape of technological innovations in the legal space.
- **RegTech:** The landscape of technological innovations in the space of regulation.
- **ComplianceTech:** The landscape of technological innovations in the space of compliance.
- **Legal ontology:** A knowledge base of legal concepts.
- **Upper ontology:** A knowledge base of common-sense concepts.
- **Model:** A representation that is constructed to capture aspects of a reality.
- **Computational contract:** A perspective of contract that emphasizes its computational aspect.

9.1 From Legal Informatics to Computational Law

9.1.1 *What is Legal Informatics*

Legal informatics is the discipline that is concerned with legal information.

A perspective inclined towards informatics will have a boundary drawn around algorithms, processes, and systems that handle data with legal content. Such an approach may require nothing more than a superficial link between informatics and law. Any database that is capable of handling generic data well will probably handle legal data reasonably well. Any search algorithm whose performance is dependent on the set of keys on which it is trained will probably perform reasonably well when trained with keywords from the legal domain.

In recent developments involving computational law (CL) and artificial intelligence (AI), the focus is on how legal reasoning may be modeled with data structures embedded in programming languages. This will require deeper levels of interaction between informatics and law.

The intertwining of informatics and law is not unique as it is also observed in finance where information, previously deemed to be simply a record to convey some fact, has recently been brought innovatively into smart contract platforms, which can potentially support the development of financial institutions on the internet, hence disrupting the conventional financial industry.

A proposed delineation of legal informatics into subfields that reflects either an emphasis on the informatics or the law is as follows (Saarenpää and Sztobryn, 2016):

- Legal Information;
- Legal Information Processing;
- Information Law;
- ICT Law.

Legal information refers to the management of information in law, while legal information processing refers to the methods by which data can be processed and analyzed for extracting the information necessary for legal decisions. Information law refers to the law that regulates the generation, deployment, management, dissemination, and protection of information. ICT law is concerned with the technological means by which information is generated, deployed, managed, disseminated, and protected.

Legal informatics is also associated with topical concerns such as these:

- Computational Law;
- Jurimetrics;
- Lawbots;
- Legal expert systems;
- Legal information retrieval.

As mentioned, CL is concerned with the modeling of legal reasoning by computational methods. Jurimetrics refers to the application of scientific methods, namely quantitative and empirical analyses, to law. Legal expert systems refer to AI design and implementation of expert systems that encode query-answering capabilities of human experts. Lawbots refer to robots, machines or systems capable of providing answers to legal queries typically posed in natural language. Legal information retrieval refers to the methods of search and retrieval applied to legal information.

Reference/Further Reading

Saarenpää, A., & Sztobryn, K. (2016). *Lawyers in the Media Society: The Legal Challenges of the Media Society*. University of Lapland.

9.1.2 *Developments in Informatics with Legal Impacts*

In 1949, Lee Loevinger coined the term "jurimetrics" in his paper "Jurimetrics: The Next Step Forward" that started the field — an approach to legal analysis that is based on quantitative reasoning with empirical data (Loevinger, 1948). In 1950, Norbert Wiener published his book "The Human Use of Human Beings," which explored how cybernetics (the scientific study of control and communication in the animal and the machine) can benefit society (Wiener, 1988). As we now understand, quantitative methods lend themselves well to computational treatment, with data analytics being one of the manifestations of the digital medium. In light of the notion of the Internet of Things (IoT), programmable implants, and smart contracts, cybernetics is manifested through the programmatic control of devices, men (animals), and society.

The 1950s was a time when computing as an academic discipline was in its infancy and computing machines were nowhere close in power or usability to the nifty personal computers (PCs) that were to come three decades later. Experience with computing was confined to only a few who either had the rare opportunity to operate computing devices or who exercised their imaginations on computation as a concept and what its worldly manifestation would have in store for society in the future, just as what Loevinger and Wiener did.

From the 1970s to the new millennium, the period witnessed the dizzying pace at which information technology developed and became ubiquitous, transforming society into one that is truly information-centric and elevating computation to a central spot in social thinking. Landmarks provide a good glimpse of the developmental path: the advent of the PCs in the 1980s; the simmering growth of the internet from the ARPANET to the adoption of the TCP/IP protocol in 1983, and the creation of the World Wide Web in the early 1990s, which brought internetworking to the general public; the rise of the internet giants in the 2000s; and the era of mobile devices. The net effect is a global society heavily connected and reliant on the internet for its daily affairs.

From individuals to institutions, the means of information access, communication, and networking have been totally transformed in a few short decades. Legal organizations, such as parliaments, judiciaries, and legal firms are not immune from these changes. Particularly interesting are developments in informatics that have deeper impacts related to legal semantics.

In 1996, Nick Szabo published an article to describe his vision of the smart contract (Szabo, 1996). This overturned the assumption that a contract must be a written agreement that binds human participants into a relationship of rights and obligations. The smart contract is written as computer code. This opens up the possibility for it to be processed or interacted with by computers. Participants on a smart contract may themselves be computer code. Blockchain comes into the picture by enabling the creation of decentralized online communities that can, and are willing to, uphold smart contracts.

However, there is a gap for technology to fill. As legal contracts are written in natural language rather than computer code, algorithms must become sufficiently competent in the correct interpretation of the legal semantics before smart contracts can take on the role of conventional contracts more holistically. Recent developments in natural language processing and AI, such as the winning feat in the game show Jeopardy! by IBM's Watson (Kelly III & Hamm, 2013), raise the prospect for successful applications to the law in the area of legal reasoning support.

References/Further Readings

Kelly III, J. E., & Hamm, S. (2013). *Smart Machines: IBM's Watson and the Era of Cognitive Computing*. Columbia University Press.

Loevinger, L. (1948). Jurimetrics — The Next Step Forward. *Minnesota Law Review*, 33, 455.

Szabo, N. (1996). Smart contracts: Building blocks for digital markets. *EXTROPY: The Journal of Transhumanist Thought*, (16), 18(2).

Wiener, N. (1988). *The Human Use of Human Beings: Cybernetics and Society* (No. 320). Da Capo Press.

9.1.3 *Computational Law*

CL is a subfield of legal informatics concerned with computing technology applications to legal reasoning.

While legal informatics may be traced back to before 1960, CL is a relatively new discipline whose growth is aided by a surge in general interest in smart contracts and AI, and a belief in their potential to transform society.

One concern of CL is the codification of legal documents into forms that are not merely digital that aids transmission and storage, but also computational, to be interpreted by humans and computers working in tandem. An early attempt in this direction is the translation of the British National Act 1981 (BNA) into the programming language Prolog (Bratko, 2001). Prolog has been a programming language of choice in AI for work on computer reasoning and expert systems. The study indicates that while the purely logical parts of the BNA can be faithfully translated to Prolog, certain aspects of the BNA are not so well captured. Some examples are statements that depend on beliefs (...the President is satisfied that...), defaults (...unless the contrary is shown...) or relate to other parts of the law (...as defined in section 4 of...). The article has since spawned numerous research studies into related issues.

Another concern of CL is that of computational contracts. Underlying this is the notion that contracts are written directly in a programming language that can be interpreted by both humans and computers. Thus expressed, they can be stored in a node residing in a network for other nodes to interact with. The notion of smart contracts arose from the writing of Nick Szabo (Szabo, 1996). His vision has since been realized in the form of smart contract platforms, such as Ethereum (Antonopoulos & Wood, 2018).

One may attempt a far-sighted view to see where the infusion of technology into law will lead us and be assured that the development has a certain deep-rooted nature and not merely a fad. A view that machines may soon replace men in social affairs, and hence legal ones too, is likely to be premature as the current weight of evidence is in favor of machines being better or having the potential to be better than humans in focused and well-defined tasks, such as a game of Go.

In contrast, humans are much better equipped to cope in the general environment thanks to biological evolution. Cognitive computing, as espoused in Smart Machines: IBM's Watson and the Era of Cognitive Computing (Kelly III & Hamm, 2013), is a realistic and positive paradigm on which to base a vision of future development with a proliferation of interactional arenas of cooperating agencies comprising men and computers in the solution of social problems.

References/Further Readings

Antonopoulos, A. M., & Wood, G. (2018). *Mastering Ethereum: Building Smart Contracts and Dapps*. O'reilly Media.

Bratko, I. (2001). *Prolog Programming for Artificial Intelligence*. Pearson Education.

Kelly III, J. E., & Hamm, S. (2013). *Smart Machines: IBM's Watson and the Era of Cognitive Computing*. Columbia University Press.

Szabo, N. (1996). Smart contracts: Building blocks for digital markets. *EXTROPY: The Journal of Transhumanist Thought*, (16), 18(2).

9.1.4 *LegalTech, RegTech and ComplianceTech*

LegalTech refers to the landscape of technological innovations in the legal space. In particular, it encompasses the creation and use of software technology in legal services. RegTech and ComplianceTech refer to the landscape of technological innovations in the space of regulation and compliance, respectively. Pertaining to the finance industry, the terms apply to technology firms and innovations that have developed around the regulatory concerns of the central banks.

Traditional legal technology involves using software to facilitate or manage accounting, billing, document storage, information retrieval, and legal practice. In recent years, LegalTech extends the domain of traditional application into the practice of law itself to include support in legal reasoning, DIY legal assistance, and the legal marketplace.

LegalTech is nascent (as of 2020) reflected by its Wikipedia page (Legal technology, 28 August 2020) and other publicly available statistics obtainable from the Web. The number of references is 10, and the number of notable LegalTech companies and key areas of concern both amount to 17 on its Wikipedia page. On the other hand, a Google search with the keyword "legaltech" turns up 6.33 million results, with titles such as "12 Legal Tech Startup Founders in Asia to Follow in 2020" and "The Future of Lawyers: Legal Tech, AI, Big Data And Online Court" in the lead. GitHub Topics lists 58 public repositories under legaltech, nine public repositories under regtech (GitHub Topics — legaltech, 28 August 2020; GitHub Topics — regtech, 28 August 2020) while compliance tech is not currently a topic.

Another perspective of development is evident from the creation of CodeX — the Center for Legal Informatics at the Stanford Law School, the setting up of the Centre for CL at the Singapore Management University, the offering of the CL in Token Economy course at the Singapore University of Social Sciences and the inclusion of CL as a topic in the curriculum of the Chartered Fintech Professional by the Global Fintech Institute.

References/Further Readings

GitHub Topics — Legaltech. (28 August 2020). GitHub. Retrieved from https://github.com/topics/legaltech.

GitHub Topics — Regtech. (28 August 2020). GitHub. Retrieved from https://github.com/topics/regtech.

Legal Technology. (28 August 2020). Wikipedia. Retrieved from https://en.wikipedia.org/wiki/Legal_technology.

9.2 Aspects of Computational Law

9.2.1 *Legal Text Analysis*

To make sense of legal texts, one requires the appropriate concepts from the legal domain.

A concept is a notion that captures the individuation of something essential in a domain of discourse, which if grasped, affords understanding, and thereby enables eventual action in the environment. In other words, a concept is the smallest piece of information that allows for the appreciation of the meaning, where meaning is understood to have a purpose that is ultimately connected to interacting with the environment.

Philosophers and scientists, particularly psychologists and computer scientists, have attempted to make concrete what concepts are. Invariably, this amounts to the representation of concepts in various forms.

Ontology is a term that arose from philosophy to denote what is essentially there. It has been used in informatics to refer to the explicit representation of key notions that belong to a domain of discourse. While one speaks of different ontologies or ontological systems, every ontology starts from the *name* primitive.

For instance, the phrase *judicial role* can be conceived as a name that belongs to an ontology. In fact, it is a name that belongs to the e-Court ontology (Breuker *et al.*, 2002). The significance of a name is due to a certain two-sided property that it possesses. That it is a phrase from the legal domain means that legal users are able to imbue it with meaning from the wider legal context. That it is an "individual" means that it affords computational manipulation with machines.

An ontology typically comprises a collection of such names that are interrelated in a certain structure. The differences in the collection of names and the structures that inter-relate these names are the sources of differences in ontological systems. The collection of names and the inter-relations between the names reflect the concepts and their inter-relations in specific domains that the ontologies capture.

In recent years, numerous ontologies have been created. Well-known ontologies that capture general knowledge domain are BFO, Cyc, DOLCE, GFO, PROTON, Sowa Ontology, and SUMO (Muscardi *et al.*, 2007). They are also known as upper or common-sense ontologies as the names are selected to reflect concepts at the level of the common usage of general knowledge, which is above the detailed level of specialized domains.

In the field of legal informatics, examples of ontologies are LRI-Core, e-Court, DALOS, and LegalRuleML (Athan *et al.*, 2015; Breuker *et al.*, 2002; Breuker *et al.*, 2004; Francesconi, 2008). Many ontologies have an underlying network-of-concepts structure. van Kralingen's classic ontology (Kralingen, 1995) is based on frames. Each frame contains slots whose values represent concrete instances on legal acts, concepts, or norms. LUIMA (Grabmair *et al.*, 2015) is a special kind of ontology in the

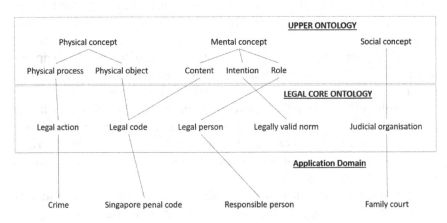

Figure 9.1:   LRI-Core ontology concepts.

legal domain known as a type system. A type system uses data structures (other than just the network kind found in common ontologies) to interpret and analyze domain data in a data processing pipeline.

Two issues that concern legal ontologies are:

(1) How is a legal ontology constructed?
(2) What are the applications of legal ontologies?

The following sections address them.

(a) Construction of Legal Ontology

We take here, for example, the LRI-Core ontology. This ontology was developed by the Leibniz Center for Law of the University of Amsterdam. It has been merged into the LKIF Core ontology (Hoekstra *et al.*, 2007).

The LRI-Core has two levels — upper ontology and legal core ontology. The upper ontology contains common-sense concepts that interface with proper legal and core concepts. The interfacing between the upper ontology and the legal core ontology is realized through the "is-a" relationship. Thus, a legal person belongs to the legal core ontology, *an agent that is both a physical object and* a mental object, both of which belong to the upper ontology. Within each level, there is also the "part-of" relationship that links two notions together when one is a part of another.

A snapshot of the LRI-Core ontology is shown in Figure 9.1.

(b) Applications of Legal Ontologies

A legal ontology may be seen as belonging to a legal knowledge base from which resources may be drawn for informatics work in the legal domain. The ontology is stored in a digital form that machines can easily manipulate. At the same time, the ontology comprises concepts at a level of common usage in the legal domain or in more specialized subdomains.

The names of concepts and the inter-connectedness thus encoded are meant to map consistently with real-world usage. This facilitates the transformation process required in the pipeline from raw data to output in general workflows. That an ontology is understood and manipulable by both humans and machines implies the potential to build systems in which men and machines cooperate towards given goals.

In the area of statutory reasoning, a legal ontology may be applied to the construction of statutes. The resulting article may be part-programming code in nature. This allows machines to be used in reasoning about the various aspects of the statute.

In the area of legal argumentation, a legal ontology may be a basic component in a legal tutoring system in which a law professor instructs students in the construction of legal arguments. The tutoring system functions as an aid to manage the parts of the interaction that is difficult to handle by human beings, such as processing a multitude of cases or handling the tedious and boring aspects.

References/Further Readings

Athan, T., Governatori, G., Palmirani, M., Paschke, A., & Wyner, A. (2015, July). LegalRuleML: Design principles and foundations. In *Reasoning Web International Summer School* (pp. 151–188). Springer, Cham.

Breuker, J., Elhag, A., Petkov, E., & Winkels, R. (2002). Ontologies for legal information serving and knowledge management. In *Legal Knowledge and Information Systems, Jurix 2002: The Fifteenth Annual Conference* (pp. 1–10).

Breuker, J., & Hoekstra, R. J. (2004). Epistemology and ontology in core ontologies: FOLaw and LRI-Core, two core ontologies for law.

Francesconi, E., & Tiscornia, D. (2008). Building semantic resources for legislative drafting: The DALOS Project. In *Computable Models of the Law* (pp. 56–70). Springer, Berlin, Heidelberg.

Grabmair, M., Ashley, K. D., Chen, R., Sureshkumar, P., Wang, C., Nyberg, E., & Walker, V. R. (2015, June). Introducing LUIMA: An experiment in legal conceptual retrieval of vaccine injury decisions using a UIMA type system and tools. In *Proceedings of the 15th International Conference on Artificial Intelligence and Law* (pp. 69–78).

Hoekstra, R., Breuker, J., Di Bello, M., & Boer, A. (2007). The LKIF core ontology of basic legal concepts. *LOAIT*, 321, 43–63.

Kralingen, R. W. V. (1995). *Frame-Based Conceptual Models of Statute Law.* Kluwer Law Intl.

Mascardi, V., Cordì, V., & Rosso, P. (2007, September). A Comparison of Upper Ontologies. In *WOA* (Vol. 2007, pp. 55–64).

9.2.2 Computational Models in the Legal Domain

A model is a notion that arises in science, engineering, mathematics, and everyday language. Models in science capture certain aspects of real-world phenomena with equations or computer simulations to explain the phenomena and derive value from the possibility of prediction as a result of the explanation (Frigg and Hartman, Spring 2020 Edition; Frigg and Nguyen, Spring 2020 Edition; Winsburg, Winter 2020 Edition). Models in engineering capture certain aspects of an object in a more manipulable form than the object itself as a means to guide an implementational process towards the realization of the object (Kleppe *et al.*, 2003; Wymore, 2018). In mathematics, the central feature of model theory is a model, which takes the form of a mathematical structure in which propositions are evaluated to be true or false (Hodges, Fall 2018 Edition). In everyday language, a model is an entity that represents another, bringing certain features into focus through the representation.

The unifying concept is thus a representation that is constructed to capture aspects of a reality, from which meaning is derived, and reasoning is carried out, and to produce an output downstream. When applied to the legal domain, a model is a computer algorithm, program or app that captures certain key aspects of legal data. Analyses may be performed to eventually produce relevant legal information downstream.

The pervasiveness of information technology means that the legal community, like any other knowledge-based communities, has been using technology to facilitate information handling as soon as it became widely available. The difference between how technology was used and how it is expected to be used currently in CL lies in constructing rich computational models that reflect legal knowledge. In some sense, modeling is an internal development in contrast to an external development associated with jurimetrics that is concerned with measurements.

A key aspect of legal documents and activities is the underlying reasoning that leads to conclusions, decisions, and judgments. A major concern of CL is, therefore the computational modeling of reasoning in the legal domain. Successful modeling helps to create apps or systems that can facilitate the analyses of legal documents, synthesis of legal information, and the interaction of legal professionals, clients, and machines in a digital economy.

References/Further Readings

Frigg, Roman and Stephan Hartmann, *Models in Science*, The Stanford Encyclopedia of Philosophy (Spring 2020 Edition), Edward N. Zalta (ed.). Available at: https://plato.stanford.edu/archives/spr2020/entries/models-science/.

Frigg, Roman and James Nguyen, *Scientific Representation, The Stanford Encyclopedia of Philosophy* (Spring 2020 Edition), Edward N. Zalta (ed.). Available at: https://plato.stanford.edu/archives/spr2020/entries/scientific-representation/.

Hodges, Wilfrid, *Model Theory*, The Stanford Encyclopedia of Philosophy (Fall 2018 Edition), Edward N. Zalta (ed.). Available at: https://plato.stanford.edu/archives/fall2018/entries/model-theory/.

Kleppe, A. G., Warmer, J., Warmer, J. B., & Bast, W. (2003). *MDA Explained: The Model Driven Architecture: Practice and Promise*. Addison-Wesley Professional.

Winsberg, Eric. *Computer Simulations in Science*, The Stanford Encyclopedia of Philosophy (Winter 2019 Edition), Edward N. Zalta (ed.). Available at: https://plato.stanford.edu/archives/win2019/entries/simulations-science/.

Wymore, A. W. (2018). *Model-Based Systems Engineering* (Vol. 3). CRC Press.

9.2.3 *Computational Contracts*

Contract is a central area in law.

Recent developments in technology, particularly smart contracts, will impact on the form and delivery of legal contracts. This compels a cross-disciplinary look at the notion of a contract for a deeper understanding.

In an article that foretold the development of smart contracts (Szabo, 1997), Nick Szabo calls a contract a set of promises agreed to in a meeting place of minds and discusses the dimensions of contract design in a list of objectives:

- • Transaction Costs
- — Mental
- — Computational
- • Contracting Phases
- • Observability
- — Hidden Knowledge
- — Hidden Actions
- • Verifiability
- — Online Enforceability
- — Verifiability by Adjudicators
- • Privity
- — Protection from Third Parties

Nick Szabo built his list by expanding on and extending the economic theory on contracts. In the design of a contract, these objectives need to be traded off against one another.

In economics, the concern in a contract lies in the function of contractual agreements to bind agents together to produce an economic outcome. Hence, the need to layout the issues that may affect the process (Salanié, 2017). Economic analyses typically model agents as decision-makers who may be incentivized and take actions to optimize their utilities. In the context of contracts, each actor bound to a contract will attempt to optimize his personal utility, while the contract designer will attempt to optimize the social utility that the contract is required to produce for those involved. Moral hazard, adverse selection, and signaling are three well-known situations involving agents under contractual agreements. Models are derived for reasoning towards economically optimal contract design. In the sub-branch of economics known as mechanism design, contracts are studied in a framework in which agents are bound together in a game setting, interacting in a prescribed manner according to the rules of the game while optimizing personal gains at the same time (Börgers *et al.*, 2015).

In computing science and engineering, contracts are software components that bind other components together in agreements to guarantee that planned outcomes are produced. In the paradigm known as design-by-contract or contract programming, interfaces between software components are required to declare pre-conditions, post-conditions, and invariants required to be satisfied or checked. The Eiffel programming language is an implementation of this idea (Meyer, 1988). Contracts also constitute a topic in the modeling and computation of cyber-physical systems as a means to specify safety requirements (Platzer, 2018).

In the legal domain, a contract is a document that legally binds its participants to interact in a manner that is recorded in the document prescribing the rights and obligations of those involved. The contract must be drafted in a way that appropriately invokes legal principles so that it may be enforced by the law of the jurisdiction in which the contract is formed. Aspects of contract formation (e.g., offer, acceptance, consideration, mutual intent), formalities (e.g., oral, writing, deeds), and the segment of law from which the legal principles apply are distinguished (Poole, 2016).

With these perspectives, we may now reflect on the development in smart contracts' space for legal contracts.

Smart contracts are computer programs that reside on machines functioning as nodes in a network that runs on the internet. These computer programs allow several users to bind and interact with one another according to the specifications found in the program. An underlying blockchain and token network uphold the program itself and its changes as the contract phases unfold. The public readability of the program enables mutual intent as it is found on the blockchain, while the trust that the contract will function as it is written is attributed to the robust communication mechanism that is found in the consensus protocols of the network. The rules that bind the smart contract with its participants are those found in the network protocol and the semantics of the language in which the smart contracts are expressed. Whether smart contracts are legally binding outside the network is an outstanding issue.

The development that brings about smart contracts fits into the wider picture in which we find the ideas of the IoT and a digital economy. Agent interaction is a constant feature of society. This interaction will evolve to become a mix involving physical, social and digital networks in the current informatics landscape. Furthermore, agents in the networks may not necessarily be people or even just physical things as it is commonly portrayed in IoT, but may also include software agents such as AI robots and smart contracts.

It is in this context that the future development of legal contracts should be assessed. The traditional forms that legal contracts take are documents or deeds, both of which are frequently expressed in writing. Even non-writing-based artifacts can have digital representations, which can function in the same manner as the physical artifacts regarding rights and obligations when accepted by the participants involved. It is only a matter of time when substantial volumes of legal documents are in digital form and expressed in such a manner, likely by choice of suitable languages, both humans and machines can understand that. This will pave the way for other aspects of contracting to be operationalized through digital means.

A notion of contract that can capture some of the key features and concerns arising from the various perspectives above is that of a computational contract. The primary idea is that the essence of a contract lies in the computation required internally to produce an outcome externally, viewed equally in computational terms. The contract is expressed in a suitable programming language that facilitates human expression and understanding and easy processing by machines in a fashion that enables computer-assisted reasoning and support through machine learning (ML) and artificial intelligence (AI).

The relevance to the legal domain is that the computational contracts may contain clear legal content and may themselves be regarded as sources of law rather than mere representations. The possibility for a computational contract to include operational aspects allows the reduction of transaction costs in the monitoring and enforcing aspects of contracting.

References/Further Readings

Börgers, T., & Krahmer, D. (2015). *An Introduction to the Theory of Mechanism Design*. Oxford University Press, USA.

Meyer, B. (1988). Eiffel: A language and environment for software engineering. *Journal of Systems and Software*, 8(3), 199–246.

Platzer, A. (2018). *Logical Foundations of Cyber-Physical Systems* (Vol. 662). Cham: Springer.

Poole, J. (2016). *Textbook on Contract Law*. Oxford University Press.

Salanié, B. (2017). *The Economics of Contracts*. MIT press.

Szabo, N. (1997). *Formalizing and Securing Relationships on Public Networks*. First Monday.

9.3 Sample Questions

Question 1
A smart contract is distinguished from a traditional contract because

(a) It has AI components embedded for intelligent processing.
(b) It is written in computer code.
(c) It is written in computer code and embedded in a context that facilitates the interaction that is specified therein.

Question 2
Which of the following is the most fruitful goal of computational law?

(a) To develop cognitive computing legal platforms.
(b) To automate legal processes.
(c) To convert legal documents into computer code.

Question 3

Legal technology involves _____.

(a) The use of software to facilitate or manage accounting, billing, document storage, information retrieval, and legal practice
(b) Support in legal reasoning, DIY legal assistance, and legal marketplace.
(c) Both of (a) and (b)

Question 4

Which of the following is not a legal ontology?

(a) LRI-Core
(b) SUMO
(c) DALOS

Question 5

The power of computational models in the legal domain lies in

(a) The ability of models to represent aspects of the legal reality.
(b) The representation of models in computational forms that permits machine support in reasoning and processing.
(c) Both of (a) and (b)

Question 6

Which of the following is incorrect regarding a computational contract?

(a) Computational contracts are smart contracts
(b) Computational contracts constitute a view of contracts that emphasizes computation
(c) Computational contracts may be used as building blocks in cognitive computing

Solutions

Question 1

Solution: Option **c** is correct.

Any document can be expressed in computer code. The outstanding feature of a smart contract is the specification therein and the facilitation of the prescribed interaction. "Smart" does not equate to "AI."

Question 2

Solution: Option **a** is correct.

It is not realistic in the near future to expect legal documents and processes to be converted into computer code in a wholesale fashion because human interpretation of law is pivotal. Cognitive computing platforms facilitate legal interaction between humans and machines. Such platforms already exist. Hence it is a practical and fruitful goal of computational law to further develop such platforms. This should be the justifying reason for converting any aspect of existing legal code into computer code for computational handling.

Question 3

Solution: Option **c** is correct.

Refer to the reading.

Question 4

Solution: Option **b** is correct.

Refer to the reading.

Question 5

Solution: Option **c** is correct.

Models are useful for their ability to represent aspects of reality. Computational ones allow for machine processing.

Question 6

Solution: Option **a** is correct.

Computational contracts emphasize a view of contracts that emphasize computation. It includes the notion of smart contracts. Contracts will be necessary to build platforms for cognitive computing to coordinate interaction between agents. As the agents will be humans and machines, the contracts must be computer-coded and computational.

Chapter 10

Impact of AI, Data, and Blockchain

Learning Objectives
- Identify the impact of the convergence of technologies at country, enterprise, and societal levels.
- Review the definition of financial inclusion in the digital age; Identify the broadband and mobile technologies as solutions.

Main Takeaways

Main Points
- Many countries launch national AI strategies and set up appropriate registries for blockchain.
- The innovative technologies of AI and blockchain pose both unprecedented opportunities and challenges for enterprises.
- AI and blockchain have broader impacts on social implications, including disruption of future jobs and challenges for employees.
- Financial inclusion provides universal access to financial services for the unbanked and the underbanked market.
- Broadband has the potential to fundamentally address the cost concerns faced in delivering financial services.
- Mobile technologies can expand digital financial inclusion by delivering financial services to bridge the gap between physical, and the digital use and the access to money.

Main Terms

- **Liquid Democracy:** A type of delegation democracy in which people can delegate the authorized proxies they trust for their votes on specific issues.
- **Singapore's Personal Data Protection Act:** An Act passed in 2012 to govern the personal data collection, use, and disclosure by organizations.
- **Hyper-personalization:** A technology to use AI and real-time data to show the users the most relevant content, product, and service information.
- **Unbanked:** Refers to people who do not use banks or banking institutions.
- **Underbanked:** Refers to people who have a bank account but do not use mainstream financial services to manage their assets.

10.1 Country-Level, Enterprise-Level, and Social-Level Implications

The following reference is selected to provide a comprehensive overview of this topic. You are required to read the listed study materials.

Reference/Further Reading

Lee Kuo Chuen, D., Chong, G., & Ding, D. *Artificial Intelligence, Data and Blockchain in a Digital Economy* (Chapter 4, pp. 127–148).

10.2 Financial Inclusion

The following references are selected to provide a comprehensive overview of this topic. You are required to read the listed study materials.

References/Further Readings

Lee, D., & Deng, R. (2018). *Handbook of Blockchain, Digital Finance, and Inclusion* (Vol. 1, Chapters 4–6, pp. 58–144). Elsevier.
Lee, D., & Deng, R. (2018). *Handbook of Blockchain, Digital Finance, and Inclusion* (Vol. 2, Chapters 14–18, pp. 361–462). Elsevier.

10.3 Sample Questions

Question 1
Which of the following is the key factor for developing sophisticated data-driven Hyper-personalization?

(a) Available abundant data
(b) AI algorithms
(c) Both of (a) and (b)

Question 2
For India, which of the following could be a key priority given India's overarching goal to leverage AI for inclusion?

(a) Inclusion
(b) Social well-being
(c) Both of (a) and (b)

Question 3
The assertion that "the adoption of AI will alter work for blue-collar workers and disrupt the future work lives of white-collar workers the most" is ___ according to the MIT Technology Review study.

(a) True
(b) False
(c) Mainly unresolved

Question 4
Which of the following is/are key regulatory issues that will take center stage as digital financial services delivered on broadband channels become more available?

(a) Transparency and disclosure
(b) Borrower education and awareness
(c) Both (a) and (b)

Question 5
Which one of the following statements is not true?

(a) Smartphones are playing an increasing role in the next generation of digital financial services.
(b) Profitability from financial inclusion is the main concern from the government's perspective
(c) Many unbanked and underbanked individuals are financially unhealthy.

Question 6
The progress of financial inclusion in the Latin America and Caribbean region is constrained by

(a) High costs of providing and accessing financial services
(b) Politics concern
(c) Both of (a) and (b)

Question 7
Relative to traditional infrastructure, what can broadband channels offer?

(a) A shift from large fixed costs to smaller unit transaction costs
(b) The automated collection of a larger set of data on customers
(c) Both of (a) and (b)

Solutions

Question 1

Solution: Option **c** is correct.

With available abundant data and AI algorithms, businesses are moving towards sophisticated data-driven marketing strategies to develop products and target customers with products that interest them and cater to their specific needs, which are also referred to as hyper-personalization.

Question 2

Solution: Option **c** is correct.

Refer to the reading about inclusion and social well-being.

Question 3

Solution: Option **a** is correct.

Refer to the reading of *Jobs and Skills* in Section 10.1.

Question 4

Solution: Option **c** is correct.

Financial regulators can expect five sets of issues to take center stage as digital financial services delivered on broadband channels develop: Transparency and disclosure; Borrower education and awareness; client data protection; regulatory reporting and oversight; regulation and supervision of digital market platforms.

Question 5

Solution: Option **b** is correct.

Making profit is not a major goal of the government on financial inclusion.

Question 6

Solution: Option **a** is correct.

According to the reading of Section 10.2, the progress of financial inclusion in the Latin America and Caribbean region is constrained by the high costs involved in providing and accessing financial services. Politics is not a major concern.

Question 7

Solution: Option **c** is correct.

Relative to traditional brick-and-mortar infrastructure, broadband channels can offer: (i) a much greater sense of immediacy and ubiquity; (ii) a shift from large fixed costs to smaller and variable unit transaction costs; and (iii) automated collection of a much larger set of data on customers and transactions.

Chapter 11

The Future Trends

Learning Objectives
- Understand how different countries with different culture and policies can collaborate in developing future digital economy.
- Review the landscape of insurance technology and its potential from the perspective of enablement for financial and insurance services.
- Review the current development of cutting-edge technologies.
- Understand the transformation of AI application in banking and finance

Main Takeaways

Main Points
- Develop regional e-commerce standards to facilitate paperless trade across the region.
- Singapore and China can complement each other's approaches to the digital economy.
- Insurance technology offers future solutions to life risks by using data analytics, sensors, and wearables.
- Quantum technology is still at the infancy developmental stage to solve problems using different kinds of quantum computations.
- Quantum computing has practical applications for any situation that would require any form of computer or smartphone.
- Fintech unicorns can use the information to deliver services and value in a better way than traditional banks.

Main Terms
- **RCEP:** Regional Comprehensive Economic Partnership. It is a free trade agreement between the Asia-Pacific nations.
- **Insurtech:** A shorter technical name for Insurance Technology; It is applying technology to address the long list of problems currently facing the insurance industry.
- **Mobile Revolution:** Mobile devices are changing how people work, travel, read, communicate, shop, and engage in many other lifestyle pursuits.
- **Mutual aid:** Describes a structure or organization that everyone is free to join and free to participate.
- **Qubit:** Quantum computer bits. It is the basic unit of quantum information.

11.1 Technology Culture and Policy

Learning Objectives
- Understand other countries' technological culture and policies are crucial in advancing digital economic cooperation.
- Observe how countries mutually respect the differences in their blockchain and token policies and focus on the complementarity of their approaches.
- Appreciate the collaboration on central bank digital currencies and other projects and how countries lead the way regionally and globally in building digital economies of the future.
- Analyze the trade and technology wars of the current day and understand the differences in culture and policy of different countries.

Long-planned advances in China — in 5G, blockchain, central bank coins, and SME superapps — have coalesced into a new world of digitized, tokenized, and tradable assets. New digital mega-projects like the Blockchain Service Network, smart cities, and new foreign exchange digital rails are animating physical assets: offices, warehouses, homes, and farms. Powered by a network of sensors, AI, and distributed trust, the property has digitized wings. The resulting inflow of data from every part of the "built" world will create new industries, uproot traditional finance, and transform cities.

The global trade war is not just a re-ordering of technology: it's a re-ordering of cities. Nations that export this digital technology first will alter the digital fabric of the developing world. The articles and chapters explore the many people and companies, large and small, blazing new trails in China's "Internet of Everything" to transform the way we live, buy, and move.

References/Further Readings

Pei, S., Lee, D., & Li, Y. (2020), Token Economics: How Singapore can Boost Synergy with China in Building Digital Economies. Retrieved from https://www.thinkchina.sg/token-economics-how-singapore-can-boost-synergy-china-building-digital-economies.
Schulte, P., Sun, D., & Roman, S. (2021). *The Digital Transformation of Property in Greater China* (Chapters 1–3, pp. 1–88). World Scientific.

11.2 Insurtech

Learning Objectives
- Survey the landscape of insurance technology and its potential from the perspective of enablement for financial and insurance services.
- Understand how insurtech companies disrupt the multi-trillion dollar industry.
- Analyze how the insurtech will change the landscape of insurance and the underlying reasons.

Digital revolution is occurring in a sector that has hardly changed over the last 300 years. Surprising to many, recent innovation in China's digital finance space has shown that emerging entities can and will disrupt the multitrillion-dollar industry. With big data and Blockchain, the impact on the insurance sector will be a lot faster and more significant than most people will anticipate.

The lack of innovation in the product space of the insurance sector and the failure to cater to market needs have created a situation of disappointing experience for many. With the advancement in technology, it is now known that "The person is now the product" in the insurance space. By that, it means that InsurTech, a shorter technical name for Insurance Technology, offers individual, bespoke, customized solutions to life risks using data analytics, sensors, wearables and cell phone data in ways that were impossible only a few years ago. It is conjectured that agent-like insurance brokers may disappear slowly, then suddenly, as in insurance disruption that we have seen so far in China and elsewhere.

Reference/Further Reading

Tan, C., Schulte, P., & Lee. D. (2018). Insurtech and Fintech: Banking and Insurance Enablement. In *Handbook of Blockchain, Digital Finance, and Inclusion* (Vol. 1, pp. 249–282). Elsevier.

11.3 Quantum Computing, 5G, and Cloud

Learning Objectives
- Understand the basics of Quantum Computing (QC).
- Analyze the landscape, companies, and projects in QC
- Survey the software and hardware developments in QC.
- Compare the different projects in QC.
- Understand how QC will affect finance, especially in fintech, block-chain, and cryptocurrency that rely on cryptography technology.
- Learn the Grover and Shor Algorithms.
- Understand finance and business applications using QC.
- Learning the cloud business landscape and competitions.

Quantum computing is perhaps the most expensive innovative technology and the most difficult to understand because it has been on the Gartner Hype Cycle up-slope for more than ten years! Since 2005, quantum computing has been mentioned as an emerging technology, and in 2017, it is still considered emerging.

The foundation of quantum computing is the understanding that theoretical methods of computing cannot be separated from the physics that govern instruments of computing. Specifically, the theory of quantum mechanics presents a new paradigm for computer science that drastically alters our understanding of information processing and what we have long assumed to be the upper limits of computation.

This chapter will cover technology, algorithms, software, hardware, businesses, and the impact of QC on fintech, especially those that use cryptography to secure trust. Cloud business is another essential aspect as data must be stored, and the cloud is an important technology besides Distributed Ledger Technology.

Reference/Further Reading

Lee, D., & Schulte, P. (2019). *AI & Quantum Computing for Finance and Insurance* (Chapters 11–12, pp. 309–370). Elsevier.

11.4 Global Leadership in the Transformation with AI in Banking and Finance

Learning Objectives
- Analyze the competition among the tech giants in their country of origin and other markets.
- Analyze Huawei's strengths and weaknesses from the technology perspective.
- Understand the business strategies of tech companies and onshore and offshore.
- Understand the Merger and Acquisition strategies of giant tech companies.

This part of the course covers the competition between Alibaba, Tencent, and Ping An, in the fintech industry. It also covers the global landscape in 5G and Cloud with an emphasis on Huawei. India is another huge market for Fintech besides China and ASEAN and a competition ground for Indian, Chinese and USA technology companies.

Reference/Further Reading

Lee, D., & Schulte, P. (2019a). *AI & Quantum Computing for Finance and Insurance* (Chapters 7–10, pp. 161–308). Elsevier.

11.5 The Race for 5G Supremacy

The following reference is selected to provide a comprehensive overview of this topic. You are required to read the listed study materials.

Reference/Further Reading

Groves, A., & Schulte, P. (2020). *The Race for 5G Supremacy: Why China Is Surging, Where Millennials Struggle, & How America Can Prevail.* World Scientific.

11.6 The Digital Transformation of Property in Greater China

The following reference is selected to provide a comprehensive overview of this topic. You are required to read the listed study materials.

Reference/Further Reading

Schulte, P., Sun, D., & Roman, S. (2021). *The Digital Transformation of Property in Greater China* (Chapters 1 to 3, pp. 1–88). World Scientific.

11.7 Sample Questions

Question 1
Which of the following is not true?

(a) Singapore's competitive edge mainly relies on a comprehensive regulatory framework
(b) Building a legal infrastructure is crucial to the development of the digital economy
(c) Singapore and China can be mutually complementary for blockchain and token policies

Question 2
Why is the insurance sector lack innovation?

(a) Because of the complexity and the heavily regulated nature of the industry
(b) Because of the profitability of incumbents that provides few incentives to change
(c) Both of (a) and (b)

Question 3
Which of the following is not a fundamental trend for InsurTech?

(a) Personalization
(b) Simplification
(c) Localization

Question 4
Which of the following is the quantum computer which specializes only in optimization calculations?

(a) Adiabatic quantum computer
(b) Universal quantum computer
(c) None of above

Question 5
Which of the following is not true?

(a) Amazon is creating a world-class "farm to market" infrastructure
(b) Amazon and Alibaba are two dominant companies in the Indian e-commerce market
(c) Amazon's revenue in Indian mainly comes from advertising and marketplace sales

Question 6
Which consortium platform below has the backing of the highest industry and government apparatus in China?

(a) Hyperledger
(b) Multichain
(c) BSN

Solutions

Question 1

Solution: Option **a** is correct.

Singapore's competitive edge comes from its comprehensive, robust, and innovative regulatory framework and an effective and in-depth interpretation of the technological developments and policy contexts of various countries.

Question 2

Solution: Option **c** is correct.

Refer to the reading of Section 11.2.

Question 3

Solution: Option **c** is correct.

Three fundamental trends are personalization, connectivity, and simplification.

Question 4

Solution: Option **a** is correct

Refer to the reading of Section 11.3.

Question 5

Solution: Option **b** is correct.

Flipkart (Walmart) and Amazon are two dominant companies in the Indian e-commerce market.

Question 6

Solution: Option **c** is correct.

Refer to the reading of Section 11.6. Blockchain-Based Service Network (BSN) has government support in China. The rest two choices are not Chinese projects.